THE ENLIGHTENMENT

NORMAN HAMPSON

PENGUIN BOOKS

PENGUIN BOOKS

Published by the Penguin Group
Penguin Books Ltd, 27 Wrights Lane, London W8 5TZ, England
Penguin Books USA Inc., 375 Hudson Street, New York, New York 10014, USA
Penguin Books Australia Ltd, Ringwood, Victoria, Australia
Penguin Books Canada Ltd, 2801 John Street, Markham, Ontario, Canada L3R 1B4
Penguin Books (NZ) Ltd, 182–190 Wairau Road, Auckland 10, New Zealand

Penguin Books Ltd, Registered Offices: Harmondsworth, Middlesex, England

First published in Pelican Books 1968
Reprinted with new Bibliographical Note 1982
Reprinted in Penguin Books 1990
3 5 7 9 10 8 6 4

Printed in England by Clays Ltd, St Ives plc
Set in Monotype Bembo

To the memory of my father

CONTENTS

PREFACE

THE historian who writes about a concrete subject, such as the battle of Waterloo, begins with what might be considered an advantage: however interpretations of the causes and consequences of the battle may differ, there is general agreement that it did exist, that it occurred in a specific place, at a particular time, and that the French lost. The Enlightenment, on the other hand, only existed to the extent that it appears meaningful to isolate certain beliefs and ways of thinking and behaving, and to regard these as especially characteristic of a particular period. At most, it can only be regarded as a significant statistical concentration, not as an event. However one defines 'Enlightenment', some of its characteristics have been present in most ages and no period of history has seen the general acceptance of them all. Moreover, these characteristics were not 'facts' but attitudes, and a book like Montesquieu's *De l'esprit des lois* admits of more interpretations than a peace treaty or a budget. The attitudes which one chooses to regard as typical of the Enlightenment therefore constitute a free, subjective choice, which then, in turn, determines the shape of the synthesis one constructs for one's self. It may be argued with equal plausibility that Rousseau was either one of the greatest writers of the Enlightenment or its most eloquent and effective opponent. After weighing what the writers of the time thought of themselves and their period, one must finally impose a personal pattern on the rich anarchy of the evidence. Within limits, the Enlightenment was what one thinks it was. This book embodies one particular synthesis, one personal point of view. It will have failed in its purpose if the reader simply endorses this interpretation as his own. I hope he will be stimulated, and if necessary provoked to disagree and to seek his own synthesis.

There does not seem to me much point in attempting any general definition of the movement. Such a definition would have to include so many qualifications and contradictions as to be virtually meaningless, or else prove so constricting that logic would continually be trying to debar what common sense insisted on including. I would, however, assert that whatever is meant by the Enlightenment refers to ways of thinking and behaving that permeated many aspects of life. It was an interlacing pattern in which the 'facts' of history, the creations of the arts, the discoveries of science and the speculations of philosophy reacted upon each other and in turn affected men's attitudes to history, the arts, science, philosophy and religion. Any one of these strands may be followed in isolation, but to appreciate the causes and consequences of its peculiar convolutions one must try to attain some kind of simultaneous perception of the pattern as a whole. If one is to have any chance of doing so, one must take liberties with chronology. In the arrangement of the book I have therefore concentrated on themes rather than on individuals. Part One deals with ideas and attitudes that originated early in the period and follows them through to the second half of the eighteenth century. The attitudes studied in Part Two arose, in part at least, from the problems raised by the early Enlightenment, but the two overlapped in time and the same man might well have a foot in each camp. Such a plan may make it difficult for the reader to appreciate at once the particular contribution of someone like Montesquieu or Diderot, but the alternative appeared to me to be even more confusing.

To do justice to all the various ramifications of such a diverse movement, throughout the whole of civilized Europe, would require a rare combination of talents, to which I make no pretensions. No one, I hope, is more aware than I of the limitations which time, space and my own ignorance have imposed on this essay. Whole subjects on which I do not consider myself competent to express an opinion, such as music, painting and architecture, have been excluded. With comparatively unimportant exceptions, I have restricted myself to the movement of ideas in England, France and Germany. Even so, the subject covered is far too wide for me to advance any claims to exhaustive scholarship. Time and again, I have had to rush in where specialists, quite properly, fear to tread. My justification is quite simple. The Enlightenment was, to a remarkable degree, a period when the culture of the educated man was thought to take in the whole of human knowledge. A writer like Voltaire attained a European reputation as dramatist, poet, historian and philosopher – at a time when philosophy could not be divorced from theology. He was also the man who introduced Newtonian physics, on which his own philosophy was largely based, to the educated French public. In dealing with an age which would have regarded the conception of 'two cultures' as equivalent to no culture at all, there is perhaps as much distortion in the specialist investigation of one subject in isolation from its contemporary context, as in the more superficial survey of the period as a whole. I certainly feel that whatever insight into the Enlightenment I have been able to attain is directly due to this kind of synthetic approach.

The question immediately arises of the relationship between the different parts of this integrated whole. The reader may well ask how social and economic factors conditioned, or were conditioned by, the ideas of men who were shaped by the society in which they lived, and which they themselves helped to modify. An introductory essay of this kind is no place for the microscopical examination which would be necessary to arrive at even the most tentative answer in any specific instance. I have therefore not felt justified in doing more than throw out occasional hints of a possible relationship. At a superficial glance, the political stability of the period from 1715 to 1740 seems to fit the confident deism of some of the writers of the time and the increasing doubt of the intellectuals appears to coincide with the European wars of 1740-63 or the unrest that culminated in the French Revolution. But any such hasty parallels break down on examination. It would be absurd to attribute to the philosophy of the Enlightenment the invasion of Silesia by Frederick II of Prussia in 1740 which began the series of wars. The darkening of the intellectual horizons did not begin until some time later, and the greatest upheaval of all, the French Revolution, at first seemed to vindicate the optimists and to announce a period of European peace. The same year – 1749 – saw the publication of Condillac's 'Newtonian' *Traité des systèmes* which attacked teleological science, Buffon's assertion of the fixity of species, Diderot's *Lettre sur les aveugles*, which pointed towards materialist determinism, and the prize essay in which Rousseau began his assault on the accepted values of his age. It would be an ingenious dialectician who could harness four such dissimilar horses to the chariot of historical necessity. In more general terms, the attempt to relate the ideas of the Enlightenment to some hypothetical 'rise of the bourgeoisie' seems to me, as I have indicated elsewhere, to rest on very insecure foundations. I am far from suggesting that causal relationships between economic developments, social attitudes and intellectual speculations did not exist. On the contrary, everything appears to me to suggest such a symbiosis, but one whose nature and mode of operation is almost inconceivably complex if not actually incomprehensible.

On a more technical matter, I feel that I should perhaps apologize for the absence of specific references to the sources I have used. To have identified every quotation, in a general survey of this kind, would have been like using an artillery barrage to shoot rabbits. Rather than include some and not others, by some arbitrary process of selection, I have omitted them all, though I have tried to indicate the particular work to which I refer, whenever this seemed appropriate.

The object of this book, in other words, is not to attempt a scholarly and systematic investigation of this or that aspect of the Enlightenment. My aim is to convince the general reader that the authors I have quoted are well worth his reading for himself and my ambition, to help him towards a better understanding of what they were saying. I trust he will regard it, not as intellectual nourishment in its own right so much as an invitation to a banquet of his own.

I should like to acknowledge my debt to the University of Manchester for leave of absence and for the rich resources of its library. I am particularly indebted to Professor J. H. Plumb for inviting me to embark on a venture that has proved so rewarding and enjoyable, and for allowing me to steer my own course. Professor A. Goodwin, with his customary generosity, despite many pressing calls on his time, very kindly read my manuscript and put his wide knowledge of the eighteenth century at my disposal. I have also benefited from the fraternal help of Dr Frank Hampson, especially where scientific matters were concerned. I am happy to pay tribute, in a more general way, to the many authors whose books have delighted me and whose ideas I have so often appropriated. The mistakes and misunderstandings, however, are entirely original.

N. H.

Introduction

THE INTELLECTUAL BACKGROUND TO THE EIGHTEENTH CENTURY

HISTORIANS, in their search for origins, always tend to push back the beginning of whatever they are studying. In *The Crisis of European Consciousness* (1935), Paul Hazard suggested that the first flowering of the Enlightenment should be sought, not in the eighteenth century, but in the second half of the seventeenth. More recently, Christopher Hill, in *The Intellectual Origins of the English Revolution* (1965), argued that, in England at least, attitudes generally attributed to the Enlightenment were widespread in the late sixteenth century. At this rate the Enlightenment looks like linking up with the Renaissance, itself receding in the direction of the twelfth century! This is a useful warning against mechanical attempts to divide historical evolution into self-contained and homogeneous periods. European societies developed at different rates, responding both to national traditions and to the influence of their neighbours; foreign influences varied in direction and extent from one country to another and from one generation to the next; within a given society different elements of the same social class varied in their receptiveness to new ideas and ideas themselves changed more rapidly in some aspects of thought and taste than in others. Any historical synthesis has therefore to be something of a bed of Procrustes, but without synthesis history disintegrates into its innumerable and individually meaningless atoms. When due allowance has been made for all the exceptions, it is, I think, helpful to regard the seventeenth century as an age which saw a transition from one intellectual climate to another. In order to understand whatever is implied by the Enlightenment, one must consequently first appreciate the assumptions, attitudes and values against which it reacted.

The cultural horizon of most educated men in western Europe in the early seventeenth century was dominated by two almost unchallenged sources of authority: scripture and the classics. Each in its own way perpetuated the idea that civilization had degenerated from a former Golden Age. The most rational preoccupation for contemporary man was, therefore, by the study of the more fortunate ancients to move back towards the kind of society which the latter had known. Recent European movements, the Renaissance and the Reformation, had reinforced this attitude and enhanced the authority of the sacred texts. The Renaissance and the humanist educational movement had been largely based on a revival of Greek and Latin learning. The Reformation had taken the form of a revolt against the Roman Church, accused of having departed from the true faith as revealed in the Bible. Protestant scholars, from Luther onwards, therefore stressed the supreme authority of scripture. The Roman Catholics fought back with rival interpretations and by stressing the authority of the Christian Fathers. In this bitter conflict there was no room for the allegorical latitude which some medieval churchmen had permitted themselves in their approach to scripture. The sixteenth century had thus strengthened the reverence with which men approached the texts that enshrined the twin sources of European civilization.

It is virtually impossible for us today, whose acquaintance with Latin authors is generally limited to the reluctant translation of texts 'prescribed' for reasons not always obvious, to appreciate the eager veneration with which the sixteenth and seventeenth centuries approached the classics. During the long agony of the Roman Empire these were the brightest lights that shone across the dark seas of ignorance from a more civilized shore. The new confidence with which the men of the

Renaissance claimed the kinship of these illustrious ancestors had been a liberating force. The secular attitudes of Greece and Rome, their conception of civic virtue and the life of active public utility was a useful corrective in a society which, officially at least, assumed the wickedness of man, extolled the contemplative life and believed the destiny of nations to be the prerogative of God. A good deal of classical learning, however, was absorbed into an intellectual order that was assumed to reflect the divine purpose – and therefore carried the sanction of the Church behind it. This was especially true of Aristotle who had been, as it were, canonized when his philosophy was grafted on to Christian theology in the middle ages. The Church's approval had been extended in a general sort of way to cover his scientific, as well as his philosophical ideas. The sixteenth-century radical, eager to move on to new discoveries, was therefore faced by a double barrier: psychologically, it required a bold man to believe that his own reason – for as yet there was little experiment and no conception of the sovereignty of experimental evidence – had penetrated further than that of the Master. In the second place, perseverance in his presumption might cost him the goodwill of a conservative academic 'Establishment' and might bring him under suspicion of heresy. As late as 1636, in Protestant England, archbishop Laud was enforcing the authority of Hippocrates, Galen and Aristotle. One must not exaggerate this reverence accorded to the ancients; their texts represented no more than human wisdom and it was at least theoretically possible to argue that they had been wrong in matters of detail. Nevertheless the intellectual world which they had created still imposed its perspectives on the learned, whose commitment to the classical viewpoint was in many respects so automatic as to be unconscious.

However great the authority of classical authors, the one unquestionable voice of knowledge and duty was that of God himself, as recorded in the Bible, and particularly in the Old

Testament. Here was contained both the history of the human race and the explanation of the divine purpose. The first chapter of Genesis bolted the door against any optimistic interpretation of human nature or man's prospect of creating a satisfactory society on earth. The early history of all humanity was known, so far as it could ever be known, from the Old Testament account of the events before the Flood. Thereafter the Jews, the chosen people under the direct guidance of God, had been the teachers of all antiquity; Plato, for example, had been a pupil of Jeremiah in Egypt. The solution to all such human problems as were humanly soluble was therefore to be found in biblical exegesis. Interpretation might be difficult and opinions conflicting, but the only way to certain knowledge was by establishing the exact significance of God's own statement of his will and purpose. To anyone brought up in this tradition, theology was very properly an incomparably more serious study than the gratification of mere curiosity in matters of science or philosophy. And so we find the French bishop, Bossuet, writing in the dedication of the work on political theory that he composed about 1677 for the son of Louis XIV:

Whatever was wisest in Sparta, in Athens, in Rome; to go back to the very beginning, in Egypt and the best-governed of all states, is as nothing compared to the wisdom that is contained in the law of God, whence the other constitutions have drawn all their better aspects. Therefore no state has ever enjoyed a finer constitution than that under which you will see the people of God. Moses, who shaped it, possessed all the divine and human wisdom with which a great and noble mind can be embellished, and [divine] inspiration did no more than bring to final certitude and perfection what the customs and knowledge of the wisest of all empires and its greatest ministers had already drawn in outline.

More succinctly: the answer to all problems of political philosophy was to be found in the Old Testament. Even Descartes, one of the great intellectual revolutionaries of the century, concluded his *Principes de la philosophie*, 'Above all, we will observe as an infallible rule that what God has revealed is incomparably more certain than all the rest.' Wherever its message reached, in history and philosophy as well as theology, the authority of the Bible was absolute.

As S. Toulmin and J. Goodfield have shown in *The Discovery of Time* (1965), the universe of the early seventeenth century was, by modern standards, extraordinarily circumscribed in space and time. The earth was its centre. In other words, the whole purpose of the cosmos centred upon man, the only rational being on the only inhabited planet. The stars – whether or not they were still believed to be fixed to crystalline spheres – were very near; comets and other such warnings and messengers practically brushed the earth. Man's knowledge of terrestrial geography had been revolutionized in the comparatively recent past and, by the end of the seventeenth century, world maps were tolerably accurate, so far as the great land-masses were concerned, though many Pacific islands were still unknown. Then as now, accounts of voyages of exploration made exciting reading and Hakluyt and his fellow-chroniclers commanded a wide public. Such vicarious travel no doubt helped to broaden many European minds, but the full significance of the trans-oceanic world could not be appreciated until travellers were replaced by residents with the time, interest and ability to investigate newly-discovered civilizations. It was not until towards the end of the seventeenth century that anthropological information was available in sufficient quantity to exercise a marked influence on European ways of thought.

Voyages of discovery led to an impressive knowledge of coastlines, but in the interior there were enough blank spaces on the maps for tales of monsters to be credible: a unicorn is, after all, scarcely less improbable than a giraffe or a coelacanth, and our own age has its doubts about the Abominable Snowman. But the greater part of the globe seemed only

marginally relevant to the European Christian, heir to the
traditions of Israel and the exclusive fraternity of the Church.
Beyond Europe lay the old Islamic enemy, the instrument by
which God had from time to time chastised his people. Merchants and missionaries were beginning to describe a mighty
Chinese Empire far to the East. But the greater part of the
extra-European world contained only 'savages' whose conversion was one of the more unexpected duties imposed by
the unfolding of the divine purpose. The educated European
had therefore virtually no standards of comparison outside his
own society and the classical antiquity on which it modelled
itself. Little was known of the ancient civilizations of Egypt
and Mesopotamia, or of contemporary societies in different
parts of the globe, and from the viewpoint of intolerant
Christendom such evidence was mainly useful as a warning
of the aberrations into which man inevitably fell when bereft
of divine guidance.

This circumscribed universe had had a comparatively
recent beginning and was hastening towards an even nearer
end. The Creation, it was generally agreed – for here Revelation silenced Aristotle and his eternal universe – took place
around 4004 B.C. The greater part of the ensuing period was
lost to human curiosity, apart from such evidence as was preserved in the Old Testament, 'for all other histories are but
late in respect of the sacred story.' Secular texts threw a dim
light as far back as 400 B.C. or thereabouts, but the rest was
darkness. Large parts of the Christian era itself were scarcely
better known, a few facts – or myths – emerging from the
shapeless sands of time. Although it was generally regarded
as fruitless, if not actually impious, to try to determine when
this brief universe would come to its apocalyptic close, there
was general agreement that the fatal date could not be far
distant. This was a theme that contemporary writers seem to
have found particularly moving. For Raleigh, for example,
'the long day of mankind' was 'drawing fast towards an

evening and the world's tragedy and time near at an end.'
Sir Thomas Browne sounded the same note of pessimistic
resignation:

We cannot hope to live so long in our names, as some have done in
their persons, one face of Janus holds no proportion unto the other.
'Tis too late to be ambitious. The great mutations of the world are
acted, or time may be too short for our designs.

The new telescopes, which had revealed the existence of sun-
spots, suggested that decay was already well-advanced in the
heavens themselves – for scientific evidence can only answer
the questions that scientists think fit to ask.

If man's share in the history of the universe, both as individual and as species, seemed incomparably greater than
would now be recognized, his narrower horizons offered
little for his comfort. Corrupted almost from the beginning
of time, his brief sojourn in a vale of tears was a mere prelude
to that Last Judgment where many would be called but few
chosen. The destiny of the vast majority of mankind was an
eternity of torment. Sir Thomas Browne, who seemed
reasonably confident that he himself would 'bring up the rear
in heaven', regarded this future prospect as the only thing
that made earthly existence tolerable. 'Certainly there is no
happiness within this circle of flesh, nor is it in the optics of
these eyes to behold felicity.' 'Were there not another life
that I hope for, all the vanities of this world should not en-
treat a moment's breath from me: could Death work my
belief to imagine I could never die, I would not outlive that
very thought.' Others, less sanguine about their more distant
prospects, shared his disparaging view of their present
existence. Everyday occurrences were in many respects incomprehensible and often regarded as the sinister product of
maleficent occult forces. Superstitious fear had spread its poison
over Europe since the more rational days of the later middle
ages. The sixteenth and early seventeenth centuries were the

great age of witchcraft trials; in Languedoc alone, 400 sorcerers were burned in 1577. There were, it is true, some sceptical voices, but they risked accusations of heresy, for to dispute the existence of pacts with the Devil seemed to cast doubt on the existence of the Evil One himself. In 1584 Bishop Jewell preached before Queen Elizabeth that witchcraft had increased enormously in the previous four years. The storms which delayed the return of James I to Scotland a few years later were an obvious product of sorcery for which many were burned. Recurrent outbreaks of plague in England and the frightful destruction of the Thirty Years War in Germany afforded more tangible reminders of the wrath of God and the vulnerability of fallen man, for whatever happened was evidence of the divine scheme. Bossuet spoke for his generation when he wrote,

This long sequence of particular causes which make and break empires, depends on the secret commands of divine Providence. . . . What our uncertain councils mistake for chance is a design elaborated in a higher council, in that eternal council which comprises all causes and effects within a single unity. In this way all things work together to the same end and it is because we fail to understand the whole that we see chance and irregularity in particular occurrences. That is why all who govern feel themselves subject to a more powerful force. What they do is always more or less than they intend and their plans never fail to have unforeseen consequences. There is no human force which, despite itself, does not serve other intentions. Only God knows how to make all things subservient to his will.

Even a courtier like Saint-Simon, in the eighteenth century, considered that the number of tactical mistakes made by otherwise competent French generals before the battle of Blenheim was explicable only in terms of divine intervention.

It may well be that, for ordinary people, 'this circle of flesh' had more compensations than Sir Thomas Browne was prepared to concede, but as they picked their precarious way through an incomprehensible world, hell gaped literally

beneath their feet and their every thought and action was
under the scrutiny of a deity more just than merciful, en-
throned in a heaven that was very near.

During the seventeenth century these pessimistic certainties were gradually eroded by new knowledge and new ways
of looking at experience which brought first doubt and then,
gradually, unprecedented optimism concerning the nature of
man and his ability to shape his material and social environment to his own convenience. It has often been suggested
that advances in science, particularly in astronomy, were the
most effective agents of this change and the names of Galileo
and Newton have at times been brandished like battle-stand-
ards in the Holy War of science against superstition. This is at
best a most misleading over-simplification. It would be ridi-
culous to deny that the new heliocentric theory of the solar
system, expounded by Copernicus in 1543 and developed by
Galileo almost a century later, had far-reaching implications.
The question was not merely who revolved around whom,
nor were the occasional Old Testament texts that implied a
geocentric universe the real crux of the matter. The astronomical argument concerned the relationship between man
and nature. If the earth was in fact the centre, then man was
the lord of the universe, as the Greeks had assumed and the
Jewish-Christian tradition preached. If, on the other hand, the
earth was merely one planet orbiting a local star, it was an
easy transition to postulate innumerable similar planets scattered throughout the heavens. As astronomical observation
and calculation pushed back the limits of space to unimaginable dimensions and revealed myriads of unsuspected stars,
the idea of man as a uniquely significant being appeared increasingly presumptuous. The logical corollary to the new
astronomy was the publication in 1686 of Fontenelle's *De la
pluralité des mondes*.

To consider seventeenth-century science in this light, while

not wholly misleading, is nevertheless a modern anachronism. All, or almost all, the cosmologists were sincerely religious men, deeply convinced that their discoveries glorified
God by revealing the unsuspected grandeur of his Creation.
Galileo, in 1614, published *The Authority of Scripture*, in which
he tried to reconcile science with Revelation, and Newton
devoted many years to biblical studies. It is quite true that the
Roman Catholic Church, provoked by Bruno, an ex-Dom-
inican who had renounced Christianity, and perhaps by
Galileo too, unwisely threw its spiritual authority behind the
geocentric theory and thereby committed itself to a hopeless
battle which it might perhaps have avoided. If it had been
prepared to concede that the occasional passages in the Old
Testament which implied that the sun went round the earth
were no more than figures of speech, or homely simplifica-
tion for the ignorant, the new cosmology might have become
the new orthodoxy, with Galileo a second Aristotle. The
Protestant Churches – certainly no less devoted to the literal
interpretation of scripture – experienced no insuperable difficulty in coming to terms with Copernicus. In England at
least, his theory seems to have been regarded in the early years
of the century as an interesting paradox. Donne, in *Ignatius his
Conclave* (1611), whilst including Copernicus amongst the
troublesome innovators, rejected his claim to pre-eminence
in hell on that account.

What cares he [Lucifer] whether the earth travel, or stand still?
Hath your raising up of the earth into heaven brought men to that
confidence, that they build new towers [of Babel] or threaten God
again? Or do they out of this motion of the earth conclude that there
is no hell, or deny the punishment of sin? Do not men believe? Do
they not live just, as they did before? Besides ... those opinions of
yours may very well be true.

It is difficult to quarrel with Donne's conclusion. Seventeenth-century science seemed to reinforce religious faith by
revealing new principles of order in natural phenomena,

suggesting the presence of a divine architect of infinite virtuosity. Harvey's explanation of the circulation of the blood could be – and later was – interpreted in a mechanistic sense. It certainly challenged the authority of Galen. But so long as there was no evolutionary theory to explain how complex forms of life could evolve from more simple ones, each new proof of ecological balance or functional harmony seemed another verse in the hymn of nature to its omniscient creator. In implication at least, the most disturbing scientific discoveries were those in geology. Evidence of the rise and fall of the earth's surface was difficult to fit into the 6,000-year span that the Old Testament allowed. Fossil remains of extinct species were equally disconcerting. These first hints of a new chronology and of evolution concerned aspects of life about which a head-on confrontation of science and Revelation was eventually inevitable. For the moment, however, the discovery of marine fossils far above sea-level looked more like scientific proof of the Flood, and Burnet's *Sacred Theory of the Earth* (1681) reconciled science and scripture to most men's satisfaction for another century.

More immediately unsettling was a growing tendency to see European (i.e. Christian) civilization in a world (i.e. pagan) context. The sixteenth century had been excited by discovery, as the limits of the known world were driven back. But merchants, seamen and military adventurers were on the whole indifferent anthropologists. Soon, however, others settled in the new lands, acquired the local language, investigated these alien cultures and eventually published their findings in Europe. Works of this nature had an enthusiastic reception – one might almost regard them as the science-fiction of the seventeenth century – and under their influence scholars began also to look in a new way at civilizations with which they had long been familiar, such as Islam. What is significant for our present purpose is not so much the new information itself as its relation to European standards, the new attitudes which it helped to foster and which in turn prompted new enquiries.

It is impossible here to do more than hint at the complexity of these distant influences, which have been affecting European art and thought ever since, and will recur throughout the present book. We may, for convenience, divide the alien cultures into two crude categories, the 'primitive' and the 'civilized'. Of the latter, China was unquestionably the most important. The very existence of the enormous 'middle kingdom', heir to a longer tradition of continuous civilization than Europe itself, and from 1644, under the vigorous new Manchu dynasty, asserting once more its view of itself as the world's centre, posed unprecedented problems for Europe. Bossuet, in his *Histoire universelle* (1681), one of the synoptic histories in which the century delighted, deployed considerable erudition to show how gentile and Jewish-Christian history were interwoven to serve as a vehicle for the operation of divine providence. His readers may well have asked themselves what was the 'purpose' of the Chinese. An idealized Confucianism came to be equated with the pagan values of ancient Rome, and free-thinkers, disconcerted by the fall of the Roman Empire, could now point to China for proof that their secular values were no less politically effective than Christian ones. The Chinese millennia themselves constituted another problem for, to quote Voltaire, 'authentic histories trace this nation back, through a sequence of 36 recorded eclipses of the sun, to a date earlier than that which we normally attribute to the Flood'. From whatever angle one regarded the Chinese phenomenon, it was impossible to reconcile it with the traditional picture of European history and society.

Primitive societies posed different, but equally disturbing problems. It was something of a strain on credulity to imagine the Flood operating on the far shore of the Atlantic. The issue was not so much what was possible – for the Flood in any event required a miraculous explanation – but what seemed probable. Raleigh reported of the American Indians, 'We found the people most gentle, loving and faithful, void of all guile and treason, and such as live after the manner of the golden age.' Lahontan, in 1703, launched the conception of the *bon sauvage* leading a moral life by the light of natural religion. Original sin, which conformed to the ideas European society entertained about itself, seemed almost to have spared these more fortunate sons of Adam. Equally disquieting were the ideas Europeans were beginning to form about primitive religions. Awkward resemblances to classical mythology and Jewish or Christian antecedents raised doubts about the unique, God-given character of European faith.

As the cosmologists reduced the status of the earth to that of one planet among many, in a similar way these early anthropologists and their more philosophically-minded readers reduced the classical-Christian civilization and its history from being the story of the divine will made manifest, as Bossuet conceived it, to an account of one of the more fortunate branches of a numerous family. *Homo Europeensis* came gradually to believe that neither the world nor the universe revolved entirely round his collective person. Anthropological evidence provided grist for many mills. Descartes invoked the example of China, in his *Discours de la méthode* (1637), to prove that social habits varied, or, as Pascal was to put it twenty years later, 'three degrees of latitude reverse the whole of jurisprudence, a meridian decides about truth.' Locke, in particular, in his *Essay concerning Human Understanding* (1690), relied heavily on such evidence in order to deny the existence of innate ideas. Such examples suffice to show the extent to which educated opinion was aware of the intellectual challenge of non-European societies, a much more direct and fundamental challenge to traditional Christian beliefs than any which seemed likely to come from the scientists.

No less alarming was a new tendency for philosophers to

assume that human reason had no need of the supporting arm of theology to find its way to truth. Descartes, in his revolutionary *Discourse*, announced his intention of beginning by accepting nothing as true unless he himself had a clear and distinct perception of its veracity. What mattered to the defenders of orthodoxy was not the motivation of the philosophers, most of them – with the conspicuous exception of Hobbes – devout men who aspired to glorify God in their own way. From the viewpoint of the Christian churches their dismissal of the authority of the past was likely to bring down upon them the fate of Lucifer, as they presumed to weigh eternal truth in the balance of their own judgement. Such fears were, in fact, well-founded. However orthodox men like Descartes, Locke and Leibniz might be, their Christian orthodoxy was tacked on to systems of thought which were as logically viable without it. Granted the society in which they lived, philosophers who set about reconstructing the universe on the basis of reason and logic were likely to emerge with 'proofs' of the existence of God, the architect of the whole integrated pattern of experience. What was not logically deducible was the Jewish-Christian religion, with all its unique characteristics, still less the dogmatic niceties that distinguished one sect from another. And so we find the French Protestant refugee Pierre Bayle, whose personal beliefs are still the subject of controversy, proclaiming 'every individual dogma . . . is false when refuted by the clear and distinct perceptions of natural reason.' Descartes might have winced at such blasphemous progeny but he would have found it hard to deny his paternity. He himself, by the separation of life into spiritual and material categories, seemed to have excluded God from a material world regulated exclusively by secondary causes. In Descartes' mathematical universe, sin had almost been reduced to a miscalculation, 'since our will only exerts itself to pursue or avoid something, in proportion as our understanding represents the thing to the will as good or bad, good judgement suffices to ensure right action'. He repeated in a letter of 1644 that if we perceive something to be evil, 'it would be impossible for us to sin during the time that we see it in this way.' One is tempted to think that Bossuet had Descartes in mind when he wrote of the temptation of Adam and Eve, 'This is where the spirit of revolt begins: men argue about precept and their obedience is called into question. [Satan says] "You will be like gods, free and independent, wise and contented by your own efforts. You will understand good and evil; nothing will be beyond your comprehension." It is from these motives that man's mind challenges the order of creation and sets itself above the rule.' The Jewish philosopher, Spinoza, whose Cartesian reasoning led him to pantheism, affirmed that the Old Testament was no more than a history of the Jews, and no more accurate than any other history. Hobbes, in England, eliminated religion altogether as a source of moral values, and based ethics, as well as political theory, on the purely human urge towards self-preservation. Everyone found Hobbes an embarrassing ally, but Descartes and Spinoza were devout men who considered their reason as enlisted in the service of God. The Roman Church put all Descartes' works on the Index of prohibited books, but his influence permeated much of Christian Europe to an extent that would have been impossible if he had been an adversary of the faith. In Protestant states religious speculation penetrated far beyond the No Man's Land that theology had formerly permitted. Within Catholic Europe the defences of orthodoxy were less easily penetrated, especially by heretics, but the defenders themselves were so divided and confused by the rival claimants to leadership that faith became more a source of conflict than of unity. It was this dissension, rather than any onslaught from unbelievers, that contributed most to the decline of the intellectual authority of the churches in the seventeenth century.

One further aspect of the new learning deserves separate

mention since it affected both biblical and secular studies. Stimulated, perhaps, by the growing conviction that mere tradition conferred no authority, scholars began a more systematic scrutiny of the texts on which that tradition reposed. So far as the history of the Church was concerned, such studies were not altogether new. It was nevertheless significant of the new climate when Pierre Simon set about the examination of the scriptures themselves. His demonstration that the Old Testament was a much-rewritten work was bound to impair its authority as the product of Revelation and the literal word of God himself. So once again a writer who protested his Catholic orthodoxy found his work on the Index, and Simon's translation of the New Testament was also banned. Where secular history was concerned, the new scepticism had for some time been challenging the myths which more credulous generations had accepted as a matter of course. Brutus the Trojan, founder of Britain, had disappeared in the sixteenth century and now it was the turn of Arthur, whose exploits had until recently furnished the 'Matter of Britain'. The positive side to this *Götterdämmerung* was a new devotion to the collection and study of historical texts, typical of the age in its stern pursuit of accurate knowledge based on evidence, logic and probability, in preference to the colourful confusion of myth and legend that had satisfied a less critical age.

Such influences as these, and no doubt others besides, reinforced and modified each other. Unsavoury myths or ceremonies of primitive tribes, which resembled those of the classical world, provided ammunition for the Moderns in their significant attempt, towards the end of the century, to prove that contemporary writers had nothing to fear from comparison with those of Greece and Rome. Charles Perrault, for the Moderns, pointed to the dethronement of Aristotle, Hippocrates and Ptolemy by contemporary scientists, as further proof of the same thesis. The development of mathematics, on which astronomers relied, more than on their primitive telescopes, for their new syntheses, provided an instrument for the philosopher, an apparently infallible ladder of truth. Spinoza's *Ethics* was arranged entirely in terms of definitions, axioms, propositions and corollaries. The historian of an oriental people might find his researches conflicting with the accepted chronology of the Old Testament or challenging the cultural seniority of Israel. These various currents swirled in different and sometimes contradictory directions, as in the conflict between Cartesian and Newtonian physics. The one thing they had in common was their rejection of traditional assumptions and attitudes. This did not make for clarity. It was – and still is – impossible to detect a steady advance by the forces of any particular cause. We may, as historians, pronounce inevitable the victory of those who were going to win, but this is not very illuminating. For contemporaries, the picture was one of a confused *mêlée*, each protagonist lashing out at his particular opponent, where the dust of controversy and the claims of victory by almost all the contestants prevented anyone from having a clear idea of what was happening.

*

Signs of a loss of confidence were visible in much seventeenth-century writing. This was, of course, by no means true of everyone, and writers such as Pascal and Milton are a warning against trying to compress an age within an epigram. Nevertheless, men found it increasingly hard to offer rational justification for traditional beliefs, both secular and religious, and as the century wore on there were fewer who could accept Sir Thomas Browne's cheerful *Certum est quia impossibile est*. Reactions varied according to individual temperament, but there was a widespread preoccupation with the death and decline of empires, and of the globe itself. Donne, in *Ignatius his Conclave*, directed his censure against those who 'had so attempted any innovation in this life, that they gave an affront to all antiquity, and induced doubts, and anxieties, and scruples, and after, a liberty of believing what they would; at length established opinions directly contrary to all established before'. By the latter half of the century, faith and tradition were calling in the barbarian forces of reason to man their threatened frontiers. Bossuet commended royal succession by primogeniture in the male line not merely because such had been God's dispensation for Israel, but on grounds of practical expediency as well, apparently unaware that to invoke the second argument was to cast doubt on the sufficiency of the first.

Those who had no hesitation in preferring new knowledge to traditional credence found themselves little better off than the defenders of tradition. In this transitional age it was impossible for anyone to distinguish between science and superstition, except perhaps in his own specialist field of study. This is, of course, partially true of all ages. The present writer, who would be hard put to it to prove the heliocentric theory, confesses that in many parts of this book he has relied on information which he lacked either the time or the knowledge to verify for himself. He assumed the accuracy of what was reported as true by men who enjoyed the respect of colleagues in a position to challenge them – which is more or less what scholars have always done. In the seventeenth century there was a new concern to explain, that is, to account for phenomena in terms of natural causes instead of invoking the designs of providence. But in every chain of causation there were liable to be links that were untrue, or at best no more than probable. No one could be sure what to believe or how to establish criteria that would distinguish fact from fiction.

As Milton wrote at the beginning of the *History of Britain* which he published in 1670, 'The beginning of nations, those excepted of whom sacred books have spoken, is to this day unknown. Nor only the beginning, but the deeds also of many succeeding ages, yea, periods of ages, either wholly unknown, or obscured and blemished with fables.' Uncertain what to do about Brutus the Trojan and his numerous progeny, Milton finally decided to include them, on the ground that 'Relations heretofore accounted fabulous, have been after found to contain in them many footsteps and relics of something true, as what we read in poets of the Flood, and giants little believed, till undoubted witnesses taught us that all was not feigned.'

The extraordinary combination of what appears to us sense and nonsense, which was the best that an intelligent man could hope to achieve, is well illustrated by John Swan's *Speculum Mundi*, published by the Cambridge University Press in 1635. Swan denounced attempts to predict the end of the world as 'doting froth of some men's idle fancies' – but he was prepared to date its creation as precisely as 26 or 27 October! He believed in unicorns and mermen but not in the phoenix – since Noah would not have accepted in the ark an animal of which only one specimen existed. He was on the whole receptive to new knowledge. 'Although I be no Stoic to tie God's mighty hand to second causes, yet I verily suppose that all things are not beyond the course of nature which seem to be extraordinary: but even many strange seeming things are wrought by the power of nature.' As far as possible, he attempted to reconcile first and second causes; thus the rainbow was both a divine signal and the product of the refraction of light – which, as he saw, implied that there were rainbows before the Flood. The sensitivity of their organs might enable mermaids to foretell storms but they could not cause them. Swan welcomed recent astronomical discoveries, about which he was well-informed. He rejected the theories of Copernicus not from prejudice, but in part at least because he realized that Copernicus was mistaken in believing the rotation of the earth to be the cause of tides. Swan himself considered it 'not improbable that the waters are drawn by the power of the Moon'. One could go on almost indefinitely multiplying such examples of intelligent reasoning which often led to erroneous conclusions, such as his pithy comment that comets – correctly located in outer space – produce 'not only change of air but change of heirs also'.

From such reasonable absurdity not even the paladins of the 'scientific revolution' were exempt. Bacon shared Swan's belief in the maleficent influence of comets and Newton believed that Moses knew all about the heliocentric theory and the law of gravity. It was wholly typical of the age that Newton should have devoted years of study to an attempt to establish a scientific basis for the chronology of antiquity by applying his accurate knowledge of the precession of the equinox to defective documentary material. His conclusion was that the first celestial sphere was drawn in 939 B.C. by Chiron the centaur for the benefit of the Argonauts. It was Newton who wrote, 'If any question at any time arise concerning his [Christ's] interpretations we are to beware of Philosophy and vain deceit and oppositions of science falsely so called and to have recourse to the Old Testament.'

Not only were the findings of 'reason' fallible and controversial; where most successful in destroying accepted beliefs it had often no immediate answer to the problems which it raised. The indefatigable Bayle demolished all dogma with impartial enthusiasm only to arrive at the uncomfortable conclusion that 'the grounds for doubting are themselves doubtful; we must therefore doubt whether we ought to doubt'. Such was also the total scepticism of Molière's Don Juan, whom Sganarelle accused in a pregnant phrase of being *impie en médecine*. Anglican clergymen, grappling with the problem of reconciling divine mercy with the damnation of the great majority of men, were inclined to challenge the conventional attitude to hell. In so doing they upset the scheme of 'recompensive justice' on which, for Sir Thomas Browne at least, all morality depended. Growing scepticism about hell did not produce the popular saturnalia which were predicted in warnings similar to those directed nowadays against the abolition of capital punishment, but it did call in question the literal accuracy of the scriptures, which bishop Burnet (cautiously writing in Latin for private circulation amongst his friends) ventured to suggest contained an esoteric meaning hidden beneath tales intended merely for the vulgar. The demolition of historical myth looked like carrying away all of the early history of antiquity. If Greek and Roman authors were to be subjected to the criterion of seventeenth-century common sense, it was difficult to know where to stop. At which chapter did Livy turn from fable into history? Even the twentieth century does not seem quite sure. What was urgently needed in the seventeenth was a criterion of truth, a system by which the reliability of evidence could be checked and a new model of the universe gradually assembled from elements which had passed the new tests of credibility.

*

Looking back on the seventeenth century in the light of what followed, one can notice the evolution of certain attitudes which were gradually to spread and to fortify themselves with new evidence until they became the conscious principles of most educated men. The first problem was not so much the acquisition of knowledge, as of the means of distinguishing truth from plausible error. As science seemed to establish itself on an impregnable basis of experimentally verified fact, doubt and confusion eventually gave way to self-confidence, the belief that the unknown was merely the undiscovered, and the general assumption – unprecedented in the Christian era – that man was to a great extent the master of his own destiny. It will, I hope, already have become clear that this gradual and complex shift in the intellectual climate is not simply to be equated with a 'scientific revolution'. A generation after he had published his *Principia*, Newton was struggling to discover the exact plan of Solomon's temple, which he considered the best guide to the topography of heaven. One is at first tempted to regard the sudden scepticism about the existence of witchcraft, which spread rapidly in the second half of the century, as an indication of a more secular-minded approach to life. But laymen, rather than clergy, had been the most active witch-hunters; Puritanism, which is sometimes linked with the progress of science, had not distinguished itself in the matter of witchcraft; and the Spanish Inquisition had shown itself more judicious and sceptical. The remaining part of this chapter makes no pretence of explaining why, as the Marquis of Halifax complained, 'the world is grown saucy and expecteth reasons, and good ones too, before they give up their own opinions to other men's dictates, though never so magisterially delivered to them.' What follows is merely an attempt to draw attention to three men whose opinions were regarded by eighteenth-century opinion as particularly significant.

Francis Bacon (1561–1627), although his contemporaries were unaware of it, provided the following generation with a method of experiment and induction that seemed to offer an infallible means of distinguishing between truth and error. Bacon began by rejecting the authority of tradition in all branches of learning. His biography of Henry VII, in which the emphasis was on human causation rather than the unfolding of providential purpose, included the significant manifesto: 'Men have been kept back, as by a kind of enchantment, from progress in the sciences by reverence for antiquity, by the authority of men accounted great in philosophy, and then by general consent.' Bacon's radicalism was deliberately optimistic. He complained that the devotees of traditional learning 'tend to nothing less than a wicked effort to curtail human power over nature and to produce a deliberate and artificial despair. This despair in its turn confounds the promptings of hope, cuts the springs and sinews of industry, and makes men unwilling to put anything to the hazard of trial.' Although he himself was a sincere Christian, Bacon even hoped that applied science might free man from some of the burden of original sin. The Fall had involved the loss of man's control over nature which science could partially recover by 'a restitution and reinvigorating (in great part) of man to the sovereignty and power ... which he had in his first state of creation'. Full of confidence in the transformation that could be effected within a few years by an intensive national programme of scientific and technological research, Bacon already held many of the beliefs and assumptions that were to dominate the eighteenth century.

Sir Isaac Newton (1642–1727), although his greatest discoveries were perhaps the product of intuition, synthesis and mathematical calculation, rather than of induction from experiment, seemed to vindicate Bacon's view of the possibilities of science. Our concern here is less with Newton's contribution to physics than with the influence which he exerted on the intellectual climate of Europe. For this purpose, we may concentrate on his law of gravity. The beautiful simplicity of a single law which appeared to explain the operation of every kind of earthly and celestial movement was a triumphant example of the possibilities of the new learning. Human reason, operating by means of careful observation and checking its conclusions by further observation or experiment, could for the first time in the history of man reveal the mechanism of the natural world in which he had lived for so long like a fearful and wondering child. Nature, instead of being a mere collection of phenomena, a hotch-potch of occult influences or the canvas on which an inscrutable Providence painted its mysterious symbols, was a system of intelligible forces. God was a mathematician whose calculations, although infinite in their subtle complexity, were accessible to man's intelligence. What was still unknown could eventually be discovered. Pope's famous epigram

> Nature and Nature's laws lay hid in night,
> God said 'Let Newton be!' and all was light.

was only a half truth. Much still remained in darkness, but after Newton it seemed reasonable to hope that human effort would eventually penetrate every corner of the universe. Newton's friend Halley may be excused the abominable verse of the dedicatory ode with which he greeted the *Principia*:

> Here ponder too the laws which God,
> Framing the universe, set not aside
> But made the fixed foundation of his work. ...
> Matters that vexed the minds of ancient seers,
> And for our learned doctors often led
> To loud and vain contention, now are seen
> In reason's light, the clouds of ignorance
> Dispelled at last by science.

The new currents of thought all seemed to flow together in Newton's friend, John Locke (1632–1704). As a politician, Locke, a refugee in Holland from 1683 to 1688, was concerned in the movement which overthrew James II and put an end to Divine Right monarchy in England. Locke's second *Treatise on Civil Government* (1690) provided the theoretical justification for the contractual view of monarchy as a limited and revocable agreement between ruler and ruled, which had triumphed in England in 1688. Other works, on education, on toleration and on the reasonableness of Christianity, indicate the direction of his interests and the first in particular exercised a good deal of influence on succeeding generations. But perhaps the most important of all Locke's works, from the viewpoint of eighteenth-century Europe, was his *Essay Concerning Human Understanding*, first published in 1690. The essay sets out to discover what one might almost regard as the law of gravity controlling the formation of human ideas. Locke began by rejecting Descartes' assertion that ideas were innate. To prove his point he made intensive use of anthropological evidence from non-European societies. He then substituted his own view that ideas were either the direct products of sense-impressions – as a photographic film responds to light – or else of the reflection of the mind on such evidence as the senses provided. Moral values arose from sensations of pleasure and pain, the mind calling 'good' what experience showed to be productive of pleasure. Although Locke himself, like Bacon, Descartes and Newton, was careful to fit his theories within a Christian framework, the way was open for followers who made no such reservation to formulate an entirely mechanistic theory of moral values. The implications of Locke's philosophy were to dominate much eighteenth-century thought: toleration (since beliefs were largely a product of environment); acceptance of the potential equality of man, except as regards natural intelligence (since human differences were not due to hereditary distinctions of 'blood', but to differences of environment); the assumption that society, by the regulation of material conditions, could promote the moral improvement of its members; a new psychology and a new attitude to education, based on the belief that human irrationality was the product of erroneous associations of ideas, that had become fixed in childhood. Just as Newton had seemed to substitute a rational law of nature for unpredictable and often malevolent forces, Locke appeared to have disclosed the scientific laws of the human mind, which would allow men to reconstruct society on happier and more rational lines. As the influence of these two Englishmen spread through western Europe, men might well feel that they had crossed the threshold into a new age. The words of Locke, reflecting a new confidence in man and his future, spurred them on in pursuit of the modern Grail.

INTRODUCTION

The floating of other men's opinions in our brains makes us not one jot the more knowing, though they happen to be true. What in them was science, is in us but opinionatrety; whilst we give up our assent only to reverend names, and do not, as they did, employ our own reason to understand those truths which gave them reputation. Aristotle was certainly a knowing man, but nobody ever thought him so because he blindly embraced and confidently vented the opinions of another. ... In the sciences, every one has so much as he really knows and comprehends; what he believes only, and takes upon trust, are but shreds, which, however well in the whole piece, make no considerable addition to his stock who gathers them. Such borrowed wealth, like fairy money, though it were gold in the hands from which he received it, will be but leaves and dust when it comes to use.

PART ONE

A New Heaven and
a New Earth

Chapter 1

THE SOCIAL AND POLITICAL ENVIRONMENT, 1715-40

THE generation that separated the wars of Louis XIV from those of Frederick the Great was not, in any meaningful sense, an age of transition. It was an age of stability. There were constitutional and social conflicts in Sweden and Russia and dynastic changes in parts of Italy, but in most of Europe men expected continuity rather than change and their ambitions were conceived in terms of rearrangement rather than of transformation. This is not, of course, to imply that European society was static, but merely to reduce to their proper proportions the forces of change which were gradually inclining it in new directions. The identification of these forces and the assessment of their importance involve the kind of historical judgement which varies with the individual and the pre-occupations of his age; many present-day historians, however, would probably agree that three of the main factors were changes in population, economic developments and the growth of more professional government. None of these was new, and their influence at the time is easily exaggerated.

With relatively few exceptions, most European countries in the early eighteenth century produced slightly more food than was required for the subsistence of their populations. Demographic history is still in its infancy; the enormous fluctuation in the death rate from one village to another and from year to year, and the lacunae of the evidence make local studies arduous and sometimes inconclusive and generalizations tentative at best. It is likely that in much of Europe the population tended to rise until a bad harvest, or more catastrophic-

43

ally, a succession of bad harvests, reduced it abruptly by famine or the diseases which battened on malnutrition. A society of this kind had nothing in reserve to deal with calamities of natural or human origin. Some kinds of war produced a drastic fall in population, due not so much to casualties in battle as to the devastation of crops and the epidemics spread by soldiers and refugees. Plague was a haphazard but particularly deadly killer which seems to have been most virulent in the comparatively urban societies of the Mediterranean area.

Between 1715 and 1740 the general decline in the European population during the previous century seems to have been reversed. In Spain, Italy, Sweden, Germany, Hungary and Russia numbers began to grow again, although in most cases the 1740 figures were perhaps still below those of the early seventeenth century. In England, both birth and death rates rose quite steeply, allowing for only very slow growth. But after about 1730 the death rate began to fall sharply and the population gradually increased, a rate of growth that was to be maintained for generations. In Europe as a whole, the ground gained by 1740 still seemed to have been precariously won. Outbreaks of plague were fewer, but no one was to know that the great epidemics would not recur. A generation without warfare on the destructive scale of the past was, in fact, drawing to an end. What had happened seemed no more than the latest swing of the immemorial pendulum. Population was still, almost everywhere, regulated by the harvests and as vulnerable as it had been in the past. Contemporaries, less inclined than formerly to attribute whatever happened to Divine Providence, and increasingly convinced of the advantages of a rising population, became concerned at an increase so inconspicuous that many mistook it for a continuing decline. But facts, even if not recognized, produced certain inevitable consequences. Demand grew with numbers, prices began to rise again – especially towards the end of the period – and the economy of Europe recovered some of its lost buoyancy. All this, however, was so gradual, and the controlling factors were so familiar and uncertain that those who benefited from the turn of the tide had no means of guessing that it was about to flow with unprecedented force and for generation after generation.

The economy of every country with the partial exception of the Netherlands was predominantly agricultural and that of many almost wholly so. Towns, especially in eastern Europe, were few, small and isolated by poor communications. As late as 1780 the combined population of all the towns of Hungary was no more than 356,000: slightly more than half that of Paris and considerably less than half that of London. In Bohemia no town except Prague had 10,000 inhabitants. Warsaw, the capital of an extensive, if ramshackle state, had a population of less than 30,000. The urban population was much higher in the west, where France had a dozen towns of over 30,000 and Spain and Italy each nine over 40,000. Even in France, however, eighty-five per cent of the population lived in villages of 2,000 inhabitants or less, and the inland towns do not seem to have been expanding much.

Farming, the main preoccupation of all Europe, the one shield against famine and the source of such capital as was available for buying manufactured goods, was still conducted on traditional lines that had altered little since the Middle Ages. Yields were very low, not more than five or six times the original seed. Crop areas were limited by the shortage of manure which obliged farmers to leave a third or more of the land fallow. Livestock were of poor quality and few could be kept over the winter. Communal cultivation led the peasant to think in communal terms: the village community acted as a unit when it performed the customary labours of the seasons. The free villagers of western Europe, though acutely aware of their private ownership of land, were inclined to regard the harvest itself as in some sense collective property. Manorial

45

obligations, for some of which their liability was collective, perpetuated a certain medieval vagueness as to the individual's exclusive right to the disposal of his own property. Newer and more individualistic methods of farming were already practised in parts of the Netherlands and were spreading to England, whence they were eventually to return to the Continent. But by 1740 little had been done, certainly not enough to suggest that any 'agrarian revolution' was at hand. Enclosure Acts in England still averaged no more than three or four a year.

Industry was almost equally traditional in its methods, organization and outlook. Guild regulations, designed to regulate a static economy, perpetuated customary processes, restrained production and protected established interests. Large cities, which were generally capital cities supplying the needs of growing Courts and their increasingly urbanized nobility, contained as many domestic servants as artisans. Here and there examples of large-scale production were to be found, whose exceptional nature attracted the attention of gentleman-travellers: van Robais' textile factory at Abbeville, or the Lombe brothers' silk mill at Derby. These were numerically unimportant exceptions to the general rule. More significant was the creation of an important iron industry in the Urals by Peter the Great, as a deliberate act of state policy. Rulers fostered war industry, such as the great naval arsenals at Toulon and Brest. Nobles developed industry for profit. It has been said of the revival of the Bohemian glass industry that it 'increased the influence of the aristocracy and retarded the liberation of the bourgeoisie'. There was as yet no serious evidence of the rise of any manufacturing class with its ambitions linked to machinery and an indefinite increase of production. Even in England, the expansion of industrial output between 1715 and 1740 has been estimated at less than one per cent a year.

Only in oceanic commerce was there any indication of a

rate of change so considerable as to suggest a modification in
the balance of social forces. British overseas trade increased by
about one-half during this period. French foreign trade, beginning at a very much lower level after the wars of Louis
XIV, more than doubled in the next forty years. The new
development, which was eventually to stimulate domestic
industry – for example, in order to compete with fine-quality
Indian cotton goods – seems to have been felt most strongly
along the Atlantic and Channel coasts and to have had less
effect in the Mediterranean. Ports such as Liverpool and
Bristol, Nantes and Bordeaux, sprang up or were transformed. In them, as in London, wholesale merchants developed a new self-confidence that matched their standard of
living and awareness of their increased importance to the
national economy. The opening scene of George Lillo's
London Merchant, published in 1731, includes the significant
claim, 'As the name of merchant never degrades the gentleman, so by no means does it exclude him', and goes on to
observe that the state and bank of Genoa 'prefer the friendship of the merchants of London to that of the monarch who
proudly styles himself King of both Indies'. Socially as well as
economically, commercial developments accentuated the
growing difference between the maritime areas of the west
and the inward-looking mass of eastern Europe which was
following a different path.

From about the sixteenth century the landed aristocracy
of most of eastern Europe had begun to reverse the general
trend towards the emancipation of a formerly servile peasantry. Encouraged by a growing market for corn, they increased
the labour-service of their serfs and used their local influence
to deprive free peasants of their status. In weak monarchies
such as Poland they exploited their political influence to become virtual rulers over their estates; where monarchy was
gaining in strength and efficiency, as in Brandenburg-
Prussia, they were able to strike a bargain, surrendering their

traditional claim to a share in the control of central policy in return for exemption from new taxation and a relatively free hand on their own estates. In Russia, somewhat different causes produced similar effects, serfdom being much extended by Peter the Great, partly to facilitate the taxation of elusive peasants and partly to compensate nobles for the state service that was now required of them. East of the Elbe the whole economy came to be dominated by the special conditions of serfdom and an alliance of political power with the economic interests of a landed aristocracy. Over-taxed, faced with fiscally-privileged competition from the serf-industries of the great noble estates, unable to attract tied labour from the countryside, the towns failed to develop or actually declined. The forces of economic competition were arrested or distorted and the artificial system tended to perpetuate itself. Capital cities grew with the exigencies of encroaching government, but elsewhere conditions were highly unfavourable to the growth of an educated urban society with more than parochial interests. Magnates came within the cultural attraction of Courts, but the rural squirarchy was left to its bucolic pursuits – the Squire Westerns were, in fact, mostly eastern – and the middle classes of the vegetating towns had rarely the opportunity or the incentive to join in the growing intellectual exchanges of the West.

Probably the most active of the forces of change, certainly the one most visibly effective at the time, was the development of more professional forms of central government. This was a complicated process, each country evolving at a different pace and in ways peculiar to itself. Normally associated with the victory of royal absolutism, the trend could accommodate itself to a political movement in the opposite direction, as happened in Britain. Whatever its political complexion, the state was increasingly asserting itself as an impersonal force with its own machinery directed by its professional servants.

In most of Europe government had ceased to be a partnership between rulers and great magnates whose birth conferred office as well as economic power and social status. Leading Ministers might be noblemen or princes of the Church but they owed their position to the unfettered choice of the ruler, and their power to the efficiency of the administrative machine which they controlled. By present-day standards the bureaucratic process had not developed very far. Court life implied the possibility of courtiers by-passing the administration by a direct appeal to the ruler, whose Divine Right was superior to any legal precedent. It was wiser, even in the eighteenth century, for the prince to deal cautiously with great territorial magnates whose influence in their own areas might frustrate, if it could no longer defy, the authority of the state. The more humble the origin of Ministers, the more their borrowed plumage trembled in the fickle winds of royal favour. Some might unwisely triumph in their hour but many would attempt to safeguard the future by judicious favours and marriage alliances to nobles whose positions rested on more enduring foundations. Most aspired to place their children high in the social rather than the bureaucratic order. The most striking change was perhaps to be seen at a lower level, in the organization of government and the assumptions behind it. The state service was increasingly becoming a career for able men. Its steady expansion inclined it to undertake new activities suggested by the changing attitude to government itself. Gradually it began to accumulate the statistical evidence which made domestic policy possible. A new dimension was added to the ruler's customary preoccupation with war, foreign policy and the management of his own estates and traditional sources of revenue. As the state's agents established themselves throughout the land they provided new sources of information and the means of influencing what had previously to be left to tradition, nature and Providence.

As governments became more powerful they were able to

embark on more ambitious – and more expensive – policies. From the mid-seventeenth to the mid-eighteenth centuries in particular, their administrative potential was inclined to exceed their fiscal resources. The immense palace that housed both Court and government at Versailles, which cost Louis XIV about eighty million livres (roughly four million pounds), is the most obvious example of royal magnificence, imitated on a smaller scale by many petty German princes. As early as 1689 the silver furniture of Versailles had to be melted down to pay for the costs of war. The new professional armies, of unprecedented size, cost more than the palaces, and it was even more difficult to retire from military than from architectural competition. By the early eighteenth century, Britain and France were the only major Powers that could wage sustained war without foreign subsidies.

If the new states failed to cover their expenses by taxation, it was not for want of trying. State taxation increased enormously – in France the main tax on the peasantry, the *taille*, was quadrupled during the seventeenth century – while the billeting of the new armies imposed a very heavy additional burden. The administrative revolution took place within a socially conservative society in which the peasantry continued to pay manorial dues to lords whose protective role had been assumed by the state. The result of such heavy taxation and economically unproductive expenditure was probably to restrict growth, especially in states such as Prussia where the efficiency of government contrasted most harshly with the poverty of local resources. Over much of Europe there was a running fight between governments and the medieval Estates which claimed the right to assent to new taxation. These Estates were in most cases dominated by the nobility who resented both their increasing exclusion from political power and the state's competition for the taxable surplus of the peasants. The aristocratic reaction was strong enough to resist and sometimes temporarily to reverse the trend towards bureaucratic absolutism; in France, Russia and Sweden the death of an autocrat was followed by an attempt to put the clock back, while in Hungary the Magyar nobility waged a continuous war of attrition against Habsburg centralization. But where the nobility fought a purely defensive battle it could do no more than postpone its defeat. In the one country where it succeeded in permanently asserting the claims of a traditional elected body, the English nobility was less socially and fiscally separate from the rest of the community and perhaps more ready to adapt itself to the new forms of government and the burdens which they involved.

It will have become apparent that these forces of change reacted upon each other to create a bewildering variety of combinations defying any simple theories of historical causation. The 'natural' development of one society threw up industrial techniques or forms of government whose efficiency might lead rulers to attempt to impose them on quite different societies, creating in the process new tensions and unique developments. To imprison this living reality within the fetters of a materialist or idealist explanation is to deprive it of much of its meaning. By the use of foreign advisers Peter the Great transformed the administrative structure of Russia which in turn enabled him to modify the economic development of the country. Population was affected by state policy: Bourbon centralization led to the flight of Protestant refugees from France, who were settled in Brandenburg by Hohenzollern absolutism. Moreover, similar forces could produce very different results in different societies. Increasing demand for the products of industry might attract free labour from the country to the towns, whereas serf-labour could merely be transferred from farm to manorial factory. A rise in food prices might benefit the yeoman farmer in the West; in the East it would tend to increase the labour-services imposed on the serf and the pressure to reduce free peasants to servile status. As the effective power of despotic monarchy increased, the importance of the ruler's own character tended to grow with it, for the state machinery still depended for its dynamism, if not for the routine business of administration, on the man who wore the crown. One of the main reasons for the relative stability of the early eighteenth century derived from the unadventurous policies pursued for different reasons by Walpole in England, Fleury in France, Frederick William I of Brandenburg-Prussia, Charles VI the Habsburg Emperor and the successors to Peter the Great in Russia. These rulers, however sympathetically they responded to new ideas, were primarily concerned with the specific problems of their own states, each the product of a unique historical evolution. To appreciate the receptivity of the various European states to the ideas of the Enlightenment it is therefore necessary to look briefly at some of their outstanding characteristics which led them to respond in different ways to the influence of new attitudes and new material forces.

*

France, although ineffectually ruled for most of the century, remained potentially the most powerful state in Europe, on account of its size, relative unity, fertility and consequent population. The development of its overseas trade and colonial empire exposed it to some of the influences which were characteristic of the Netherlands and, to a lesser extent, of Britain, while official social attitudes, especially the entrenched privilege of the nobility, aligned it with the Continental monarchies. It was in France that the new form of bureaucratic government was most highly developed. A swollen civil service, an extraordinary proliferation of law courts and a numerous and relatively educated clergy provided a considerable literate public. A dozen *parlements*, or appeal courts, maintaining a vociferous fight against royal absolutism, kept alive a spirit of controversy whose wider political implications were never far below the surface. The disgruntled *parlements* and a divided Church weakened the authority of the state and offered at least the possibility that critical writers might find protectors amongst their disunited opponents. Censorship was theoretically strict and could prove ferocious to the man without connexions, but by publication abroad, by a pretence of anonymity and the manipulation of influence, the enterprising writer could generally thread his way through. The Paris salons then assured the dissemination of his ideas with remarkable speed.

For most of the century France was the cultural dictator to Continental Europe, and to a lesser extent, to Britain also. Court society, and increasingly, bourgeois society also, looked to France as the model of taste in literature, art, architecture, in the new refinement of social behaviour that had grown up at Versailles with all its ancillary arts of furniture, dress and cuisine. A French architect was to write in 1765, 'Travel through Russia, Prussia, Denmark, Württemburg, the Palatinate, Bavaria, Spain, Portugal and Italy, everywhere you will find French architects in the highest places. . . . Paris is to Europe what Athens was to Greece.' The dolls of the French fashion-designers were awaited with impatience throughout well-dressed Europe. Everyone who could afford it employed a French chef. French had replaced Latin as the common European language. Even Frederick William I, who is usually regarded as the embodiment of the Prussian spirit, spoke better French than German. The Habsburg government often wrote to its ambassadors in French and the German used at the Viennese Court was absurdly distorted by French importations. As a Sussex landowner wrote to his son, 'A man who understands French may travel all the World over without hesitation of making himself understood, and may make himself perfectly agreeable to all Good Company, which is not the case of any other Language whatever.' What was doubly a *lingua franca* ensured the rapid dissemination of ideas. Anything published in French was immediately accessible to educated Europe, and what was not originally written in French was soon translated into the universal language.

In Britain, royal absolutism had been successfully tamed by aristocratic and popular resistance and the resulting compromise guaranteed to all a degree of civil liberty that was the envy of the rest of Europe. The nobles were too few to constitute a ruling class – for most of the century there were less than two hundred peers. Britain differed significantly from the rest of Europe in limiting hereditary nobility to a single heir. One consequence of this was the existence of the typically vague British category of gentleman, so different from the specifically noble French *gentilhomme*. Gentlemen might be great landowners connected with the peerage by birth and marriage, prosperous merchants, or impecunious writers like Dr Johnson. All shared in the observance of a code of honour and none enjoyed the kind of formal privileges which divided noble from commoner in Continental Europe. The point was well made by Smollett: Peregrine Pickle, at the theatre in Paris, was incensed to see a respectable citizen humiliated by a *musquetaire* who 'turned to one of his companions, and with an air of disdainful ridicule, told him he was like to have had an affair with a Bourgeois; adding, by way of heightening the irony, "Egad! I believe he's a physician."' This was too much for the irascible Pickle, who intervened with the very British comment, 'Sir, a physician may be a man of honour.' British society gained enormously in cohesion – and in ability to resist change – from the fact that men of education and influence were not divided from each other by a crucial hereditary barrier. There remained, of course, a very pronounced social hierarchy, and the pursuit of places, favours and influence by the cultivation of connexions was one of the main activities of the ambitious gentleman, but this was a means to advancement that did not involve any admission that the owner of the ante-chamber where one kicked one's heels belonged to an order of society that was almost biologically distinct from one's own. Where the code of honour did not apply, British attitudes were nearer to those of the rest of western Europe, if we can take as typical the philandering of Peregrine Pickle and his friend Gauntlet. 'Our adventurers, wild and licentious as they were, governed their actions by certain notions of honour. ... Among the lower class of people, they did not act with the same virtuous moderation, but laid close siege to every buxom country damsel that fell in their way; imagining that their dalliance with such Dulcineas could produce no fatal effects, and that it would be in their power to atone for any damage these inamoratas might sustain.'

Wealth, lack of censorship, freedom from the cultural domination of an overpowering Court and informal social relationships in country areas where the gentry were mindful of the need to cultivate an electorate, produced an unusually wide dissemination of culture. London had its first daily newspaper as early as 1702 and there were a score more in the capital by the end of the century. By 1727 there were twenty-five newspapers printed in the provinces and in 1753 stamp duty was paid on over seven million newspapers. The *Gentleman's Magazine* had a circulation of 10–15,000. The 'moral weeklies', which were a marked feature of the first half of the eighteenth century, appear to have begun in England, where over 200 were founded. The *Tatler* and the *Spectator* had a nation-wide readership and contributed to the refinement of manners as well as to the dissemination of literary news. Many of the gentry had good libraries and circulating libraries were already springing up in the more important spas. Even the daughters of substantial farmers were being educated at boarding schools by the end of the century and the general level of literacy was, by European standards, very high. This lively society was partially shielded from French cultural domination by national rivalry and by the vigour of its own literary and intellectual tradition. In Newton, Locke and Pope it had produced three men of the first stature and by mid-century its novelists were popularizing a new genre throughout Europe. Links with the Continent, especially with France, were, however, probably closer than at any subsequent period. English men of letters were almost as much at home in Paris as in London. When Gibbon began to write a history of Switzerland, he composed it in French, 'because I think in French and, strange as it may seem, I can say, with some shame but no affectation, that it would be a matter of difficulty to me to compose in my native language.' European works of consequence were translated into English over and over again – ten English translations of Montesquieu's *De l'esprit des lois* appeared within twenty-five years of its publication. Britain was an integral part of the European cultural movement and Britain and France together provided the main impetus behind the Enlightenment.

Across the North Sea, the United Provinces, a federation of seven states, of which Holland was by far the most important, presented a strange contrast of economic pioneering and political antiquarianism. Holland, in particular, was a highly urbanized mercantile community of immense wealth. Its cities, renowned both for commerce and learning, were linked by cheap and frequent transport along the canals which were both an example of successful technology and a stimulus to economic development. Although the Dutch had lost their overwhelming predominance in the European carrying trade, their East India Company, as late as 1743, was considered by an English writer to be 'undoubtedly richer and more powerful than the English'. Amsterdam, a city of 200,000 whose construction over marsh and water was itself no mean technical achievement, remained the financial capital of Europe. Politically, however, the Union still seemed to be living in the Middle Ages. The old struggle between the House of Orange and the patrician oligarchies which ruled the towns showed no signs of leading to any conclusion. Their 'High Mightinesses', the members of the Estates General, despite their title, were no more than ambassadors from their provinces, to which they had to refer back all important business. The provincial Estates in turn were weak federal bodies, real power residing in the more important towns. Representative government, in the Netherlands even more than in England, was based on respect for traditional rights rather than on any conception of popular sovereignty. The mere idea of majority rule was alien to a community which evolved its policies by a laborious process of compromise between local interests.

The Netherlands in the early eighteenth century were still one of the most active intellectual centres of Europe. At Leiden they had a university with a Continental reputation. Stimulated by French Protestant refugees, the Dutch publishing industry supplied fine type and Asiatic characters to the rest of Europe, besides printing some of the most famous books of the century for French authors intent on evading censorship. But although the special contribution of the Netherlands to the cultural life of Europe remained much the same, Dutch society itself was losing some of its peculiar characteristics. The thrift and sobriety of the seventeenth-century Calvinists were giving way to more aristocratic habits. Dutchmen were more ready to invest their savings abroad and a wealthy rentier class felt fewer inhibitions about letting its affluence show in country houses, luxurious yachts – the local equivalent of carriages – and fine clothes. Economic activity, taste and way of life all brought the wealthy society of the Netherlands into closer contact with the rest of Europe and Dutch idiosyncrasy increasingly conformed to the general pattern of European culture. The anonymous English writer of 1743 reported that the Opera House at The Hague was 'more frequently used for French comedies'.

South of the Pyrenees one seemed almost to enter a new

continent, although a Bourbon ruled in Madrid, and Spain was increasingly drawn into the French political orbit. Since the reign of Philip II political power had been centralized under the king, as it was later to be in France, but the social structure of the two countries was very different. Four great Spanish families owned one third of the cultivable land of the entire country. Over most of Spain the gap between the magnates (*titulos*) and the *hidalgos* or squirarchy suggested eastern rather than western Europe. The proportion of nobles, most of them impoverished, was about three times that in France. Since these nobles tended to prefer town life, Spain had a relatively high urban population, but little industry or commerce and an insignificant middle class.

Many factors made the country somewhat impervious to foreign influences, not least its memories of past greatness and native literary tradition. The French language found it harder to penetrate than in almost any other civilized country. Lord Chesterfield, who thought it rather odd that Lord Huntingdon should go to Spain at all, advised him to take a Spanish master before crossing the Pyrenees since 'even the people of quality speak no other languages'. Translations into Spanish were relatively few and Spanish isolation from the main cultural trends of Europe had brought intellectual stagnation. When Newton was ousting Descartes over most of the Continent, Spain was still finding Copernicus too revolutionary. The university of Salamanca, indeed, had eliminated the study of both Newton and Descartes in favour of Aristotle, who was more easily reconciled with Revelation. Until 1763 no Greek, Hebrew or Arabic type had been cast in Spain. The Church, the main source of such intellectual life as there was, tended to identify foreign with heretical and to wield its effective censorship with more thoroughness than discrimination. Contemporaries were perhaps a little too sweeping in their condemnation: the French ambassador in 1759 described Spain as 'at least two centuries behind every other country' and

Chesterfield a few years earlier had been even more violent: 'Spain is surely the only country in Europe that has been barbarizing itself every day more and more in proportion as all the other countries have civilized themselves.' The second half of the century was to show that centres of education and enlightenment did exist, but they were few and scattered and never succeeded in imposing their influence on the country as a whole. For the writers of the rest of Europe Spain was essentially the country of the Inquisition, a dreadful compound of poverty, ignorance and fanaticism.

Across the Rhine from France, the situation was much more varied and complex. Germany consisted of a few sizable states and hundreds of petty principalities, free cities and Imperial Knights. The Holy Roman Empire did not exactly correspond to the areas inhabited by German-speaking peoples and the Habsburg territories sprawled well beyond both. In a region so wide and so politically fragmented, conditions varied almost from one extreme to the other. Hamburg was a great trading city and Hanover came under the influence of the dynastic link with Britain; in the south-west the agrarian economy was similar to that of France and the rulers looked to Paris for protection and subsidies; east of the Elbe a servile peasantry symbolized a very different economic and social structure.

Despite so much diversity, some common characteristics were to be found in most of Germany. Signs of economic development were harder to perceive than in Britain and France. Most towns declined or stagnated as economic units, though Vienna and Berlin grew in importance as the administrative centres of major Powers and a few cities maintained a precarious activity as the artificial creations of petty Courts. Almost all the remaining towns were dominated by patrician oligarchs who owned most of the urban property and had frequently bought estates in the surrounding country and retired from trade. The guilds which provided for the social life as well as the economic interests of their members, were forces of resistance to change. In Court-towns such as Stuttgart, with 250 tailors to a population of 18,000, or Munich, where there were more goldsmiths than cloth-makers, the domination of urban life by princes and nobles must have seemed almost a law of nature. Many of the German nobility lived no better than British tenant-farmers and it was perhaps this which led some to compensate for their shortage of acres by stressing the length of their lineage. Candide's master, the Baron of Thunder-ten-Tronckh, 'one of the most important lords of Westphalia, for his château had both a door and windows', was suspected of rejecting a suitor for his sister's hand who could prove no more than 71 quarterings. If Voltaire's caricature seems dubious evidence, other sources are not lacking. 'I am a great prince and have adopted the forms of government which befit a great prince, like others of my kind.' This champion of the new absolutism was Eberhard Louis, Duke of Württemberg, who ruled over a population equal to that of Paris. These Lilliputian rulers took a serious view of their dignity; there were 200 officials at the tiny Court of Weimar and the financing of armies of a few hundred men formed a source of endless contention between these would-be despots and their medievally-minded Estates.

In some respects the fragmentation of Germany proved culturally stimulating, universities and Court orchestras serving as symbols of status: there were no less than 37 universities within the Holy Roman Empire and another 5 in the German-speaking territories beyond; Saxony, with a population of only two million, maintained three universities. In the brilliant Saxon Court at Dresden, the Elector boasted in 1716 an orchestra of 65, a French choir of 20, a French ballet of 60 and a theatre company of 27. Some of his Ministers also had their own private orchestras. Musicians probably benefited most from the competition for their services and their ability to move from one patron to another, music being the only branch of the arts in which fashionable society accepted German talent as superior to French. Even the Prussian martinet, Frederick William I, who regarded Courts and Court culture as wasting precious money that could have been spent on the army, made an exception where music was concerned. Writers found the political climate less congenial. Courtiers must have French literature and French plays. Contempt for German culture reached its peak with Frederick the Great, who excluded Lessing from his Academy and rejected the proposal to offer the direction of the royal library to Winckelmann at a salary of 2,000 thalers, on the ground that 'one thousand are enough for a German'. The urban middle classes provided a public of sorts for local newspapers, literary reviews and 'moral weeklies', but the best-known literary review, the *Litteratur-Zeitung*, had a circulation of only 2,000 and most of the 'moral weeklies' were ephemeral productions. As late as the 1760s the total number of books printed in Germany was no higher than it had been at the beginning of the seventeenth century. Serious authors, whose successful works were unprotected by any effective copyright, found it impossible to live by their pens. One of the best-selling books printed in Germany was, typically enough, Peplier's French grammar. The German cultural revival did not really get under way until the second half of the century.

Two predominantly German states stood out from the rest: the Habsburg dominions and Prussia. The Habsburg lands ranged from the essentially western Austrian Netherlands to Hungary – where a Turkish pasha had maintained his harem and slave-market at Buda until almost the end of the seventeenth century. Conditions varied as much as might have been expected in lands ranging from the Oder to the Po, and the efforts of the Habsburgs to enforce some unity on their disparate dominions were never to be very successful. Bohemia had been crushed and apparently absorbed after the Thirty Years War, but the Magyar nobility continued to exercise a good deal of local autonomy in Hungary. The Magyars, isolated by their language – their Diet still conducted its business in Latin – and the suspicions of a country squirarchy mistrustful of Vienna and its German colonists, were quite beyond the gravitational pull of France, and as yet scarcely touched by German influence. But even here the tenacious if inefficient centralization of government by the Habsburgs was leading the magnates to build themselves palaces at Vienna. The great cosmopolitan capital drew together the upper aristocracy of the whole empire and subjected it to the civilizing influences of a Court which had now shaken off the semi-barbarity of its former dwarfs and jesters. Although Vienna did not become an important centre of cultural initiative and a relatively efficient clerical censorship isolated it to some extent from the west, the French language and French fashions conquered Court society, and many of the army of civil servants became well-acquainted with the movement of ideas in the rest of Europe.

Prussia, much smaller, but almost as widely-scattered as the Habsburg Empire, since it stretched from the Rhine to Lithuania, was organized on a primarily military basis. The revenue from Crown lands, high taxation and rigorous parsimony enabled Frederick William I to maintain a standing army comparable in quality, if not yet in numbers, to that of the Habsburgs. In Prussia the new trend towards more professional government had made conspicuous progress, as exemplified by the imposition by the king of a land tax based on a new land census, an active state policy of economic development and an attempt to compile a single code of law for the entire state. The men responsible would probably have felt flattered by the comment that the result was a barracks. The nobility officered the growing army or lived on their estates. Frederick William kept nothing that the rest of Europe would have recognized as a Court. His interest in education was essentially utilitarian and the university of Halle existed primarily for the production of civil servants. When its most distinguished professor, Christian Wolff, was exiled on suspicion of unorthodoxy, he moved to more congenial Saxony and refused all invitations to return during the king's lifetime. Even in Prussia, however, the growth of Berlin, whose population increased from 20,000 in 1688 to nearly 70,000 by 1740, and the influence there of a lively colony of French Protestant refugees, provided a small oasis in a desert of poverty, militarized authority and rigorous social subordination.

The Italian peninsula provided so much contrast as to make generalization more than usually misleading. On the one hand it was the site of an ancient urban civilization. Naples was one of the half-dozen most populous cities of Europe, and Rome, Venice, Milan and Palermo all had over 100,000 inhabitants, with Genoa, Florence and Bologna above 50,000. But Naples and Palermo formed part of a backward kingdom in which real power belonged to a landed aristocracy entrenched behind its extensive seigneurial rights, whereas Venice and Genoa were the relics of mercantile republics that still dominated their hinterland. Parts of the peninsula were under foreign rule, notably Naples and Sicily, Milan, and for most of the century, Tuscany. The 'states' themselves were sometimes ramshackle agglomerations of territories acquired by their rulers at different times, and each the more or less willing prisoner of its own traditional customs and privileges. The Papal States, strung across central Italy, were regarded by Rome as the temporal shield of its spiritual power, but were just as likely to provide the Pope's enemies with a means of blackmailing him. Although the more fertile parts of the peninsula exported corn; disunity, misgovernment and limited natural resources left most of the region in no position to compete with the more extensive and efficient states beyond the Alps. For much of Italy, unlike the rest of western Europe, the first half of the eighteenth century was a period of upheaval, as Habsburg and Spanish Bourbon challenged the peace settlement of 1713. It was not until mid-century that the peninsula settled down to a long period of peace and political stability.

Various factors kept Italy in close contact with the rest of Europe. To the Catholic, Rome was the centre of Christendom. To the Protestant, especially to the English gentleman on the Grand Tour, it was more important as the inspiration behind his classical education and, with Florence, the home of the new learning of the Renaissance. For Catholic clergy, gentlemen, scholars and artists, Italy exerted a unique attraction and a unique influence, of which Gibbon and Goethe provide two of the best-known examples. The Italians themselves, with their partially urbanized society, their proud cultural tradition and still famous universities, were active participants in the intellectual and aesthetic commerce of Europe. With the exception of music, however, and to a lesser extent, of painting, theirs was not now a markedly original contribution. Individuals such as Vico and Beccaria obtained – or at least merited – a European reputation, but on the whole the Italians do not seem to have rebelled against the appropriation of the Roman tradition by classical France. Galiani, for example, found his spiritual home in Paris and published his celebrated treatise on the corn trade in French.

Poland deserves perhaps a brief mention, if only for its size. Through its Saxon rulers it maintained a tenuous link with central Europe, but the elective monarchs had little power or influence. Real authority rested with a handful of great families whose estates were almost self-sufficient, leaving room for little commerce and no towns of any size. A multitude of impoverished petty nobles lived in conditions which seemed to belong to another century. Strict ecclesiastical censorship and the official monopoly of the Warsaw Gazette left little room for an independent press, even assuming the readers to be there. Such newspapers as there were, written in

German for the German population of the towns, had a minimal circulation. There were to be important developments later in the century but in 1740 Poland was still almost a cultural cipher.

Russian society showed stronger contrasts than that of any other European state. Peter the Great, who died in 1725, had accelerated the westernization of the state itself, borrowing forms of political organization, creating a relatively modern army and fleet and beginning in the Urals what was to become the most important iron industry in Europe. The Russian nobility, pressed into unwilling state service, were brought into forcible contact with an alien way of life. The new royal city of St Petersburg, built in a western style that from the beginning set it apart from Moscow and the native tradition, was intended to point the way to the new Russia. After Peter's death, however, there was nothing remotely western about the extravagant barbarity of Anna's Court. Aristocratic society was eventually to be permeated by western, and especially French influences, but there was little sign of this by 1740. Peter the Great had had technical works translated and printed in Russian at Amsterdam, but the lack of a Russian technical vocabulary made them virtually unreadable and the majority remained unsold. His Academy of Science, founded in 1725, originally consisted entirely of foreigners. Such European influences as penetrated Russia during Anna's reign were more or less confined to the members of this Academy, who read each other's works in manuscript.

The peasants had paid the main price for Peter's reorganization of Russian society. When they had been fixed on the land to prevent their escaping taxation and conscription, the land-owner's responsibility for both obligations enabled him to reduce free peasants to serfdom. Each new grant of Crown lands to a favourite included the peasants liable to services which became more oppressive as the century advanced. Granted the unimportance of almost all Russian towns, society tended to split, both socially and culturally, into a noble minority that was soon to become French-speaking, and an abject and illiterate mass. The unwritten popular culture of the peasant evolved in its own way, based on folk-tales and religious legends, while the peasants' masters quite literally spoke – and read – another language. The full consequences of this division within Russian society were not to become obvious for many years, but its origins were becoming visible in the first half of the eighteenth century.

*

To most people during this period, the fact that something had been done for a long time was both sufficient proof of its legitimacy and adequate reason for going on indefinitely doing it in the same way. Those who were satisfied with their position in the traditional order, the nobility who controlled the various local Estates and, on the whole, the town oligarchs, believed themselves to be upholding traditional constitutions and 'liberties' in the medieval sense. The main force of change was the determination of the ruler and his advisers to introduce more effective forms of government. As Eberhard Louis said, 'these forms are now utterly different from what they used to be, 30, 50 and 60 years ago.' To justify the abrogation of practices sanctioned by prescription, rulers invoked their Divine Right to absolute power, which made them accountable to God alone. One suspects that their professional agents, men whose entire careers were given up to administration, were also motivated by a kind of bureaucratic common sense that was soon to be dignified with the name of Reason. Traditional particularism made for inefficient administration. It would be a mistake, however, to assume that the conflicts which arose between rulers and their more powerful subjects often assumed such abstract clarity. When governments proposed 'improvements' they were opposed by Estates on the ground that they were exceeding their 'constitutional' powers, and the ensuing *dialogue des sourds* generally produced a muddled compromise that became the basis for new disputes.

The peasantry, who formed the great majority of every state, were totally unrepresented in these contentions, which tended to be settled at their expense. In one sense, indeed, the object of the constitutional wrangling was precisely to determine who should have the lion's share of the peasants' surplus. Their condition was probably worst where their immediate lords successfully asserted their own authority. The new concern for efficient administration was beginning to affect the manor as well as the palace and the century saw a more rigorous exploitation of the almost unlimited possibilities open to the noble who was often both landowner and judge in his own court. Where the monarch prevailed, his concern was less to protect the peasant than to tax and conscript him. With the partial exception of Britain, where the power of the gentry did not imply serious manorial obligations for the farmer, his poverty and illiteracy virtually excluded him from the international exchange of ideas.

The urban middle class, generally literate and served by main roads which, however uncomfortable and unsafe, did maintain some sort of commercial contact with distant places, was much more favourably situated. But there was no 'rise of the middle class' in any general sense. Over most of Europe towns were small and their interests strictly parochial. The influential guildsman was generally as conservative as the nobility whose ranks he aspired to enter. Town life was often dominated by resident nobles or a cathedral chapter who constituted the main market for the burghers and set the tone for urban society as a whole. In Court towns in particular, and in centres of provincial justice and administration, it was the professional men and civil servants, generally aspiring to personal nobility, who led the middle class. Only in the great seaports of Hamburg, the Netherlands, Britain and France was there an active, wealthy and educated body of merchants with the will and means to assert their identity and their corporate interests. Even they were as yet content to accept the values of an essentially aristocratic society.

Aristocratic values, which predominated from Portugal to the Russian frontier, were based on a code of honour that implied military origin. To quote de Brosses, in the Remonstrance which he prepared for the *Parlement* of Burgundy in 1762, 'honour is a law that no power may oppose. Over the upright man [*l'homme vertueux*] it exercises the first and most irresistible of all powers.' The man of honour was thus bound by a personal code which was independent of, and might conflict with, his obligations as a subject, and even as a Christian. If his personal honour was questioned, he must fight his accuser or incur social ostracism. The conflict between the demands of honour and the law of the state seems to have troubled few consciences, perhaps because rulers, who themselves shared such values, would normally pardon the too-successful duellist after a decent interval. In the Netherlands, however, where social values were least influenced by the aristocracy, the law imposing the death penalty on the provoked partner who killed his opponent was habitually enforced. But even in this burgher republic university students carried swords. The negation of Christian values which duelling implied was a more serious source of argument. As the lieutenant explained to Tom Jones, 'I love my religion very well, but I love my honour more. There must be some mistake in the wording of the text, or in the translation, or in the understanding it, or somewhere or other. But however that be, a man must run the risk for he must preserve his honour.' The virtuous Mr Thornhill, in *The Vicar of Wakefield*, obviously felt that a man of honour would not hesitate to commit the necessary sin. Even the sanctimonious Johnson concurred: 'I could wish there was not that superfluity of refinement, but while such notions prevail, no doubt a man may lawfully fight a duel.' Boswell exemplified the parallel of personal and political obligation when he justified duelling as a form of private war. The moral paradoxes that could arise from the need to defend one's reputation were amusingly illustrated in Cumberland's *West Indian*, where the hero felt obliged to fight his beloved's brother though admitting the justification for his adversary's calling him a villain.

Duelling, however convenient a device for writers, was no more than the obvious sanction behind aristocratic values. The essential point was that the man of honour was, for better or worse, expected to behave in accordance with the social and moral rules of his own code. He was, for example, to live in a manner appropriate to his station – which might well be inappropriate to his income. The pursuit of wealth was not excluded, but it must be sought in the approved ways: by office, marriage or careful estate-management, and its object was to provide the means for suitable present consumption rather than for investment. Generalizations of this kind can never do justice to the complexity of social practice, but there was nevertheless a basic contrast between the thrifty virtues of a later bourgeois society intent on expansion and an aristocracy which valued wealth as a means of maintaining visible present status. Social status was still almost everywhere equated with land-ownership. Successful merchants bought estates and lived up to the incomes which they had formerly saved to accumulate. How far admission to 'society' depended on birth varied from one country to another. Lord Chesterfield, a connoisseur, offered his own definition: 'Good company ... consists chiefly (but by no means without exception) of people of considerable birth, rank and character; for people of neither birth nor rank are frequently, and very justly, admitted into it, if distinguished by any peculiar merit, or eminency in any liberal art or science.' An interpretation so liberal probably applied more to capitals than to provincial towns and certainly more to maritime and western Europe than to Spain, Germany and regions farther east. Accession to the favoured ranks was easiest in Britain, where formal nobility was least important. Elsewhere rulers insisted on ennobling their servants and creditors – and aristocratic society on despising the parvenus. The situation in France towards the end of the century was brilliantly described by Rivarol:

The wealthy and the men of education considered noble rank to be intolerable, most of them found it so intolerable that they ended up by buying it; but then they began to undergo a new form of torture; they were *anoblis*, men of noble rank, but they were not *gentils-hommes*; for the kings of France, when they sold titles, never thought of selling the time which parvenus always lack. . . . The kings of France cured their subjects of humble birth in the same sort of way that they cured them of the King's Itch, on condition that the signs remained.

In some countries, such as Prussia, commoners were forbidden to buy manors and the rulers supported the efforts of the nobility to remove the social ladder up which most of them had climbed. In general, rulers, however they might oppose the political aspirations of their nobles, considered themselves as standing at the apex of a social pyramid whose values they respected. It was probably for this reason as much as any other that there was no alliance between monarchs and the middle class, to base a more efficient despotism on the destruction of aristocratic privilege and particularism. Frederick the Great, for example, wrote in his Political Testament, 'If commoners own land they open up to themselves the road to every form of employment. The majority think basely and make bad officers; one cannot send them anywhere on diplomatic missions.' How far the aristocratic code of values should reach, and how far the club should admit new entrants, were sources of noisy contention in many parts of Europe, but everywhere the distinction between those within and those without was a social fact of the first importance.

Despite the enormous variations within European society, the gentlemen of Europe formed more of a social club in the eighteenth century than at any time before or since. Court society almost everywhere, and the gentry in the more civilized areas, shared a common language and a common culture. If the society of Paris and Versailles was regarded as the finest finishing school, Chesterfield also insisted on his son's graduating at Rome and Turin. Professional armies might oppose each other in complicated and bloody evolutions, but there was an almost total absence of the divisive passions that had fanned the religious wars of the previous two centuries and were to brutalize the national wars of the next two. In polite society, an assertion of national superiority would have appeared a confession of parochial ill-breeding. Voltaire was to describe Europe as a 'great republic divided between several states', Rousseau to claim 'there is no longer a France, a Germany, a Spain, not even English, there are only Europeans. All have the same tastes, the same passions, the same way of life.' Sterne's comment in his *Sentimental Journey*, 'I had left London [for Paris] with so much precipitation, that it never entered my mind we were at war with France', is almost credible.

This cosmopolitan society, with its ties of kinship and patronage criss-crossing Europe like telephone wires, afforded infinite possibilities for the communication of men and ideas. Travellers and their books abounded – and the eighteenth-century traveller was no hasty tourist, insulated within his national capsule. Once arrived at his immediate destination, his letters of introduction procured him access to local society. Chesterfield, it is true, complained of young Englishmen on the Grand Tour who saw only each other's company in Paris, but for those who chose to enter, the doors of society stood wide open – to the right people. Even the wrong people, if they could afford to buy books and knew how to read them, had the *entrée* to an international exchange of ideas that gathered momentum as the century progressed. During its first half, in particular, the new thought was mostly generated within the triangle, London–Paris–Amsterdam. Its influence varied with distance, national wealth, urbanization, the effectiveness of ecclesiastical censorship and occasionally, as in Hungary, with a linguistic barrier. Perhaps it would be more accurate to assess cultural penetration in terms of speed rather than intensity, for it was eventually to reach from Lisbon to Moscow. How far down the social scale the message could be felt as something that mattered will be discussed in a subsequent chapter.* We must now turn to the ideas themselves.

* See below, pp. 132–41.

Chapter 2

NATURE AND NATURE'S GOD

WHEN the Sorbonne gingerly began coming to terms with Descartes, in the first half of the eighteenth century, the majestic edifice of Cartesian physics was already derelict. Experimental science, aided by its new tools, the telescope and the microscope, had shown more things in heaven and earth than were dreamt of in Descartes' philosophy. The microscope revealed the extraordinary complexity of those animals which the great philosopher had assumed to be relatively simple machines. It was now obvious that the functional organization of the house-fly was as complicated as human physiology had been assumed to be a century earlier. More generally, microscopes showed that the 'clear and distinct perceptions' received through the eye, which Descartes had taken as his criteria of truth, were sometimes a mere product of low magnification. The deductive method was most effective when the problem was to explain a collection of phenomena that had not been radically extended since the time of Aristotle. When every year brought new and unpredictable discoveries, there was a natural tendency to begin with the discoveries themselves and thence to induce the laws which regulated their functioning.

Particularly important were the discoveries relating to the reproduction of mammals that were made between 1660 and 1680. The research of several biologists detected the production of eggs by viviparous animals, and the self-taught Dutch microscopist, Leeuwenhoek, identified spermatozoa. Descartes' mechanistic interpretation of conception, which implied that different particles of male and female semen locked on to each other – which had never won much support from his

73

contemporaries – was completely discredited. The new discoveries, however, raised problems beyond the capacity of seventeenth-century biology, which took refuge in the 'pre-existence' theory, first formulated by Swammerdam in 1669, that became orthodox belief for the best part of a century. According to this explanation, the seed of all living creatures had been formed at the creation of the world, each generation being contained in the one before, like a series of Chinese boxes. However offensive to the 'common sense' of the twentieth century, and despite its inability to explain heredit-ary resemblance to the families of both parents, this theory had obvious theological attractions. All life was created by God, as indicated in the Old Testament, and the Fall of Man, entailing the corruption of the entire species by original sin, acquired a new biological foundation. Descartes' mechanical approach to the animal world and to human bodies, which had offended the pious as savouring of materialism, seemed to have been happily demolished by science.

At the other extreme of the natural scale, observation of the heavens and Newton's law of gravitation also discredited the Cartesians. If, as Descartes had assumed, following the Greeks, nature 'abhorred a vacuum', the movement of light, due to the pressure of one light-particle on another, should have been instantaneous. In 1675 the Danish astronomer, Roemer, measured the velocity of light with reasonable accuracy, and his calculations were confirmed by Bradley in 1727, using a different method. Newtonian gravity, which implied that the rotation of the earth in an empty, or almost empty space, would flatten it slightly at the poles and create a bulge at the equator, was confirmed experimentally by observations in Lapland and Peru in 1736–40. By this time Cartesian science had become untenable and informed opinion had transferred to Newton the veneration formerly given to his French predecessor.

The implications of this revolution were far-reaching indeed. For Descartes, as for almost everyone in the seventeenth century, science, theology and metaphysics were inseparable ways of looking at a unified human experience. The Cartesian philosophy had assumed that men were endowed with the knowledge of certain basic principles whose authenticity was guaranteed by God. By the application of logical argument to these given truths it was possible to arrive at the certain understanding of the world of experience, to discover, not merely scientific laws, but the reason why they were necessary. Locke, as we have seen, had discredited the entire concept of innate ideas, for which he had substituted merely human sense-impressions. The new scientist, in his turn, used experiment as his starting-point and not, as Descartes had done, to confirm the product of deductive reasoning. The result was, or seemed to be, the removal of final causes beyond the cognizance of man, whose realm was henceforth circumscribed to laws, without hope of attaining the reasons behind them. As Hume wrote in his *History of England*, 'While Newton seemed to draw off the veil from some of the mysteries of nature, he showed at the same time the imperfections of mechanical philosophy, and thereby restored her ultimate secrets to that obscurity in which they ever did and ever will remain.' Fontenelle, who remained an unregenerate Cartesian, was perhaps influenced in his loyalties by the dusty answers that seemed all the Newtonians had to offer: 'It is quite definite that if one wants to know what one is talking about, there is only impulsion [as Descartes had asserted]. If one is not worried about that, there is attraction and anything you like, but in that case nature is so incomprehensible to us that the wisest course is perhaps to leave it alone.'

All knowledge was subjective, in the sense that it was, at best, relative to the sense-perception of man, and could attain to no wider reality. By the middle of the eighteenth century this had become a commonplace, as defined by Condillac in his *Traité des sensations* (1754): 'Ideas in no way allow us to know beings as they actually are; they merely depict them in terms of their relationship with us, and this alone is enough to prove the vanity of the efforts of those philosophers who pretend to penetrate into the nature of things.' Réaumur, who devoted his life to the study of insects, asserted that all systems of classification in the natural sciences were matters of human convenience.

Knowledge of essences and of final causes was excluded. All knowledge, in fact, was reduced to probability, since a scientific law whose ultimate reason is unknown can be no more than a statement of what has regularly happened in the past and may therefore be presumed likely to go on happening. As Voltaire wrote in 1738, 'from the stars to the earth's centre, in the external world and within ourselves, every substance is unknown to us. We see appearances only; we are in a dream.' The limited empire of man appeared even more circumscribed than it need have done because of the backwardness of chemistry, which had made little progress since antiquity. Where chemical reactions were concerned, it was not merely the final causes, but the processes themselves that were completely unknown, and Stahl's invocation of phlogiston, the fire-spirit, to explain combustion, was probably more of a hindrance than a help. Voltaire might well exclaim, 'Has anyone ever been able to explain exactly how a log on the hearth changes into glowing embers, and by what mechanism quicklime enters into combustion with cold water?' He does not appear to have appreciated that science might legitimately aspire to explain *how*. What it now renounced was *why*. He was on surer ground when he wrote, 'The only way in which man can reason about objects is by analysis. To begin straight from first principles belongs to God alone.' Buffon expressed the same idea in more philosophical language in the methodological introduction to the first volume of his *Histoire naturelle* in 1749: 'We must therefore resign ourselves to describing as cause what is a general effect, and abandon the attempt to push our knowledge any further. These general effects are, for us, the true laws of nature'. There was a general revulsion from what Newton had denounced as 'hypotheses' and what the French scientists and philosophers vilified as 'systems'. Condillac attacked them in his *Traité des systèmes* in 1749 and, a few years earlier, Maupertuis had written in his *Vénus physique*, 'One constructs for one's self a satisfactory system while one is ignorant of the characteristics of the phenomenon to be explained. As soon as these are known, one sees the inadequacy of one's reasoning and the system fades away. If we think we know anything, this is merely because of our extreme ignorance.' Newton, who saw himself as a small boy playing with pebbles by the shore of a great unknown sea, would probably not have disagreed.

The replacement of the Cartesian by the Newtonian world involved more than the abandonment of men's efforts to understand the causes of causes. To the seventeenth-century scientist, gravitation smacked of magic, or at least, of a return to the 'occult qualities' of earlier days, which clothed ignorance in scholastic definitions. Once concede the existence of invisible forces acting across a vacuum, and the way seemed open to attribute to matter whatever unknown qualities one wished. It was perhaps for this reason, as we have seen, that a sceptic like Fontenelle remained true to the reassuring mechanism of Descartes. Moreover, even its partisans admitted that gravitation did not work. Newton himself, to his own satisfaction, discovered that his law, which explained so much, did not seem to provide the basis for a self-regulating universe. According to his calculations, motion 'is much more apt to be lost than got and is always upon the decay', the earth's axis was slipping from its proper place, and such defects could be remedied only by the direct intervention of God. If God said, 'Let Newton be!' Sir Isaac returned the compliment. We can distinguish two issues here, which tended to be confused at the time. Newton was shown by Laplace to have exaggerated

the 'perturbations' in the solar system. Some of its peculiari-
ties, however, such as the fact that the orbits of the planets
were all in one plane, were not necessarily implied by gravitation itself, and if they were not to be ascribed to mere chance,
or an unknown physical cause, seemed evidence of divine
order. The God of Newton, one can scarcely emphasize too
much, was not a vague First Cause, a divine watchmaker who
first wound up the celestial mechanism, or the prisoner of his
own laws, as Leibniz implied. He was a free agent, whose
periodic intervention was necessary if the 'laws of nature'
were to function at all. Newton seemed to have provided
scientific proof, if not for Christianity, at least for a Supreme
Being whose continuing presence was more immediate than
many Deists had imagined. As Jacques Roger wrote in his
admirable book, *Les Sciences de la vie dans la pensée française au
dix-huitième siècle*, 'The god of the English scientists at the end
of the seventeenth century is much closer to the God of the
Bible than to the god of the philosophers.'

Where the Cartesian philosophy – whatever the personal
position of Descartes – encouraged a mechanistic view of the
physical universe, the Newtonians stressed the impossibility
of man's attaining to an understanding of final causes, and the
dependence of the material world on divine regulation. Their
viewpoint was to be continually reiterated by Voltaire, from
his *Lettres philosophiques* in 1734 to the end of his long life,
over forty years later. Atheists, said Voltaire, had been misled
by Cartesian ideas, whereas 'Almost all the Newtonians I have
seen, accepting the vacuum and the finite nature of matter,
accept as a result the existence of God.' 'Physicists have become the heralds of Providence: a catechist proclaims God to
children and a Newton proclaims him to the wise.' It was no
accident that the first chapter of his *Éléments de la philosophie
de Newton* (1738), which first introduced the English scientist
to a wide French public, should carry the title 'Of God'. In
this chapter, Voltaire writes:

The whole philosophy of Newton leads of necessity to the knowledge of a Supreme Being, who created everything, arranged all things of his own free will. ... If matter gravitates, as has been proved, it does not do so by virtue of its very nature, as it is extended by reason of its nature. Therefore it received gravitation from God. If the planets rotate through empty space in one direction rather than another, their creator's hand, acting with complete freedom, must have guided their course in that direction.

Voltaire went further than Newton himself, who had conceded that gravitation might be a quality inherent in matter. It is most striking to see how the French writer, whenever he thought of God, tended to think of Newton at the same time. Sensationalism itself – which might seem to point in the direction of materialism – was for Voltaire a proof of the divine presence, with Newton's name as a reassuring talisman: 'A divine power shines out in the sensation of the lowest insects, as in the brain of Newton.' The great anti-clerical assumed the accents of the preacher as he proclaimed the presence of the Newtonian God in language that might have graced an eighteenth-century pulpit.

For a very long time people mocked at occult causes. We should rather ridicule those who doubt them. ... Vegetables, minerals, animals, where is your first principle? It is in his hand who made the sun turn on its axis and clothed it in light. ... What corpuscular physics, what atoms determine the nature [of the elements]? You know nothing. The reason will for ever be occult, so far as you are concerned. All that surrounds you, all that lies within you, is an enigma whose key it is not given to man to discover.

*

At about the same time that Newtonism was establishing itself in physics, a new attitude began to permeate much of Europe. This was the assumption that a principle of benevolence or *bienfaisance* animated man himself and the divine order around him. It is with the latter aspect alone that we are concerned in the present chapter, but the assumption involved was common to both. The new outlook seems to have been more or less co-terminous with the frontiers of the Enlightenment, as these were roughly sketched in the first chapter. It cannot be explained as the product of a particular social environment, religion or philosophy, since it embraced them all. It was as marked in autocratic France as in constitutional Britain. Its devotees included Protestants, Catholics and Deists, Newtonians such as Voltaire and anti-Newtonians like Leibniz and the abbé Pluche. The historian, however impatient with a feeling so ill-defined and apparently gratuitous, must resist the temptation to 'explain' it as a by-product of other factors which respond more easily to his methods of analysis, and accept it as an independent agent in its own right.

To the twentieth-century mind, the difficulty is not immediately apparent. The Newtonian revolution, with its emphasis on the limitations of human knowledge and the immediacy of God, might seem to imply faith in a divine order that was *ipso facto* omniscient and benevolent. But this would be to ignore the whole temper of seventeenth-century religious feeling, as I have tried to suggest it in an earlier chapter. The cardinal fact in religious experience had hitherto been the Fall. Man, born in sin, made his erring way through this vale of tears, with eternal damnation the final destination of the great majority. There was nothing in Newtonian physics, with its revelation of man's inability to explain the laws which regulated the course of nature, that implied the contrary. The fact that the divine purpose seemed more inscrutable did not make it more reassuring. Ignorance of final causes was no ground for assuming that they took account of man's convenience, and advancing scientific knowledge of the animal world and its intricate functional adjustment suggested the ingenuity rather than the goodness of its assumed creator. And yet the assumption was made that the earth was designed for man's terrestrial happiness, and made in the teeth of much evidence to the contrary. The orthodox Pluche, when he called his educational textbook on man and nature, *Le Spectacle de la nature*, assumed that the divine show was intended for the delight of man. The tables were turned so radically that it was now the Christian rather than the Deist writers whose interpretation of the human predicament offered the more comfort to the ordinary man.

The word *bienfaisance* was apparently coined in the eighteenth century. 'Providence' had a longer ancestry, but its use in the modern sense did not become common until the seventeenth century. When Leibniz asserted that the goodness of God necessarily implied that this world was the best that could possibly have been created, it was easy to assume that what was 'best' from the divine viewpoint was also most acceptable to man, and therefore most conducive to his immediate happiness – and so the word *optimiste* was added to the French language. Providence, as the agent of divine benevolence towards man, was common ground for both Christians and Deists, but the former interpreted it in a more anthropocentric sense. 'It is for him', said Pluche of Man, 'that the sun rises; it is for him that the stars shine.' The extraordinary conclusions of some of those who sought to unravel the infinite helpfulness of Providence did more credit to their ingenuity than to their judgement. Almost everything could be pressed into service, from the density of water, which Fénelon considered exactly calculated to facilitate navigation, to the shape of the water-melon, which makes it easy to slice. Bernardin de Saint-Pierre admired the forethought which ensured that dark-coloured fleas should be conspicuous on white skin – an example, incidentally, of the predilection of Providence for Europeans. A typical specimen of the interpretation of scientific evidence in a providential light was that of Clément de Boissy, who wrote in 1782, 'The heavenly body that gives us light varies its course to provide us with the advantages of changing seasons . . . the distance between the sun and the earth is also calculated in accordance with our needs . . . all the metals are placed at convenient distances . . . the most useful are those nearest to the surface of the earth.' The abbé Pluche was such a virtuoso in this genre that it is only fair to point out that he did not claim, as Voltaire and subsequent writers have misquoted him as doing, that tides were created to enable ships to enter ports. He merely pointed out that this was one of their advantages. Pluche, however, extended the long arm of Providence throughout the animal world. Domestic animals '. . . are not merely docile, but they naturally love us and come to us spontaneously to offer their various services.' The carnivores perform their part by inhabiting what would otherwise be deserted areas, and by punishing the wicked when required. Even the humble teredo-worm has its role in the divine economy: 'if one did not have to be continually caulking, and from time to time renewing the ships and the piles of Amsterdam harbour, the Muscovite and the Norwegian would tap the resin of their firs in vain, in vain the Swede would fell the oak and pine of his forests.' One could multiply such examples almost indefinitely. Behind them all lay the new assumption that, irrespective of the Fall – which Burnet had believed to have wrecked the face of nature, and even Pluche conceded had thrown the earth off an original axis that had ensured eternal spring, to Europe at least – the earthly felicity of man was the constant and over-riding concern of God.

The Deists adopted a more chilly viewpoint on outer space, from which the convenience of man and the affairs of his planet lost their claim to any special significance. Taking up an idea that Montesquieu had already expressed in the *Lettres persanes*, the hero of Voltaire's fable, Zadig,

... wondered at those vast globes of light that seem mere sparks to our eyes, while the earth, which is in fact an imperceptible point in nature, seems to our greed so great and noble. He visualized men then as they are in fact, insects that devour each other on a little atom of mud. This true image seemed to annihilate his troubles by reminding him of his own nothingness. .... His soul leapt out into the infinite, and, detached from his senses, beheld the unchangeable order of the universe.

In *Micromégas* (1752), Voltaire, viewing man *sub specie Saturni*, goes out of his way to reduce *homo sapiens* to Lilliputian proportions. Nevertheless, though man might misinterpret the cosmic order from the viewpoint of his limited experience, Voltaire never doubted that such an order existed, that it was the result of a free act of creation, and that a purposive harmony underpinned the whole structure. He denounced the 'atheism' of Spinoza who 'did not recognize any Providence. He makes no attempt to examine whether eyes were made to see.... How is it that he did not glance at these mechanisms, these agents, each of which has its purpose, and investigate whether they do not prove the existence of a supreme artisan?' Voltaire teased the '.... estimable author of the *Spectacle of Nature*' for assuming that Providence watched over the creation of man, but his own position was not far from that of Pluche. Believing in a static universe, he accepted that whatever existed, essentially unchanged since the beginning of time, reflected a providential arrangement. Mountain ranges, for example, are '... a chain of high and continuous aqueducts, which by their apertures allow the rivers and the arms of the sea the space which they need to irrigate the land.' This happy dispensation, he continues, is proof of the 'wisdom and benevolence' of God.

Newtonian science and the general acceptance of a beneficent Providence, as these ideas were understood in the early eighteenth century, combined to divert attention from the materialist followers of Descartes, most brilliantly personified by the English philospher, Hobbes, in the previous century. Challenging Hobbes with his own rational and scientific weapons, scientists seemed to have relegated atheism to the lumber-room of discarded classical speculation. Hobbes's pessimistic psychology, in which the dominant urge of self-preservation manifested itself basically as fear, appeared equally irrelevant to a more tranquil society, in which Christian and Deist were agreed on the natural benevolence of man and the existence of a providential order. It was only when these assumptions came to be challenged in the second half of the century that the influence of Hobbes began to grow. Rousseau was to pay him tribute in *Du contrat social* and the whole *credo* of the Marquis de Sade might reasonably be summarized in Hobbes's dictum: *homo homini lupus*.

*

By the middle of the eighteenth century, science was well launched on its extraordinary journey. The ancients had been left far behind, in physics and zoology at least, and Pluche, who was no radical, exulted over their eclipse in the preface to his own work.

We had no thought at all of making use of what the ancients have published on some of these subjects, only too often with more credulity than examination. But the reader will be more inclined to savour what he will find guaranteed by the evidence of modern observers who have acquired a universal reputation for their precision and exactitude.

The eighteenth-century Arthur Mee did not always follow his own advice, and there are inaccurate 'facts' as well as naïve enthusiasms in his great compilation. Nevertheless, the century that separates *Speculum Mundi* from the *Spectacle de la nature* had seen more scientific discovery than any previous century in human history and Pluche's knowledge in several branches of science would shame that of many a present-day

Arts graduate. The truce between science and religion, despite the warnings of the French Jansenists in their clandestine publication, the *Nouvelles ecclésiastiques*, encouraged all to participate in the search for knowledge. The scientists, abandoning the quest for metaphysical implications, were in the main content, like Réaumur, to observe and record. Their findings were acclaimed by the divines as grist for the mills of Providence. Protestant, Catholic and Deist shared a common attitude to experience, as the Christians turned their attention away from original sin and the Deists agreed that the heavens declared the glory of God. In this atmosphere there began the intensive prosecution of scientific research, and its emancipation from theological control, that have continued ever since.

Many scientific societies had been founded in central and western Europe. Helped initially by a common international language – Latin – and later, by an almost universal knowledge of French, they provided a remarkably efficient system for the rapid dissemination of scientific discovery and speculation. Newtonian physics, which offered a disconcerting challenge to both theological and scientific orthodoxy, took some time to penetrate the Continent and still evoked the enthusiasm of the unfamiliar when Voltaire published his exposition in 1738 and de Brosses discussed the infinitesimal calculus with the Italians who entertained him during his tour in the following year. In later years the exchange of scientific information was appreciably accelerated. The Swedish botanist, 'Linnaeus', quickly established an international reputation. It is significant that his name itself has come down to us in its Latinized version, the language in which he published all his major works. By the end of the century, in the days of Lavoisier and Priestley, the network of scientific societies was so close, and contacts so frequent, that science might truly be described as international. The work of the unorthodox might still pass unnoticed, as Maupertuis found to his cost, but the incessant dialogue did ensure that experiments were checked, unwarranted conclusions challenged and discoveries quickly shared.

Since the eighteenth century regarded knowledge as a whole, rather than as a collection of separated parts, this is perhaps as good a place as any to refer to the great *Encyclopaedia*, which is often regarded as typifying the attitude of the Enlightenment. Diderot, at first assisted by d'Alembert, devoted much of his life to the production of this immense compendium of knowledge, comprising seventeen volumes of text and eleven of plates. Diderot's objectives were multiple. In the first place, the *Encyclopaedia* was to serve as a repository of technological information, which could thus be preserved and disseminated and serve as the basis for further advances. In so far as the Enlightenment was an attempt to substitute empirical knowledge for traditional practice and belief, whatever was 'scientific' and helped the individual to understand for himself was germane to its purpose. The mere diffusion of accurate and up-to-date information was itself an important part of the great offensive of knowledge against ignorance. There was, of course, more to it than that. The *Encyclopaedia* was also an anthology of 'enlightened' opinions on politics, philosophy and religion, whatever disguises contributors had to adopt in order to hoodwink their somewhat somnolent censors. The sheer number of the contributors ensured that it would not express any narrowly sectarian viewpoint, but there was sufficient agreement on a rationalist and empirical approach to ensure a certain convergence of aim. All in all, the work was reasonably typical of the general current of belief that went by the name of the Enlightenment. It was also an epoch-making – and very profitable – venture in publishing. Its 4,000 copies were widely disseminated throughout France, although the initial subscription price of 280 livres (about £14), restricted its circulation, even amongst the affluent.

The world of the mid-eighteenth-century scientist was an essentially static one. It had begun with a single act of creation that had established the terrestrial landscape and produced the fixed species of plants and animals more or less as they still existed. Voltaire clung to this belief all the more tenaciously, when it was being challenged from about 1750 onwards, since he felt that the proof of the existence of God was linked with the stability of the world. Replying to the materialist argument that, in time, matter and motion would produce every possible combination of phenomena, including the existing one, Voltaire objected,

... if everything changes, the smallest species of things would not be permanent, as they have been for so long. [The advocates of change] at least can show no reason why new species are not created every day. On the contrary, it is very probable that a powerful hand, superior to these continual changes, arrests all the species within the bounds which it has prescribed for them. So the philosopher who recognizes a God has on his side a mass of probabilities which are equivalent to certainty, and the atheist has only doubts.

By 1764, when he wrote this, Voltaire was on the defensive; his earlier works present the fixity of species not as a 'mass of probabilities' but as fact.

*

The static assumptions of European science around the 1730s were in harmony with the relatively peaceful state of most of the continent, the partial decline of religious persecution and the apocalyptic visions to which it gave rise, and the absence of acute social tension within an economy that was beginning to expand. But the question of how far such social generalizations are meaningful, if meaningful, significant, and if significant, inter-related, is one to which no 'scientific' answer is at present possible. To isolate any one factor and assume that it was the cause of the others, is an act of faith whose results may be illuminating, but cannot be conclusive.

From about 1740 there began a general change. The two great wars of 1740–48 and 1756–63 form the watershed of the century, which was henceforth marked by growing tension and a feeling of instability in much of Europe, culminating in the universal upheaval of the French Revolution. The period from the publication of Hume's *Treatise on Human Nature* in 1739–40 to the appearance of Voltaire's *Candide* in 1759, also saw the intrusion of new scientific ideas which challenged the immutability of the natural order, and of growing doubts about the management of human destiny by a benevolent Providence.

The genetic doctrine of pre-existence came under increasing attack. As early as 1719–21, Montesquieu, in two papers presented to the Academy of Bordeaux, had suggested that 'The best-organized plant is only a simple and easy consequence of the general motion of matter.' This was perhaps merely an echo of Descartes, and in any case it had a very limited public and no immediate sequel. A more serious offensive was launched by Maupertuis in his *Vénus physique* of 1745. Taking his stand on the sanctity of observed evidence, Maupertuis repudiated a theory which could not explain the known facts of heredity and the production of hybrids and 'monsters' such as Siamese twins. Three years later Needham, as a result of a faulty experimental technique, claimed to have observed the spontaneous generation of life. Maupertuis promptly took up Needham's explanation. In his *Système de la nature* (1751) he abandoned the mechanistic viewpoint he had previously held, and assumed reproduction to be due to '. . . some principle of intelligence, something similar to what we call desire, aversion, memory . . .' which was present in matter. Buffon, whose later theories will be discussed in a subsequent chapter,* had also rejected the pre-existence theory when he published the first three volumes of his *Histoire naturelle* in 1749.

* See below, pp. 222–8.

The adoption of a theory of spontaneous generation by some of the most eminent scientists of the period had two very important consequences. In the first place, it attributed to matter a form of life and implied that the spontaneous arrangement of matter could produce sentient and intelligent beings. As Buffon wrote, 'Life and movement, instead of being a metaphysical degree of existence, are physical properties of matter.' Secondly, as Montesquieu had realized a generation earlier, it removed the necessity for assuming the fixity of species, which had been implied by pre-existence. The stability of a divinely-created and unchanging order was challenged by a new conception of life as a constant and shapeless flux.

Other scientific discoveries had equally disconcerting consequences. It had been known since the beginning of the century that the lizard could replace a lost tail, and in 1712 Réaumur described how the crayfish could grow a new claw. In 1740 Trembley announced the discovery of the fresh-water polyp, which combined the characteristics of animal and plant. However these phenomena were interpreted to fit existing theories, it was clear – unless one simply denied the evidence, as Voltaire did in the case of the polyp – that nature could no longer be regarded as regulated by universal laws whose operation was always the same. This had been one of the main arguments of the providential theorists. As Leibniz had seen, and Pope had urged with anxious reiteration in his *Essay on Man*, the belief that

> The Universal Cause
> Acts not by partial, but by general laws

could provide an explanation for the existence of physical and moral evil in a world ruled by Providence. Gravity, for example, though necessary for man's survival and well-being, would destroy the individual who fell over a cliff. But if Providence could extend to lizards and crayfish special favours that were denied to man, this argument lost a good deal of its impressiveness. Moreover, if nature did not observe general laws, the demonstration by analogy, which Bishop Butler had used in his *Analogy of Religion* (1736) in order to commend Revelation to the Deists, lost much of its force.

It was gradually realized, at about the same period, that Newton had been wrong in assuming that gravitation would not keep the solar system in order without the periodic intervention of its divine creator. D'Alembert showed that the conservation of motion might be explained without invoking such intervention. Irregularities in the orbits of the planets, which Newton had assumed to be cumulative, were found to be periodical and self-correcting – a significant example of the solution of a problem in naturalistic terms by situating it within the context of time. Buffon pointed out that the formation of the solar system by the collision of a comet with the sun was the kind of natural occurrence that could account for the orbits of the planets being in the same plane. Thus the solution of some problems and the provision of possible answers to others made it easy to postulate, if not to prove, a self-regulating universal order that might be Newtonian in its laws of motion, but was significantly different from anything that the English scientist had imagined.

Although the great age of geology still lay ahead, enough was already known to raise disquieting doubts. In 1720 Réaumur observed that the evidence of marine fossils showed that they had been deposited over a longer period than the biblical Flood would allow. It was generally recognized that many such fossils in Europe were similar to contemporary warm-water animals and that Europe must therefore once have been part of the 'Indian ocean'. In 1751 Guettard realized that the hills of the Puy de Dôme area in France were volcanoes that must have become extinct in a very distant past, before legend and history could transmit any record of their activity. The geological evidence, however imperfect and puzzling, was therefore sufficient to suggest a time-scale far greater than the Old Testament permitted, and also continuous and very extensive change. It was presumably for this latter reason that Voltaire launched one passionate and ironical attack after another against the disturbing evidence.

The general trend of scientific thought in mid-century was therefore hostile to the conception of a static universe dependent on divine intervention for its creation and viability. The new attitude emphasized the complexity of matter and its apparent capacity to generate life, the existence of anomalies in nature and the revolutionary transformation of nature itself over an immense period of time. Science, in other words, seemed to have dispensed with the need for God as a necessary factor in its explanation of the universe. Diderot, in his *Interprétation de la nature* (1754), observed that if gravitation were inherent in matter, chaos was an impossibility since matter would automatically arrange itself in an ordered way. Hume, in the *Dialogues concerning Natural Religion* which he wrote about the same time, although they were not published until after his death, carried the argument a stage further. 'I would fain know', says Philo, 'how an animal could subsist unless its parts were so adjusted. Do we not find that it immediately perishes whenever this adjustment ceases, and that its matter corrupting tries some new form?' With science defecting to the enemy, the cause of a morally meaningful order now rested only on belief in a beneficent Providence.*

Men's conception of Providence did not depend on new experimental evidence, for there had always been enough facts available to justify all kinds of explanations, and the new information provided by the microscope merely made the picture more complicated without imposing any meaning of its own. The question was primarily one of attitude, and for reasons which are unexplained and perhaps inexplicable, the current of opinion was setting in the direction of pessimism.

* For a further discussion of this subject, see below, pp. 219–25.

Even Pluche had not been quite sure: 'What we call evil is *often* really good and *almost always* the occasion for the exercise of some virtue that is preferable to indolence and repose.' (The italics are mine, but the reservations were those of Pluche.) The darkening of the skies can be clearly traced in the sequence of Voltaire's fables. In *Le Monde comme il va* (1746) the conclusion is mildly optimistic: 'Though everything is not good, everything is passable.' An attitude of resigned acceptance is the conclusion of *Zadig* (1747), when the angel Jesrad informs the hero that the wicked:

... serve to test a small number of the just scattered throughout the earth and there is no evil from which good does not spring. 'But', said Zadig, 'what if there was only good and no evil?' 'Then', replied Jesrad, 'this earth would be another earth and the chain of events would represent another order of wisdom and that perfect order can exist only in the eternal dwelling of the Supreme Being which no evil can approach. ... There is no chance; all is trial, reward, punishment or foresight. ... Puny mortal, cease from challenging what you must adore.'

When Voltaire wrote *Le Blanc et le noir* and *Candide* (1759), the emphasis was very different. The change in his attitude is often ascribed to his reaction to the catastrophic Lisbon earthquake, but this seems a gratuitous over-simplification. The earthquake occurred four years before *Candide* was published and its description in the book is merely one incident amongst many. War and superstition are the main motive forces behind the anarchic violence of the story. The conclusion is still, as it always was for Voltaire, that the ultimate reason of things is unknown and unknowable, but the predicament of man has now become anything but 'passable'. When Candide's Leibnizian tutor, Pangloss, asks a wise dervish to explain the purpose of man, his only answer is

'What are you meddling with? Is it any business of yours?' 'But, holy father,' said Candide, 'there is a terrible amount of evil on earth.' 'What does it matter,' replied the dervish, 'whether there is evil or good? When his highness sends a ship to Egypt, does he worry whether the mice on board are comfortable or not?'

Even more violent was Voltaire's angry demonstration of the impeccable causal sequence that can lead to a man's dying in agony while being operated for gallstones, which illustrates his article, 'Tout est bien', in his *Questions sur l'Encyclopédie.*

Diderot ridiculed providential theories with less bitterness but equal effect in *Jacques le fataliste et son maître* (c. 1774). Jacques' master reproaches him for objecting to being stung by gnats:

When your blood is excessive or disordered, what do you do? You call a surgeon who relieves you of two or three *palettes*. Well then, these gnats that you are grumbling about are a swarm of little winged surgeons who come with their tiny lancets to sting you and draw your blood drop by drop.

JACQUES: 'Yes, but in any old way, without knowing whether I have too much or too little. ... They're thinking of themselves; everything in nature thinks of itself and only of itself. If that's bad for others, what does it matter, provided one's all right one's self?' Then he clapped his hands in the air again, crying 'Damn the little winged surgeons!'

Voltaire, even at his most pessimistic, did not doubt that some supernatural order existed, however indifferent it might be to man's convenience. Others were less sure. La Mettrie, in *L'Homme machine* (1747), put the question squarely: 'Who knows if the reason for the existence of man is not his existence itself. Perhaps chance has thrown him down at a given point on the earth's surface, without our being able to know how or why. ... We know nothing about nature: causes hidden within nature itself may have produced everything.' He developed this theme in his *Système d'Epicure* three years later:

Granted the existence of certain laws of motion, they formed eyes which saw, ears which heard, nerves which felt, a tongue sometimes capable of speech, sometimes not, according to its organization; at last they produced the organ of thought [*le viscère de la pensée*]. Nature constructed, within the machine of man, another machine which proved suitable for retaining ideas and producing new ones. ... Having made, without sight, eyes which see, it made without thinking a machine which thinks.

Maupertuis' *Essai de Cosmologie*, also in 1750, raised the same issue in less dogmatic terms. 'So many poisonous plants and harmful animals, carefully produced and preserved by nature: can these lead us to know the wisdom and goodness of he who created them?' Blake was later to put the question in more memorable language:

> Tiger! tiger! burning bright
> In the forests of the night,
> What immortal hand or eye
> Dare frame thy fearful symmetry?

It was left to d'Holbach, in his *Système de la nature* (1770) to assert bluntly that there was no divine purpose and no masterplan. 'The whole cannot have an object, for outside itself there is nothing towards which it can tend.' 'Men have completely failed to see that this nature, lacking both good and evil intentions, merely acts in accordance with necessary and immutable laws when it creates and destroys living things, from time to time making those suffer whom it created sentient, as it distributed good and evil among them.' Providence had gone the way of the Divine Artificer. There were no metaphysical lessons to be learned from the spectacle of nature, which was no more than a transient wave on the great ocean of time.

The general direction of scientific thought combined therefore with a more pessimistic view of Providence to drive mid-century writers towards an unwilling choice between complete scepticism and rigorous determinism. The great mass of the population of western Europe continued to accept the literal truth of the Bible and the existence of a Christian order. But those in the forefront of the new scientific and intellectual movements had come to recognize that Moses was an unreliable historian. Alienated from a Church that insisted on the literal truth of Revelation, natural religion no longer offered them acceptable proof of a providential order. Only two attitudes seemed to remain: to follow Hume in denying man's access to objective knowledge of any kind, or to accept d'Holbach's conception of a universe of matter in motion, in which everything happened of necessity and the answer to every question was 'because it cannot be otherwise'. Granted a static universe, or a world in random motion, conforming to no identifiable pattern, philosophy seemed to be thrown back on the classical materialism of Lucretius and Epicurus. If things were in a state of unorganized flux, the product of natural determinism was nothing more than a sequence of kaleidoscopic patterns. It was characteristic of Diderot's puzzled honesty that, in his *Interprétation de la nature* (1754), he should have stated both the materialist and the sceptical causes with equal sympathy.

If phenomena are not causally related to each other, there is no philosophy. Even if they are so related, the state of each may have no permanence. But if the state of things is in a perpetual flux, if nature is still at its work, in spite of the causal chain there is no philosophy. All our natural sciences became as transient as words themselves. What we take to be the history of nature is only the very imperfect history of an instant.

Having thus defined the dilemma of the materialist in a world of undirected motion, Diderot closed his book with a most moving agnostic prayer.

O God, I do not know if you exist. . . . I ask nothing in this world, for the course of events is determined by its own necessity if you do not exist, or by your decree if you do. ... Here I stand, as I am, a necessarily organized part of eternal and necessary matter – or perhaps your own creation. ...

Science, as the key to the purpose of God, nature and man, seemed to have come up against a door that was bolted on the other side.

Chapter 3

HUMAN NATURE: MAN AND SOCIETY

THE ideas of Locke proved as destructive to Cartesian philosophy as Newton's physics had been to Descartes' science. Contemporaries, who described science as 'natural philosophy', took it for granted that any system of thought must apply to both disciplines and that its overthrow in one would lead to its abandonment in the other. Voltaire saw the defeat of Cartesian rationalism by the inductive methods of the English in these terms:

> Descartes especially, after making a pretence of doubt, speaks so categorically about what he does not understand ... that I must suspect everything he tells me about the soul when he has misled me so badly about the body.

Voltaire's breezy account of the philosophical revolution presents the eighteenth-century view of what happened, with all the false clarity of caricature.

> Descartes, in his works of fiction, pretended that we had metaphysical ideas before we knew our nurse's breast; a faculty of theology outlawed this dogma, not because it was wrong, but because it was new; then the faculty took up this fallacy, because it had been demolished by Locke, an English philosopher, and an Englishman had to be wrong.

Descartes, of course, had not been proved 'wrong' in his philosophical assumptions, where no proof was possible either way. A more empirically-minded age, impressed by the achievement of scientific methods of observation and induction, set out to apply these methods to philosophy, in the hope of discovering the laws of human nature, in the way that Newton had discovered gravitation. As Hume expressed it,

97

with less than his usual elegance, in the abstract of his *Treatise on Human Nature*, 'It is at least worth while to try if the science of *man* will not admit of the same accuracy which several parts of natural philosophy are found susceptible of.' Not surprisingly, the philosophers, using similar methods, encountered similar difficulties to those of the scientists, and the two currents of thought – often combined in the same men – followed parallel courses.

In theory, the abandonment of Descartes' 'innate' ideas for the belief that all ideas were the product of the individual's reflection about his own perceptions, substituted for universal, eternal and God-given clarities, a chaos of subjective impressions. Berkeley, in fact, went further than Locke, asserting that human perceptions were not automatic photographs, as it were, of an objective reality. The awareness of space and distance, for example, is not something communicated directly by the eye as lens. It depends on the interpretation of vision in terms of human organs and human experience and is therefore relative in a general way to *homo sapiens*, and to some extent, to the individual experience of each of us. According to Berkeley, the mind is aware only of its own perceptions and has no means of acquiring knowledge about the objects that are assumed to give rise to these perceptions. In fact, both Berkeley and Locke, as Christians, assumed that individual sense-impressions had an objective content that was guaranteed by God. Locke believed sensation to convey objectively valid knowledge of an external world, and for him, reflection had an abstract, universal quality. Ideas were bound to differ, but experiment and reflection could expose wrong associations of ideas, and chains of reasoning formed converging subjective paths towards an ultimate objective reality. Locke's assumption that the motive force for human action was the pursuit of pleasure and the avoidance of pain, which was later to tie the materialists in inextricable knots, posed no such problems for him. As a God-given principle, its correct application was bound to result in ethically valid conduct. Berkeley's development of Locke's ideas – which continental writers tended in any case to dismiss as no more than ingenious paradox – was similarly based on what he called 'the wonted indulgent methods of Providence' which guaranteed the objective truth of 'right deductions from true principles'. He and Locke, like Newton, based their systems on a Christian foundation, the supreme 'pleasure', for Locke, being the eternal felicity that was the reward of the just.

*

The new conviction that the affairs of man were guided by a beneficent Providence permeated philosophy as deeply as cosmology. Man himself was assumed to be benevolent by nature. Shaftesbury maintained that this innate quality ensured that doing good for its own sake, irrespective of the hope of reward, was one of the forms of pleasure which were the mainsprings of human conduct. Voltaire – no sentimentalist – concurred. He asserted that, in addition to the urge towards self-preservation which he shared with animals, man 'also possessed for his species a natural benevolence which one never sees in beasts'. The most emphatic statement of this point of view is to be found in Morelly's *Code de la nature* (1755). Morelly begins by rejecting the traditional view of moralists that 'Man is born vicious and wicked'. He makes man's natural *bienfaisance* the basis of his religion, as well as the regulator of his conduct.

In the natural order the idea of active or passive benevolence precedes every other idea, even that of the Divinity. This idea alone raises men to the conception of a god, at an earlier date and with more certainty than the spectacle of the universe would have done. Benevolence gives us an idea of the Divinity truly worthy of the majesty of its object. It alone, in general, perfects all the faculties of the reason and gives them their true employment. Man's conception of God is only corrupted to the extent that his idea of benevolence withers. The primitive idea of a *beneficent* god is no idolatry; one can only describe as idolatry the belief in a God who is equally occupied in harmful and beneficent action. Any moral system which bases its doctrine on this conception of the Divinity is absolutely vicious.

We have come a long way from original sin. Towards the end of the century, Condorcet, in his *Esquisse d'un tableau historique des progrès de l'esprit humain*, was still affirming that nature had endowed all men with 'rigorous and pure principles of justice ... habitual promptings of an active and enlightened benevolence, a delicate and generous sensibility'.

The providential harmony that a Christian such as Pluche discerned in the spectacle of nature also adjusted the relationships between men in society. Long before Adam Smith expressed in economic terms the identity between enlightened self-interest and the communal good, the same point had been more generally made by Shaftesbury, and by Montesquieu who wrote, 'Everyone pursues the common good under the impression that he is following his own private advantage.' It became one of the accepted tenets of the age. Mandeville's fable of the bees implied that even private vices worked to the collective advantage. Pluche, on a somewhat similar tack, observed, 'He who feels the harmony of nature and society with revealed religion will recognize that men are not what they ought to be and that the diversity of their condition is the work of Providence's concern to diminish the evil consequences of the wickedness of human hearts and compel men to do from self-interest what they ought to do from virtue.' In *Tom Jones*, the virtuous squire Allworthy annexed the passions to the empire of all-conquering Providence in a way that would have startled Racine: 'Love, however barbarously we may corrupt and pervert its meaning, as it is a laudable, is a rational passion, and can never be violent but when reciprocal.' This was indeed the best of all possible worlds.

Perhaps the most comprehensive statement of this whole attitude of mind, and certainly one of the most widely-read throughout Europe, was Pope's *Essay on Man* (1733). Beginning with a tribute to empiricist methodology,

> Say first, of God above or Man below,
> What can we reason, but from what we know?
> Of Man, what see we but his station here,
> From which to reason, or to which refer?

Pope maintains, with a bow in the direction of Leibniz,

> Respecting Man, whatever wrong we call,
> May, must be right, as relative to all.

After enlarging on the theme that man has been endowed with those faculties appropriate to his providential role in the spectacle of nature, Pope ends his first Book with a triumphant vindication of the status quo:

> All Nature is but Art, unknown to thee;
> All Chance, Direction, which thou can'st not see;
> All Discord, Harmony not understood;
> All partial Evil, universal Good:
> And, spite of Pride, in erring Reason's spite,
> One truth is clear, WHATEVER IS, IS RIGHT.

Book II is devoted to the argument that

> Two principles in human nature reign:
> Self-love, to urge, and Reason, to restrain.

Self-love, which an earlier generation would have attributed to man's turning away from the service of God, is treated by Pope as a necessary force of nature, without which reason would remain inactive. The third Book describes the harmony of nature and the emergence of human society, which passes through a period of political conflict to the resolution, in social terms, of the implied antithesis in Book II:

> Thus God and Nature linked the general frame
> And bade Self-love and Social be the same.

The argument of the final Book is best given in Pope's own summary:

Of the Nature and State of Man with respect to Happiness . . . It is the End of all Men, and attainable by all. God intends Happiness to be *equal*: and to be so, it must be *social*, since all particular happiness depends on general, and since he governs by *general*, not *particular* Laws. As it is necessary for *Order*, and the peace and welfare of *Society*, that *external goods* should be *unequal*, Happiness is not made to consist in these. But, notwithstanding that inequality, the *balance* of Happiness among *Mankind* is kept even by Providence.

We have seen that this new conception of the relationship between God and man was, if not explicitly anti-Christian, the antithesis of what had formerly been held to constitute Christianity. The Fall, in Pope's poem, has shrunk to an episode in prehistory, the emergence of human society from a shadowy Golden Age when

The state of Nature was the reign of God.

It is not even clear that we should regret the loss of this primitive innocence, since we subsequently see man 'from Nature rising slow to Art'. So far as civilized man is concerned, reason has taken the place formerly assigned to grace, and a beneficent Providence ensures the earthly bliss of the physical man, especially of the virtuous, before opening up to his spirit the portals of immortality – for there is no longer any question of an eternity of torment for the majority. Such an attitude was not universally held by the Protestant and Catholic clergy. Anglican preachers continued to denounce human wickedness and the Wesleyans were soon to revive a more intense preoccupation with sin. In France, the oppressed Jansenists still maintained, with the bitterness of the persecuted, that nature had been corrupted by the Fall of Man, and that religious inferences from alleged natural harmony were therefore invalid. Nevertheless, the main current of the religious establishment was flowing in the opposite direction.

Anglican bishops and French Jesuits appealed to the optimistic temper of the age by demonstrating that there was no conflict between the truths of Revelation and the new faith in human reason and its inference of a beneficent Providence from the spectacle of nature. This tendency for Christianity to identify itself with the complacent justification of the *status quo* was a short-term policy, full of risks for the future. The changed attitude offered poor sustenance to religious emotion, if it did not reject it outright as 'enthusiasm', and cold comfort to those who sought in God consolation for the ills and injustices which the 'general laws' of a beneficent Providence had apparently apportioned as their lot. When the Churches were prepared for so many concessions, and seemed encumbered rather than sustained by such dogma as they retained, there was a tendency for the educated to drift by easy stages from Christianity to natural religion.

If the spectacle of nature was indeed the work of a benign Providence, then human reflection, unaided by Revelation, would lead all thinking men to the conclusions of Voltaire: 'We are intelligent beings, but such beings cannot have been created by an uncouth, blind and insensible being; there is certainly a difference between Newton and a mule's droppings. Therefore the intelligence of Newton came from another intelligence.' Man's reason was the proof of God's existence and nature's harmony the sign of his benevolence. As Voltaire wrote in 1739, no doubt with Pope in mind:

> Mortels, venez à lui, mais par reconnaissance;
> La nature, attentive à remplir nos désirs,
> Vous appelle à ce Dieu, par la voix des plaisirs.
> Nul encore n'a chanté sa bonté toute entière:
> Par le seul mouvement il conduit la matière:
> Mais c'est par le plaisir qu'il conduit les humains.

Voltaire liked to stress man's total ignorance of the divine nature, but in fact the devotees of natural religion attributed to their divinity justice, benevolence and a general conformity to the moral standards of man. Nature's god was a kind of highest common denominator of the revealed religions. The wise Zadig ended the theological disputes of the Egyptian, the Hindu, the Confucian, the Aristotelian Greek and the druidical Celt, by convincing them that their particular religious observances were all related to the worship of a common divine creator. This was to be the central theme of Lessing's play, *Nathan the Wise*. Since natural religion was universal it bound the whole of humanity in a moral law common to all. The tolerance and charity encouraged by a conception of religion free from the superstition and persecution that had been so prominent in the Christian churches, affected some of the Christians themselves. The pious German, Wolff praised Confucius and the morals of the Chinese, whereupon local bigots had him deprived of his chair at the university of Halle in 1721. Whatever its limitations, and however compromised by its persistent tendency to invoke divine justification for a social order which most of its devotees found personally convenient, eighteenth-century Deism was distinguished for its dignity and its sense of the fraternity of the human race. Its influence as a religion was to prove ephemeral, but it fostered a new respect and sympathy for man.

Many Christians shared with the Deists the conviction that religion was at least as much concerned with the welfare of man as with the worship of God. An intellectual revolution separates the traditional piety of the seventeenth century, as evidenced even by a courtier like Saint-Simon, writing his memoirs at the same time as Voltaire's earlier works, from the secularism of his younger contemporaries. Pluche urged the wealthy to devote their money to public works; he did not mention the endowment of the Church or traditional forms of charity. The anthropocentric attitude to religion can be seen in Montesquieu's *Lettres persanes* (1721): 'The first aim of a religious man must surely be to please the divinity who established the religion he professes. But the most certain way to achieve this end is without any doubt to observe the rules of society and the duties of humanity.' The conviction that social utility took precedence over dogma runs like a *leitmotif* throughout the century. Pope took it up in 1733.

> For Modes of Faith let graceless zealots fight;
> He can't be wrong whose life is in the right.

Hume, in his *Dialogues concerning Natural Religion*, has the Deist, Cleanthes, assert that 'The proper office of religion is to regulate the heart of men, humanize [sic] their conduct, infuse the spirit of temperance, order and obedience.' Even the pious squire Allworthy set human reason above Church doctrine. 'To represent the Almighty as avenging the sins of the guilty upon the innocent, was indecent, if not blasphemous, as it was to represent him acting against the first principles of natural justice, and against the original notions of right or wrong, which he himself had implanted in our minds; by which we were to judge not only in all matters which were not revealed, but even of the truth of revelation itself.' Dr Johnson concurred: 'if convents should be allowed at all, they should only be retreats for persons unable to serve the public, or who have served it. It is our first duty to serve society: and, after we have done that, we may attend wholly to the salvation of our own souls.' Johnson did not have very much in common with the Marquis de Sade, but the virtuous Gaspard, in Sade's novel, *Aline et Valcour*, says much the same thing. 'I prefer to devote to virtuous actions the time that others lose in prayer and this [divine] agent, if he is just, will be better pleased with me for being useful to men than assiduous before his altar.' Sade's philosopher-king, Zamé, spoke in language that Voltaire could have endorsed: 'O just and holy God, of what concern to you are our systems and our opinions? What difference does the manner in which men invoke you make to your own majesty? What you wish is that man should be just; what pleases you is that he should be humane.'

This perpetual insistence on the connexion between religion – natural or revealed – and the welfare of man in society, was far from fortuitous. It was, in fact, the very basis for optimism about the moral validity of all that tangle of relationships that went by the name of 'nature'. It was the guarantee that human laws and institutions, whose relativity to local conditions was becoming increasingly evident, could be justified in terms of an unwritten moral code common to all humanity. It was the origin of the 'natural rights' of man in his own society and of the superiority of the universal rights of humanity as a whole over the collective egoism of a particular state. It confirmed the benevolence of Providence, prescribed his duty to the citizen and ensured the harmonious concordance of individual self-interest and a universal moral order. For these purposes, natural religion was as efficacious as revealed, but one or the other was necessary. The coherence, as well as the confidence of the Enlightenment, rested on religious foundations.

*

Relatively free from the kind of 'deep questioning that probes to endless dole', the age turned its creative energies outwards, towards the study of man in his social environment. As in the sciences, there was a vigorous search for new information, for every kind of evidence. Physical exploration had, by the end of the century, produced reasonably accurate maps of almost all the earth's coastlines. Within the interior of continents, enormous areas remained to be explored, but as the unknown receded, the distinction between its peculiar and its mythical inhabitants could be drawn with more confidence. With the careful study of exotic flora and fauna went a new kind of interest in strange human societies. There was less inclination to judge primitive communities as heathen barbarians, in need of Christianity and European civilization. The apostles of natural religion found it easier than missionaries had done to accept unfamiliar values as legitimate in their local context; indeed they tended to idealize the American Indian or the Polynesian islander, who seemed so much nearer to 'nature' than the sophisticated European. Such an attitude was by no means confined to rebels like Rousseau. Voltaire, in *l'Ingénu* (1767), conducted his own bitter criticism of French society from the viewpoint of an imaginary Huron. Interest in extra-European values was not confined to newly-discovered peoples. Islam attracted more and more attention. Here, as in the case of India, European scholars were concerned not so much to criticize as to assimilate strange cultures within a universal framework. Men like the Président de Brosses, in his *Culte des dieux fétiches* (1760), used his extensive knowledge of the literature of travel to consider fetishism as part of the history of all religions, including Christianity, and not as a mere aberration of pagans. Most of the writers of the Enlightenment had a special regard for the Chinese, whose ancient civilization was quoted as evidence for many European theses, from the destructive social consequences of revealed religion – from which the Chinese appeared to be immune – to the virtues of agriculture. Leibniz, who thought they should send missionaries to civilize the Europeans, Wolff and Voltaire, were all enthusiastic eulogists of the Chinese, whose sophisticated mandarins, elevated by merit to the upper ranks of a conservative, hierarchical society, seemed – at least at the distance of several thousand miles – to incarnate so many of the ideals of eighteenth-century society.

The exploration of human societies in space was paralleled by new enquiries into their existence in time. Patient research into the archives of European history by innumerable forgotten scholars was gradually providing some of the documentary evidence which would at least allow future disagreements to rest on a basis of fact. Some of the most eminent writers of the age, Montesquieu, Voltaire, Hume and, later in the century, Gibbon, set themselves to produce history of a new kind, which would illustrate, in terms of human society, the kind of complex interdependence that biologists were discovering in the animal world. Montesquieu's *tout est extrèmement lié* summarized the attitude of an age. The historical revolution which Vico had already begun was not to transform man's view of his past, in a new, dynamic direction, until towards the end of the century, but in this respect as in many others the later theorists could not have gone to work without the enormous extension of knowledge that previous generations provided for them.*

Roger has suggested, in the conclusion to his survey of eighteenth-century French science, that there may be a similar relationship between the scientists' preoccupation with the accumulation of evidence and the forms taken by contemporary French literature. In this context he stressed the extraordinary shapelessness of *Le Diable boiteux*, *Gil Blas*, and the two, significantly unfinished, novels of Marivaux, *La Vie de Marianne* and *Le Paysan parvenu*. As Roger is the first to insist, parallels of this kind must be treated very cautiously and it is not difficult for the ingenious historian to find, or invent, the evidence that his argument requires. His temptation is always to look away from the work of art itself and the technical evolution of a particular genre, to 'influences' which, whatever their social importance in general, may have had little significance for the artist himself. Bearing this in mind, one may nevertheless suggest the possibility that the sudden rise of the novel in the eighteenth century was not merely a response to a wider reading public and to the greater literacy of women, but was also related to the new attitude of empiricism, relativism and the rejection of innate ideas. The male characters at least of Le Sage, the abbé Prévost, Fielding and Smollett, were generally on the move. Their travels involved them, not in miraculous adventures, but in

* See below, pp. 234 *et. seq.*

close contact with a wide variety of 'natural' experiences. Their conduct was often, as in the case of Tom Jones in the inn at Upton, only too clearly the product of their sense-impressions. On the whole, despite the long digression on the 'force of friendship' in *Le Diable boiteux*, the novelists were not greatly concerned with the problem of the choice between conflicting duties, or between passion and duty, that had played so large a part in seventeenth-century tragedy and in Addison's *Cato*. Their heroes were made of more malleable stuff, shaped by their experiences rather than seeking to impose their own fixed values on an external world. Marivaux in particular loved to lose himself in the minute analysis of a gesture or a blush and his delight in such microscopical observation was sufficient in itself, without requiring the purposive framework of a plot.

All this busy observation owed its unity and coherence to a conception of human nature that was universal and static. Natural religion implied a natural man whose values were common to all ages and every continent, however their manifestation might be disguised by exotic outward trappings. This view was emphatically proclaimed by Hume in his *Inquiry concerning Human Understanding* (1748).

It is universally acknowledged that there is a great uniformity among the acts of men, in all nations and ages, and that human nature remains still the same in its principles and operations. . . . Would you know the sentiments, inclinations, and course of life of the Greeks and Romans? Study well the temper and actions of the French and English: you cannot be much mistaken in transferring to the former *most* of the observations which you have made with regard to the latter. Mankind are so much the same, in all times and places, that history informs us of nothing new or strange in this particular. Its chief use is only to discover the constant and universal principles of human nature.

This belief induced a tendency to glorify the *status quo* as a necessary part of the providential order, a tendency which was probably reinforced by the relative stability of European society at the time. We have seen how this was exemplified in Pope's *Essay on Man*. Pluche, as might be expected, took the view that all should be content with the role that Providence had assigned them. Not many of his contemporaries would have followed him quite so far as to extol the particular merit of the 'boundaries that separate the nobility from those of inferior status'. There would perhaps have been more support from the educated for Soame Jenyns's view, in his *Free Enquiry into the Nature and Origin of Evil* (1757), that the ignorance of the poor was a 'cordial administered by the gracious hand of Providence' of which they should not be deprived by 'an ill-judged and improper education'. Most of the men of letters of the period draw a sharp distinction between their own educated public and the illiterate rabble. Even radicals such as Helvétius and d'Holbach, who viewed much of the social order with anger and contempt, were pessimistic about the possibility of improving it. Helvétius, after a passionate attack on slavery – 'not a barrel of sugar arrives in Europe that is not stained with human blood' – has no more constructive suggestion to offer than 'let us turn our eyes from a spectacle so fatal, the shame and horror of humanity'. For d'Holbach, the man of goodwill, when confronted by a society that penalizes virtue and rewards vice, contents himself with domestic happiness and retires from the conflict. 'Progress', if it was possible at all, could only take the form of a movement towards a superior form of static society based on known and immutable values. Morelly was typical in assuming it to be a *return* to 'integrity', that is the natural values which man had formerly forsaken through ignorance and could hope to maintain in the future by his awareness of the value of what he had rediscovered.

Montesquieu's *Lettres persanes* (1721) illustrate many of the attitudes of the period and their popularity helped to propagate the ideas which their author emitted or reflected with clarity and brilliance. The plan of the whole book – a series of letters mostly written by two Persian residents in Paris to correspondents at home – besides enabling Montesquieu to outflank possible censorship by the disingenuous argument that the Persians' comments merely indicated their own ignorance, had another significance. It was intended to allow the French reader to distinguish, within his own society, the local and conventional from what was 'natural' and universal. Beneath all the picturesque detail and exotic local colour runs a consistent argument. Nature intended men to live peaceably together in society and endowed them with the necessary sociability and with universal moral principles. All so-called revealed religions are at bottom anthropomorphic – 'if triangles made themselves a god they would give him three sides' – and encumbered by absurd superstitions. Beneath them all, irrespective even of the existence of God, lie universal principles of justice, binding on all men. Societies differ and the best government for each is that which adapts itself most smoothly to the particular nature of the society in question. Montesquieu's relativism has its limits: the despotism of Persian government and society, as symbolized by the harem, is the antithesis of nature and corrupts all its agents. The eunuchs – the ultimate example of the corruption of man by evil institutions – seek compensation for their sexual deprivation in the abuse of their authority; their master, Usbek, who has appeared wise and tolerant in his open-minded attitude to French society, becomes a monster when his wives revolt. In the final letter written by his favourite, Roxane, after poisoning herself, she admits that she has deceived her tyrant and 'corrected your laws in accordance with those of nature'. Where Europe is concerned, however, nature is not on the side of radicalism. The fable of an imaginary race of troglodytes, who pass from primitive society through Hobbesian anarchy to a republic of virtue, has a somewhat dubious ending. The troglodytes find that continuous self-sacrifice on behalf of the community is beyond human attainment and they finally persuade their most virtuous citizen to become their reluctant king, for in a monarchy, whatever is not illegal is acceptable. Montesquieu was perhaps too much of a realist to be unduly impressed by the arguments in favour of a providential order in which individual self-interest and the common good were miraculously and infallibly reconciled. As he saw it, to be both practicable and tolerable, government must rest on a precarious balance of interests. Monarchy, the form of government most suitable to contemporary Europe, is 'a violent state which invariably degenerates into a despotism or a republic'. The emphasis is consistently on decline rather than improvement. Where an existing government is reasonably satisfactory there is a continual danger that human meddling will upset the delicate natural harmony: 'it is sometimes necessary to change certain laws. But the occasion is rare, and when it arises one must only touch them with a trembling hand.' Montesquieu, though a cautious man, was less suspicious of change than this warning against the legislative itch might seem to suggest. The main purpose of his book was to suggest how French society might, like Roxane, correct its laws in accordance with those of nature. Thanks to his own genius, to his especial interest in government and to his legal experience in the *Parlement* of Bordeaux, Montesquieu's contribution to the ideas of his time was distinctively his own. But if one places the development of his thought, from the *Lettres persanes* in 1721 to *De l'esprit des lois* in 1748, within its historical context, it is legitimate to regard the emphasis in the earlier work on universal natural values and the need to conserve the existing European political order, as typical of the society from which they sprang and for which they were written.

*

Around the middle of the century the assumptions on which the optimism of the early Enlightenment was based began to be more and more frequently challenged. Logically, if not chronologically, the first problem arose from the extension of Locke's views of the nature of perception. As the scientists developed Newtonian physics until the intervention of God became unnecessary, Condillac, in his *Traité des sensations* (1754), denied the autonomous character of reflection which, as conceived by Locke, had given to the mind some of the characteristics of the Christian soul. Condillac insisted, like Berkeley, that perception was the result of habit and not the immediate evidence of the senses. Memory was, as it were, a library of former perceptions. Reflection was the automatic comparison of these former perceptions and therefore 'sensation, after being attention, comparison, judgement, then becomes reflection itself'. The mind, far from being a kind of principle of rationality which picked its way towards objective truth by the judicious interpretation of the evidence of the senses, was merely an agglomeration of ideas which were themselves sense-impressions. As Condillac put it, referring to the imaginary statue which he endowed with one faculty after another in order to show how the senses produced ideas, 'Its "I" is nothing more than the collection of the things which it is feeling and the things which its memory recalls.' Therefore all ideas are relative to the sense-impressions of the thinker: 'The good and the beautiful are by no means absolutes; they are relative to the character of the man who judges and to the way in which he is organized.'

Besides implying that all ideas were relative to the thinker, such a view also raised in an acute form the question of free will. This insoluble dilemma the Christian might exclude from philosophy as a 'mystery', but the Deist could not accept what was to him a mere evasion. Pope, in reply to the accusation that he had preached determinism in the *Essay on*

Man, asserted in his *Universal Prayer* of the following year that God

> binding Nature fast in Fate
> Left free the Human Will.

But this was an affirmation not an argument. Voltaire, at about the same period, had been similarly peremptory, 'proving' the existence of free will by simple common-sense arguments of whose validity he did not seem altogether convinced. Thirty years later he had surrendered to determinism, asserting in the *Philosophe ignorant* (1766), 'When I am able to do what I will, I am free; but I will what I will of necessity; otherwise I should will without reason, without a cause, which is impossible.' La Mettrie, as a doctor, was impressed by the extent to which ideas were determined by a man's physical state, for example, in delirium. Aware of recent discoveries concerning muscular reactions, even in the tissue of dead animals, he was inclined to see in such reactions a new form of motion that was a property inherent in matter, and to explain the whole of human activity in terms of such motion. 'The brain has its muscles for thinking, as the legs have muscles for walking.' Consequently, 'It is vain to protest about the empire of the will. For every order which it gives it receives a hundred.' Materialist determinism did not necessarily deny the existence of God. La Mettrie himself wrote, 'I do not call into question the existence of a Supreme Being; on the contrary it seems to me that the balance of probability is in its favour.' As early as 1734 Voltaire had affirmed that matter could think if God chose to endow it with the capacity for thought. But the god of the determinists was a being infinitely more remote than the friendly Providence of Pope or Pluche and any link between the divine will and free human aspiration had been severed.

Montesquieu, in his greatest work, *De l'esprit des lois* (1748), which revolutionized men's conception of history by showing

the interrelation of social, geographical, political, economic
and religious forces, and may be considered the starting-point
of modern sociology, fought a continuous and inconclusive
battle with himself over the question of determinism. His
conservative temperament was inclined to see in the adjustment of conditioning factors to each other a justification for
whatever existed. On the subject of ecclesiastical justice, for
example, he wrote, 'The question is not to establish whether
it was right to establish it, but whether it has been established,
whether it forms part of the laws of a country and is everywhere relative to them.' But Montesquieu had too honest and
penetrating a mind not to see the arguments for both sides,
and there were some, however logical, which his conscience
would not allow him to accept. He makes out a very strong
case for determinism. Laws are 'the necessary relationships
which are determined by the nature of things'. But already,
in the same first chapter, free will secures a humble foothold,
thanks to the human capacity for error.

Since we see that the world, formed from motion and matter and
deprived of intelligence, continues to exist, its motions of necessity
imply invariable laws. ... But the world of intelligence is by no
means as well-ordered as the physical world. For although it also has
laws which are, by nature, invariable, it does not follow them as
consistently as the physical world. The reason for this is that intelligent individual beings are limited by their nature and consequently
subject to error.

After this richly ambiguous beginning, Montesquieu goes
on to consider different types of government – republican,
monarchical and despotic – showing how each logically
implies policies and institutions appropriate to its particular
nature. At this point a second difficulty occurs, with regard
to torture. 'I was going to say that it could be suitable to
despotic governments, where everything that inspires fear is
a vital force of government. ... But I hear the voice of
nature which cries out against me.' Besides doing honour to

its author and his age, Montesquieu's moral revolt implies that nature, as a moral imperative, has an autonomous existence that takes precedence over nature as a system of conditioning forces. Henceforth his objective essay in comparative sociology becomes increasingly vulnerable and finally breaks down altogether when he comes to consider political liberty. It is at once clear that he considers this the moral criterion by which any political system is to be judged. Despotism then becomes inadmissible, however well-adapted to its environment. Liberty is secured, not by the happy accident of appropriate conditioning factors, but by human ingenuity in contriving a balance between the political ambitions of various interests, any one of which, unchecked, would impose its well-intentioned tyranny on the state. 'Virtue itself requires limitation.' There follows his famous analysis of the English constitution which, for Montesquieu, was the outstanding example of such contrivance. His next two chapters consider laws, not in relation to the three types of government, but from the viewpoint of the prime objective of safeguarding individual liberty.

When he comes to consider laws in relation to the material factors conditioning a society, Montesquieu, elaborating at much greater length ideas that Voltaire had briefly sketched in his *Traité de métaphysique* in 1734, once more seems to incline towards determinism. Climate determines human temperament and thence the kind of society appropriate to a given people. Terrain similarly regulates the passivity or belligerency of a people. But in every case nature or man has an autonomous role to play. Faced with the problem of slavery, Montesquieu finds himself in the same dilemma as in the case of torture and will not admit as logical what he deplores as abhorrent. Where terrain is concerned, there are 'countries formed by human industry' such as Holland. We are therefore confronted by a two-way process in which man is determined by physical geography, but also free, in some cases at least and to a limited extent, to shape even 'nature' in accordance with his will. It is at this stage of his argument that Montesquieu asserts that all the conditioning forces at work, 'climate, religion, laws, maxims of government, the example of things past, habits, manners', create the general spirit of a society. This *esprit général* is both passive, as the product of social determinism, and also an active agent which decides how a society will react to changes in its environment, how receptive it will be to specific new ideas, and so on. Having thus demonstrated that, from the viewpoint of social determinism, cause and effect are reversible, Montesquieu considers other factors which influence societies, notably commerce, population and religious belief. He emphasizes the extent to which opinions on these subjects are determined by material factors, explaining, for example, the Protestantism of northern Europe and the rejection of episcopacy by Calvin on climatic and political grounds and Buddhist belief in metamorphosis on geographical ones. But religious or economic beliefs, whatever their origins, are demonstrably causes of social action. If climate implies Catholicism, Catholic laws on usury will influence the development of trade. Montesquieu was far too conscious of the extraordinary complexity of human experience to look for a simple answer to any question concerning the ultimate nature of man or society. His originality consisted precisely in the patient insight with which he described the web, without claiming to isolate any particular strand and assume that it regulated the whole. He was prepared to admit that laws were in part the products of an economic infra-structure, but only if granted that the economic infra-structure was in part the product of laws. Nevertheless, to his contemporaries, the new social dimension which he added to the study of political institutions implied a more deterministic attitude than any to which they were accustomed, and his successors were soon to advance much further along this road.

One of the most successful attempts to apply the methods of inductive science to the study of human society was the emergence of economics as a subject in its own right and not a subsidiary branch of politics. The history of economics in the eighteenth century offers a demonstration in microcosm of the kind of problems that confronted the Enlightenment. Towards the middle of the century a group of French writers known as the Physiocrats claimed to have identified a 'natural order' which regulated the whole economic process. This initial vision was Providential and optimistic. The creation of wealth rested on the divine miracle by which nature ensured that plants produced a surplus of food and raw materials for Man, as well as the seed necessary for their self-perpetuation. Where human industry could merely rearrange what already existed, nature could create something from nothing. Here, as elsewhere, ignorance of biochemistry might almost be considered one of the foundations of the Enlightenment. A natural harmony regulated the circulation of the wealth that nature's bounty alone created. Man, by the application of his reason, could align his institutions with the law of nature so as to achieve, not indeed utopian perfection, but at least a progressive improvement in his standard of living.

These theories were secularized and developed by Adam Smith, whose *Inquiry into the Nature and Causes of the Wealth of Nations* was published in 1776. Smith disentangled the creation of wealth from the agrarian bias of the Physiocrats, while retaining their belief in a Providential order. In so doing, he went further than merely to postulate the almost infinite growth of wealth. His theories seemed to eliminate the traditional Christian conflict between virtue and acquisitiveness. Providence had so ordered things that 'Every individual exerts himself to find out the most advantageous employment for whatever his capital can command. The study of his own advantage necessarily leads him to prefer what is most advantageous to the society.' The awkward passage about the camel and the eye of the needle was just another example of the religious obscurantism of pre-capitalist society.

Such theories were initially regarded as liberating society from the ignorant prejudice that had crippled its 'natural' development. But it soon became obvious that there was another way of regarding economic laws whose objective reality was admitted by almost everyone. One of the conclusions of the economists was that the natural price of labour, like that of every other commodity, was determined by supply and demand. In normal circumstances, wages would approximate to the 'cost of production' of the labourer. The indefinite enrichment of society therefore rested on the payment of subsistence wages to those who had nothing to sell but their labour. Even more serious, the traditional controls by which governments tried to hold down food prices in famine years were an interference with the natural order. The long-term answer to famine, which was to encourage the investment of capital in agriculture by allowing prices to rise in years of scarcity, might involve starvation in the present, besides holding out a dismal prospect for the majority in the more distant future. This 'iron law' was too much for an economic conservative like Necker, who burst out, in a controversy with the 'progressive' Minister and civil servant, Turgot, 'I simply cannot understand this cold intellectual compassion for future generations, which is supposed to harden our hearts against the cries of ten thousand unfortunates who surround us now.' Once abstract the faith in a beneficent Providence, and the rule of nature meant the enslavement of man to the laws of matter.

On the philosophical front, the most telling blows against the self-assurance of the Enlightenment were those struck by Hume. Step by step he systematically demolished its claims to have established its values on any solid foundation. His *Enquiry Concerning Human Understanding* (1748) begins with the argument that our concept of causation rests merely on the habitual observation of the same sequence of events in time. At best, it can therefore be no more than highly probable. We can never hope to attain to the logical certainty of Cartesian deduction. We have no means of knowing 'that circumstance in the cause which gives it a connexion with its effect. We have no idea of this connexion, nor even any distinct notion what it is we desire to know when we endeavour at a conception of it.' For Hume, as for Condillac, thinking is merely the involuntary association of ideas which our past experience has connected with each other. 'All these operations are a species of natural instincts which no reasoning or process of thought and understanding is able either to produce or to prevent.' At this point he continues very reasonably, 'it would be very allowable for us to stop our philosophic researches.' Free will, in such a system, can only mean the freedom to perform what one is obliged to want. Hume then faces the issue that determinism implies either that evil is a minor but necessary constituent of the best of all possible worlds, or else represents the free choice of God. Having demolished the Leibnizian view on common-sense grounds, he dismisses the latter as 'mysteries which mere natural and unassisted reason is very unfit to handle'. The remainder of the book is devoted to a ferocious attack on revealed religions. The miracles by which each claims to prove its divine origin are dismissed on grounds of probability. 'We may conclude that the Christian religion not only was at first attended with miracles, but even at this day cannot be believed by any reasonable person without one.' Providence is rejected as the product of an anthropomorphic imagination. 'The great source of our mistake on this subject and of the unbounded licence of conjecture which we indulge is that we tacitly consider ourselves as in the place of the Supreme Being and conclude that he will, on every occasion, observe the same conduct that we ourselves, in his situation, would have embraced as reasonable and eligible.'

In his *Natural History of Religion* (1757) Hume extended his work of demolition to natural religion. He first denies the existence of any universal consensus in its favour. He then goes on to ridicule the idea that primitive man founded his religion on the argument from design. Far from regarding the harmonious organization of nature as proof of the existence of God, he would take the customary order for granted and seek a supernatural explanation only to explain the exceptional phenomena that frightened him. Primitive religion, in other words, was an insurance policy against what the insurance companies still refer to as 'Acts of God'. It was therefore polytheistic, each natural menace being assumed to have its divine controller. Monotheism arose, not from the purification of the original crudities, but from a servile desire to flatter a particular god, and it was this same motive that led to his being credited, at a relatively late stage in history, with the creation of the world. Secular morality prescribes all the rules of conduct necessary for man and society. Religion, if it is to go further, must therefore consist in what is socially useless or most contrary to man's natural instincts. 'Hence it is justly regarded as unsafe to draw any certain inference in favour of a man's morals, from the fervour or strictness of his religious exercises, even though he himself believe them sincere. Nay, it has been observed, that enormities of the blackest dye have been rather apt to produce superstitious terrors, and increase the religious passion.' Hume, it must be emphasized, was not denying the existence of God; he was asserting that the history of religion showed it to be based on superstitious fear. The Deist was entitled to his belief, but not to the assumption that it rested on foundations more logically secure than those of the Christian. Natural religion was as much a faith as any other. 'The whole is a riddle, an enigma, and inexplicable mystery. Doubt, uncertainty, suspense of judgement appear the only result of our most accurate scrutiny concerning this subject.' Hume himself might view with serene detachment the thought that he and his fellow-sceptics, 'opposing one species of superstition to another, set them a quarrelling; while we ourselves, during their fury and contention, happily make our escape into the calm, though obscure, regions of philosophy.' What he had done was to knock away the main prop from beneath the intellectual foundations of a whole system of thought.

The *philosophes*, like the scientists, were driven to a reluctant choice between complete scepticism and purposeless determinism. Voltaire, despite all his intelligence and wit, was carried reluctantly with the tide. His *Philosophe ignorant* (1766) opens with a confession of human ignorance. 'Who are you? Where do you come from? What are you doing? What will become of you? This is a question one must put to every creature in the universe, but none of them gives us any answer.' Already, in 1752, the unexpected conclusion of *Micromégas* had made the same point. The voyager from Sirius, whose faculties and intelligence far transcended those of man, offered as a parting present to his European hosts, a book of philosophy in which they could read the ultimate meaning of life. 'It was taken to Paris, to the *Académie des Sciences*. But when the secretary [Fontenelle] had opened it, he found the pages completely blank. "Ah," he said, "that's just what I expected."'

Hume might contemplate the horizons of scepticism with the equanimity of the classical patrician, but others were more aware that nature without God implied, quite literally, the law of the jungle. In 1731 the wicked apprentice in the *London Merchant* had declared, 'All actions are alike natural and indifferent to man and beast, who devour or are devoured, as they meet with others weaker or stronger than themselves.' A generation later it was not easy to dismiss such opinions as the aberrations of a criminal and anti-social mind. Diderot struggled with the problem as honestly as usual. He would have liked to believe that the 'eternal will (of nature) is that good should be preferred to evil and general to individual good' but he could write, in another mood, 'nature does nothing wrong. Every form, beautiful or ugly, has its cause. Of all living creatures, there is not one which is not as it should be.' La Mettrie, in his *Anti-Sénèque* (1750), took this argument to its logical conclusion. 'Since the pleasures of the mind are the real source of happiness, it is perfectly clear that, from the point of view of happiness, good and evil are things quite indifferent in themselves and he who obtains greater satisfaction from doing evil will be happier than the man who obtains less satisfaction from doing good. This explains why so many scoundrels are happy in this life and shows that there is a kind of individual felicity which is to be found, not merely without virtue, but even in crime itself.' In his *Bonheur* (1748) La Mettrie insisted that happiness was a psychological fact, not the reward of virtue, remorse a conditioned educational reaction of no value, since a recurrence of the same temptation would lead to a repetition of the same fault. Towards the end of the century the Marquis de Sade was to elaborate these themes with the profusion of picturesque sexual detail that has won him so many readers in recent years, but Sade's principles were already familiar to the writers of the previous generation. Nature, indifferent to man and his artificial values, requires the conflict of egoisms in order to accomplish its incomprehensible processes. As the unfortunate Justine discovered with implausible regularity, to try to regulate one's life by a moral principle is to set one's self athwart the rhythm of nature, so that one's suffering is likely to be proportionate to one's disinterestedness. Since man is a part of nature, whatever he does is 'natural', and, as Diderot had already implied, deformity, whether moral or physical, was a purely human judgement, of no objective validity.

It seemed to some writers that the only escape from this moral anarchy was to construct a system of values based explicitly on the welfare of the community. Already, in 1734,

Voltaire had written in his *Traité de métaphysique* that moral standards were determined by the communal advantage 'which can have no analogy with God'. The sheep had no ground for complaint if eaten by the wolf. But Voltaire had drawn the sting from his conclusions by assuming that God implanted a natural benevolence within the hearts of men. Helvétius, without this safeguard, made ethics purely relative – to the insect in the grass, the lion is an avenger of the innocent who preserves him from the ferocity of the remorseless sheep. 'That which procures the greatest happiness for the greatest number'—an expression apparently coined by Hutcheson in the 1730s, which appeared in his posthumous *System of Moral Philosophy* in 1755 and was taken up by one writer after another—covered a multitude of what had formerly been regarded as sins. Helvétius, who took most arguments at least as far as their logical conclusions, observed that since everything done for the public good becomes both legitimate and virtuous, cannibalism amongst the crew of a ship that runs out of food is not merely permissible but good. Man has, admittedly, to consider his actions in the context of humanity as a whole, but granted the lack of any international order, his first obligation is to his immediate society and patriotism is 'absolutely exclusive of universal love'. The escape from moral anarchy was already beginning to point towards a new totalitarian nightmare.

Utilitarianism therefore provided no satisfactory alternative to the choice between total scepticism and its apparent opposite, total determinism, which appeared to be the only tenable positions left to the rational man. The latter viewpoint is well illustrated in the *Rêve de d'Alembert*, where the radicalism of Diderot's thought perhaps explains why he preferred not to publish his manuscript.

MADEMOISELLE DE L'ESPINASSE: Since I act in a certain way, someone who can act differently is not myself, and to affirm that at the instant when I say or do something, I can say or do something else, is to affirm that I am myself someone else. But, doctor, what of virtue and vice? Virtue, so sacred a word in every tongue, so sacred an idea amongst all nations.

DR BORDEU: We must change it to *bienfaisance* and its opposite to *malfaisance*. One is happily or unhappily born; one is irresistibly carried along by the general stream that bears one man to glory and another to ignominy.

MADEMOISELLE DE L'ESPINASSE: And self-respect, shame and remorse?

DR BORDEU: Puerility based on the ignorance and vanity of a being who attributes to himself the merit or demerit of a moment of necessity.

The predicament of the determinist is nowhere shown more clearly than in *De l'esprit* which Helvétius published in 1758. This paradoxical work stands at the very turning-point of the century and contains within its self-contradictions most of the conflicting tendencies of the movement we have been examining, and the revolt against it that was to be associated with Rousseau in France and the writers of the *Sturm und Drang* (Storm and Stress) in Germany. The latter aspect will be considered in a later chapter.* Our concern here is with Helvétius as the prophet of determinism. In his preface he linked philosophy with science: 'It has seemed to me that one must treat ethics like all the other sciences and construct experimental ethics in the same way as experimental physics.' Like so many of his contemporaries he equated religion with social morality. 'Every moral code whose principles are of public utility is necessarily in conformity with the principles of religion, which is merely the perfection of human morality.' The book then begins with an exposition of Locke's philosophy of sensation, as modified by Condillac. A digression on the subject of luxury brings out his own preference for the Spartan virtues of an austere, warlike and belligerent republic. The fact that Helvétius, a wealthy retired tax-farmer whose

* See below, pp. 186-218.

father had been the queen's doctor, should have idealized qualities so alien to anything he knew or practised, is perhaps an indication of the strange fascination which a new conception of antiquity was developing, a fascination that was to go on gathering strength until the French Revolution. Returning to his main theme, Helvétius vigorously denied the existence of free will. 'All our thoughts and will must be the immediate effect or the necessary consequence of impressions we have received.' In his second *Discourse* he considered mind in relation to society. Public utility is the source of all moral values. The individual therefore finds himself faced with a conflict between the interests of his family and the state, which can only be resolved by handing over the care of all children to the state – an idea that Saint-Just was to take up in 1794. Men's conduct being determined by circumstances, it is a matter of chance whether their interests happen to coincide with the social good. Helvétius followed Montesquieu in linking the laws and customs of a society, but he anticipated the writers of the second half of the century by making law the master rather than the product of social attitudes. Government therefore helps to determine which values are, in fact, socially desirable, and if a government could succeed in identifying public utility with private self-interest, all men would be 'necessitated to virtue' (*nécessités à la vertu*.). The past is all rubbish – 'the stupid veneration of the peoples for ancient laws and customs' – but the object of government is not progress, but a return to a state of primitive virtue. How this is to be attained in a determinist world is by no means clear. In the third *Discourse*, Helvétius adopted a cyclical view of history, civilization leading through luxury to despotism which in turn produced depopulation and a return to primitive life in the forests that encroached on the relics of urban decadence. In this book he argues that men are born fundamentally equal in their faculties. 'Each has within himself the physical power to raise himself to the loftiest thoughts.'

Actual differences between men are due either to the differing strength of their passions, which alone can overcome the natural inertia of the mind, or to the accident of their education. Even the passions fall under the shadow of the state, since their intensity depends on the nature of the rewards for civic virtue which a wise legislator can manipulate – and Helvétius, whose own marital constancy seems to have been somewhat unusual by eighteenth-century standards, loses himself in an erotic dream of an improved Sparta allowing its most illustrious warriors to take their pick of the local beauties! *De l'esprit* is a confused and unconvincing book which anticipates one of the weaknesses of Rousseau's *Du contrat social* in having a free legislator manipulate the wires by which the actions of all the other human puppets are determined. Despite its limitations, however, it did suggest once again that an attempt to base a code of ethics on purely human values was likely to lead, not to the emancipation of the individual, but to his immolation on the altar of society.

By the middle of the century the efforts of scientists and philosophers to discover the purpose of nature and the rights and duties of man, by the light of unaided human reason, seemed to have led to a choice between the inscrutable and the intolerable. Blake, for whom the whole enterprise was an impious denial of the sacred truth of imagination, was to sum it all up in suitably apocalyptic language:

I turn my eyes to the Schools and Universities of Europe
And there behold the Loom of Locke, whose Woof rages dire,
Wash'd by the Water-wheels of Newton: black the cloth
In heavy wreathes folds over every Nation: cruel Works
Of many Wheels I view, wheel without wheel, with cogs tyrannic
Moving by compulsion each other. . . .

Chapter 4

THE ENLIGHTENMENT
AS A WAY OF LIFE

IN the two previous chapters I have tried to trace the development of an argument, originating with Newton and Locke in England in the seventeenth century, which by about 1760 seemed to have lost its way in either scepticism or determinism. Educated men all over Europe were affected by this argument since the men whose writings they most admired – such as Voltaire – were active participants in the debate. It must, however, be emphasized that full awareness of the controversies in all their complex evolution was limited to a very small number of men of letters. The perspective of the eighteenth-century gentleman was not that of the modern reader. Some of the works referred to in previous chapters, such as Montesquieu's *De l'esprit des lois* and Buffon's *Histoire naturelle*, were best-sellers that one might expect to find in any well-stocked library. The former appeared in twenty-two editions within eighteen months of publication, which implied sales in the region of 35,000 copies. There were eight editions of Voltaire's *Candide* in 1759 alone and 4,000 subscribers to the *Encyclopédie*. Other works, of equal interest to the present-day reader, were known to comparatively few people; for example, the entire output of La Mettrie, Condillac's *Traité des sensations* and Morelly's *Code de la nature*. Diderot was famous as the editor of the *Encyclopédie* and well known as a dramatist, but his most adventurous writings were not published until after his death and his *Pensées sur l'interprétation de la nature* did not achieve more than two editions. Any attempt to assess the diffusion of the ideas of the Enlightenment must therefore start by recognizing that even the best-informed readers, who had invested heavily in expensive banned books, had a somewhat limited acquaintance with what had been published, and *a fortiori* with works circulating in manuscript within a limited circle. On the whole, despite exceptions such as Helvétius's *De l'esprit*, which achieved considerable notoriety, it was the most radical works which took longest to reach an extensive public.

Even if we restrict our enquiry to books which enjoyed an extensive circulation, the problem of how far the ideas of their writers were in fact disseminated throughout Europe is not a simple one. It is perhaps helpful to think in terms of influences radiating outwards from the triangle of Paris–London–Amsterdam, and becoming weaker in proportion to the distance from their point of origin. Geographical diffusion of this kind must also be supplemented by a study of social diffusion: in all countries, some sections of society were more receptive than others. These two factors interacted upon each other, and as one moved further eastwards changes in social structure modified the receptivity of the different classes to the ideas coming from the west. The entire complicated process must also be considered as evolving in time. Some kinds of resistance were overcome almost immediately, others more slowly and some not at all. Moreover, while the frontier of the Enlightenment spread outwards in space and downwards through the social hierarchy, the centre itself was evolving all the time. Whatever refinements of this kind we seek to introduce, we are still left with a crude mathematical formula, more appropriate to tracing the spread of an influenza epidemic than to the infinitely subtle and varied dissemination of a complex of partially inconsistent discoveries, assumptions and attitudes, through societies which could only assimilate them in local terms, by individuals who were quite capable of unpredictable reactions. As always, the historian must choose between generalizations which are never quite true in any specific instance and an incomprehensible anarchy of individual cases. The analytical abstractions which form the first part of the present chapter are therefore not intended to be more than rather crude landmarks.

Before embarking on the voyage at all it is necessary to consider one general source of opposition to the Enlightenment which explains some of the variations in the pattern of its diffusion. As we have seen, the conclusions of the mid-eighteenth-century writers challenged views of the history and nature of man and of the universe which were endorsed by the Christian Churches, especially, perhaps, by the Church of Rome. To some extent, where the challenge came from Deism rather than materialism, the Churches were free either to try to come to terms with the *philosophes* or to reject them outright as heretical. R. R. Palmer has suggested, in his study of *Catholics and Unbelievers in Eighteenth-century France*, that there were doctrinal reasons why Protestants should stress the rationality and Catholics the mysteries of Christianity. Moreover, French writers who attacked the Catholic Church were likely to enjoy a good deal of initial sympathy from vigorously anti-papal divines in England and perhaps in Germany. In these countries the issues were less clear-cut and the progress of the Enlightenment was more a question of a gradual change of emphasis than of victory in open conflict. Where the Church was most accommodating there was least incentive to revolt. *Tom Jones* provides a good illustration of the reconciliation of many of the values of the Enlightenment with respect for Christian observance. This was helped by the flexibility of the Church of England and also by its weakness as a corporate order, which subjected the humble parson to very strong pressure from lay society. Similarly, Lessing's view of Christianity as merely one phase in man's religious history did not involve him in quite the same kind of pitched battle that would have been inevitable in France. In Catholic states one of the main factors regulating the spread of the new ideas was the effectiveness of the machinery of clerical censorship. Where, as in Spain, this was not seriously in conflict with royal power, resistance could be very strong. In France the Government was from time to time at loggerheads with the Assembly of the Clergy over the taxation of Church wealth, and royal policy fluctuated with the need to conciliate the Assembly or the desire to challenge the claims of the clergy to influence the conduct of state affairs.

It would be a mistake to consider the resistance of the clergy as a merely defensive campaign. Indeed, it is something of an historical impertinence to consider the century as the age of the Enlightenment since religion exercised a far greater hold over most sections of every society than it does today. In France there appeared ninety books in defence of Christianity in 1770 alone. Palmer has shown how vigorous and effective were the counter-attacks launched by Christian writers against works such as d'Holbach's *Système de la nature* (1770). In this book d'Holbach himself conceded that 'Where religion is concerned, there are very few people who do not share to a greater or lesser extent the opinions of the ordinary man.' Hume is alleged to have said, when a guest of d'Holbach, that he did not believe in the existence of atheists. More significantly, since Deism was much commoner than atheism, Johnson gave it as his opinion that 'There are, in reality, very few infidels. I have heard a person, originally a Quaker, but now, I am afraid, a Deist, say that he did not believe there were, in all England, above 200 infidels.' Gibbon confessed in his autobiography to being taken aback by the discovery that 'the majority of English readers were so fondly attached even to the name and shadow of Christianity.' In Germany the rebirth of a national literature and the growth of the Enlightenment rested on pietist foundations and it was no accident that the first great work of this German renaissance should have been Klopstock's epic poem, *The Messiah*. One must not exaggerate this attachment to traditional religious practices.

There were probably many like the future revolutionary leader, Madame Roland, who continued to attend church from reasons of *bienséance* when they were no longer believers. The French Revolution was to reveal the extent to which religious incredulity had taken hold. France was different from England and Germany and disbelief probably spread widely in the generation before the Revolution. To some extent, religious practice varied with age: the writer Marmontel and the revolutionaries Madame Roland and Brissot were no doubt typical of many others who abandoned the beliefs of their parents as they themselves grew up. What one can assert with some confidence is that religion remained an active force, both in terms of theological argument and of mass observance. The coexistence of different patterns of behaviour was noted by Goldoni, the Italian playwright, when he came to Paris in 1761. 'Paris is a whole world. Everything there is on the grand scale, both good and evil. Go to the theatres, the promenades, the haunts of pleasure: all are crowded. Go to the churches: every one is packed.'

*

The social diffusion of the ideas of the Enlightenment was controlled in the first instance by the high cost of books which greatly restricted possible readers, even if we reject as unduly pessimistic Grimm's estimate in 1757 that, in Paris itself, only a few hundred people concerned themselves with 'literature, the arts and healthy philosophy'. Substantial works such as Rousseau's *Émile* and the *Système de la nature* cost about fifteen to eighteen livres (roughly fifteen shillings) when they could be bought on the open market. Once prohibited by the Government, their price might well be multiplied four or five times. Anti-Christian pamphlets by Voltaire sold for several pounds each, instead of their normal price of two or three shillings. Malesherbes, who was responsible for censorship in France from 1750 to 1763, seems to have shared the view of many present-day magistrates that the social danger of a book varies inversely with its price. Sympathetically disposed towards a limited freedom of the press – too much so for some of the *philosophes* since he refused to ban the works of their opponents – Malesherbes would normally give his tacit consent to the sale of a limited number of copies of a new book. If these did not produce any public outcry, others were allowed to follow. If trouble arose the book was banned, but no unseemly rigour prevented its limited distribution at an inflated price. This practice presumably helps to explain why so many first editions of controversial works were sold out within days of publication. The question with which we are concerned, however, is not merely who could afford to pay several pounds for a banned pamphlet or fifteen shillings for an authorized book, but who would think it worth his while to do so.

The answer, in the first place, would seem to be the Court aristocracy, whose less intelligent members perhaps drew no clear distinction between philosophical and pornographic daring. Where works like Diderot's *Bijoux indiscrets* were concerned, they had some excuse, and the casual reader could divert himself with salacious passages or 'shocking' anti-clericalism in a long series of books from Montesquieu's *Lettres persanes* (1721) to Raynal's *Histoire philosophique des deux Indes* (1772). Mornet, in his outstanding survey of the diffusion of the Enlightenment – entitled, somewhat mis-leadingly, *Les Origines intellectuelles de la Révolution Française* – emphasizes the connexion between dissolute morals, irreligion and the new ideas. The social snobbery attached to sexual emancipation may be illustrated by the spiteful comment of an aristocratic neighbour, that Rousseau's protector and mistress, Madame de Warens, 'concealed her bust like a *bourgeoise*'. The old ambiguity of the word *libertin* was still relevant. Sexual morality was certainly extraordinarily lax during the latter part of the reign of Louis XV. The Parisian lawyer, Barbier, writing in 1750, regarded a concern for the Christian conception of marriage as the kind of popular superstition which the educated man quite rightly despised. 'Of every twenty lords at Court, fifteen are separated from their wives and keep mistresses. Nothing is more common in Paris amongst ordinary people.' The most striking examples of open disregard for religion – which could still be dangerous – came from the invulnerable. The comte d'Artois, the brother of Louis XVI, disregarded fast days. Conti, a Prince of the Blood, on his deathbed refused to admit the Archbishop of Paris who was trying to bring him the sacraments. Marie Antoinette herself had some of the banned books in her library. As the vicomtesse de Noailles noted regretfully, after the Revolution had broken out, 'Philosophy had no apostles more well-disposed than the quality [grands seigneurs] . . . the most active and enthusiastic pupils of Rousseau and Voltaire were courtiers, even more than men of letters.' Such men had the leisure to keep abreast of the latest censored works which were the topics of fashionable conversation, besides the means to acquire them. Their influence protected the men engaged in the illicit book trade, who sometimes carried on their business from the legally-privileged town houses of the princes, and thereby helped to frustrate the royal censorship. The ideas of the Enlightenment obviously meant different things to the dissolute trifler and the intellectually inquisitive habitué of a salon where serious questions were seriously, if not solemnly discussed, but both shared attitudes of disbelief in religion and contempt for social convention, which became so general in Court circles and in much Parisian salon society that to assert an opposite view was to appear eccentric. Outside France, in Germany and Italy, and from 1763 onwards to some extent in Russia and Poland also, French influence was predominant in Court society, and French attitudes were more evident amongst the upper nobility than in any other section of the community.

The clergy, especially in Catholic Europe, played an intellectual part second only to that of the Court nobility and proved more receptive to the Enlightenment than might have been expected. They had often entered the Church in pursuance of family policies rather than religious vocation, and Mornet quotes several examples of priests who were sceptics if not actual atheists. Far more, in all probability, effected some kind of ill-defined compromise between their faith and the new outlook of the *philosophes*. In the provinces particularly, they retained something of their traditional status as custodians of learning, educated men interested in the changing ideas of the society in which they lived and concerned to understand these ideas, if only to refute them or accept them with reservations. The lawyer, de Brosses, travelling in Italy in 1739–40, found that priests were the men with libraries, with whom he could discuss Newtonian physics. Mornet refers to a Breton *curé* whose library of 540 volumes included the *Encyclopédie*, which cost about £14. The Archbishop of Salzburg had busts of Voltaire and Rousseau in his study and another pair were to be found in a Benedictine monastery at Angers. Once again, one must guard against the temptation to over-simplify. Many of the clergy no doubt heartily endorsed the fulminations of the French Jansenists' *Nouvelles ecclésiastiques* against the whole secular temper of the age as well as the blasphemies of the *philosophes*. But there were *abbés* to be found in all the *salons*. Many of the writers of the Enlightenment, such as Condillac, Morelly, Mably and Raynal, belonged – however tenuously – to the Church. The clergy were well-represented in the provincial Academies which accepted some at least of the views of the Enlightenment: they provided between one eighth and one fifth of the members of the Academies of Bordeaux, Dijon and Châlons-sur-Marne, for example. Integrated with lay society by reason of their functions, friendships and family connexions, their intellectual training and concern for general problems made them more receptive to new ideas than the often hidebound and parochially-minded laymen with whom they mixed.

To think of the bourgeoisie, as distinct from different kinds of bourgeois, is probably to be guilty of an anachronism. Although the word itself had existed in France since the Middle Ages, it was rarely used. Contemporaries were perhaps more aware of what divided the more affluent commoners than of what they had in common. Certainly, from the viewpoint of our present enquiry, there was no identifiable body of opinion that could be called 'middle class'. At the top of the commoners' scale, wealthy financiers mixed in the Parisian *salons* with the Court nobility, maintained *salons* themselves, like Madame Necker, and were culturally indistinguishable from the nobility, to which they increasingly tended to belong. The more eminent members of the liberal professions, barristers (who might have attained nobility or be aspiring to do so), some doctors and the more important agents of the royal administration formed a cultural sub-class of their own. In the Academies of Châlons and Dijon, even in that of the prosperous port of Bordeaux, all the commoners came from this section of the middle class. These were the people who had libraries, even if small ones of a primarily utilitarian nature. Professionally concerned with public affairs, they were willy-nilly made aware of national issues and their secondary education, however dominated by Latin and scholasticism, gave them some training in logic and the handling of abstract ideas. It was from this section of the middle class that most of the leaders of the French Revolution were to be recruited and these men had been active, in subordinate positions, in the intellectual life of the provinces for a considerable time before 1789. If Madame Roland was not guilty of exaggerating the status of her family's profession, one should perhaps include in this category, at least in the capital cities, those of humbler social status who were professionally engaged in purveying the wares of the Enlightenment: publishers, printers, booksellers, engravers, actors, musicians and sculptors who were brought into daily contact with a cultivated public. She herself claimed that 'Those who live in the capital, even if they are not in the first flight, have a body of knowledge and a kind of good breeding which you would certainly not find either amongst the provincial squirarchy or amongst businessmen in a hurry to make a fortune so that they can buy a title.' During her own adolescence she does not seem to have found it very difficult to obtain access to most of the major works of the Enlightenment.

In a quite different category come the hurried businessmen. It was Madame Roland's husband who maintained that commerce had a 'harmful, degrading and destructive' influence on the character of those who lived by it. Nothing in the daily life of the small merchant or master craftsman predisposed him to intellectual speculation, or even to think in terms of social change. Contemporary educated opinion, on the Continent at least, generally treated the merchant with a barely polite contempt and his social status did not reflect his financial resources unless the latter were sufficient for him to give up his business and live like a gentleman. Most European towns were sleepy places where continuity was more obvious than change. A government official wrote of Angers in 1783, 'The present generation vegetates just as that which preceded it vegetated and the succeeding one will vegetate.' Generally excluded from active participation in whatever local cultural activity there was – Academies, literary societies and masonic lodges – people of this kind did not provide much of an audience for radical thinking, whether religious or political. Being literate, some of them read; their wives and daughters read more and more, but they supplied the public for the 'moral weeklies', the sentimental theatre and the newly-arrived popular novel, purveyors of ready emotion and conformist morality rather than the discomfort of intellectual challenge.

The urban 'working classes' consisted mainly of artisans and domestic servants. One of the main ways in which they differed from their present-day counterparts was that a high proportion lived in their employers' houses, in relatively close personal contact with people of a different social class. Journeymen and apprentices came within the field of influence of master craftsmen, while servants in a noble household would be more or less aware of the values of aristocratic society and more or less influenced by them. Madame Roland, in a very striking passage in her autobiography, describes her reception by the upper servants of a wealthy financier's family. Dressed in clothes passed on by their masters, which contrasted with the bourgeois sobriety of Madame Roland and her mother, eating the food that came down from the 'first table', they aped their social superiors in language and manners. 'I became aware of a new world in which I found repeated the prejudices, vices and stupidity of a world which was little the better for its apparent superiority.' It is more than likely that all this borrowing included the ideas, and in some cases the books, of those above stairs. The disgruntled Restif de la Bretonne complained in 1785, 'In recent times the working people of the capital have become impossible to deal with, because they have read in our [sic] books truths too potent for them.' A German visitor to Paris remarked on the universal passion for reading. 'Everyone, especially the women, has a book in his pocket. Women, children, workmen, apprentices read in the shops. On Sundays the people who sit on their doorsteps read. Lackeys read behind coaches, coachmen up on their seats, soldiers at their quarters and *commissionnaires* at their posts.' Much, of course, depends on *what* they were reading and nothing obliges us to accept the interested argument of the lawyer who persuaded the Paris *parlement* to ban the *Système de la nature*, arguing that the works of the *philosophes* were scarcely published in the capital before 'they spread like a torrent through the provinces, devastating everything in their way. Few privileged places are immune from the contagion: it has penetrated the workshops and even the cottage thatch . . . the common people used to be poor but with consolation; now they are overwhelmed with both toil and doubt.' At fifteen shillings a copy, the *Système de la nature* was unlikely to set much thatch on fire. Nevertheless, widespread literacy and the short-circuiting of social classes that occurred between some nobles and some of their many dependents and domestic officers probably did produce, not a rudimentary class-consciousness, but a fair number of individual cases of the transmission of 'advanced' ideas far down the social scale. The future general, Hoche, was reading Voltaire at seventeen, when he was a stable-boy at Versailles; but whatever else Hoche may have been, he was certainly not 'typical'.

Such evidence as there is suggests that literacy was quite widespread by the end of the century, even in the countryside, and in France facilities for a good secondary education were surprisingly abundant. A recent survey of literacy in Toulouse, as indicated by the proportion of well-written signatures on marriage contracts, in 1749 and 1785, shows that between 90 and 100 per cent of the men from the 'lower middle class' and 67–75 per cent of their wives could read and write. For the 'upper working class' the figures were 51–54 per cent for the men and 18–19 per cent for the women. At the bottom of the scale came 19–26 per cent of men and 0–4 per cent of women. The Toulouse figures imply only a very limited extension of literacy between the two dates, which is surprising and does not seem to correspond to experience elsewhere. An English bookseller, estimating that book sales had quadrupled during the previous twenty years, wrote in 1791, 'The poorer sort of farmers, and even the poor country people in general, who before that period spent their winter evenings in relating stories of witches, ghosts, hobgoblins &c, now shorten the winter nights by hearing their sons and daughters read tales, romances &c, and on entering their houses you may see *Tom Jones, Roderick Random* and other entertaining books stuck up on their bacon racks.'

For those of exceptional ability – and with understanding parents – free education was often available. Day-students could attend the university of Paris free, and one third of the boarders had scholarships. Many of the parents of boys at the excellent school of Louis-le-Grand were illiterate. In Germany there were free places for poor boys who undertook to enter the state service, and the English grammar schools were also accessible to the more favoured of the poor. So far as the cultural level of the countryside is concerned, however, the point is not that many able children could go to the towns and be well-educated, but that they so rarely came back. Literacy itself was no proof of enlightenment. R. Mandrou in a recent survey, *De la culture populaire au dix-septième et dix-huitième siècles,* has demonstrated the existence of a thriving trade in very cheap popular literature which remained completely impervious to the changing attitudes of the eighteenth century. Almanacs, magic, tales of the saints and legends of chivalry showed no appreciable evolution between 1600 and 1789. Goethe describes in his autobiography how, as a child, he delighted in the same kind of popular literature. Even the humblest level of the Enlightenment, at which Fielding and Smollett replaced 'ghosts, hobgoblins &c' was beyond the reach of the French village. In 1783, within a dozen miles of Paris, when a balloon came down it was destroyed by peasants who took it for the moon. Rivarol describes how other peasants mistook an actress for an angel, 'and that happened in the century of the Enlightenment and near to Paris, in 1788'. With the inevitable exceptions, it is probably not far from the truth to say that those who remained in the villages of continental Europe were affected by the Enlightenment only to the extent that it influenced the way in which they were treated by their social superiors.

From this very sketchy and tentative survey of the social diffusion of the ideas of the Enlightenment it is at least clear that one cannot attribute the radicalism of the *philosophes* to any growing protest of the 'middle class' against a 'feudal' social order. Many of the writers were themselves members of the privileged orders of Church and nobility. The world in which they moved and for which they wrote was the aristocratic *salon* world of people who certainly did not consider themselves victimized by anyone. The new authors had, it is true, an enthusiastic public among the professional classes, who often resented the social pretensions of the nobility, but they had fewer readers amongst the merchants and manufacturers who were subsequently to be credited with having been the standard-bearers of nascent capitalism. As we shall see later in this chapter, the *philosophes* themselves claimed that they could not be accused of responsibility for social unrest since they wrote for a very limited public of men like themselves. If a connexion must be postulated between the iconoclasm of the writers and the growth of social tension, the former, which was the first to manifest itself, has as much claim to be the cause as the consequence of the latter. If a 'rising middle class' was conscious of any *economic* frustration, which seems doubtful, there is no good reason to assume that this had any direct connexion with a movement of ideas that had reached its climax twenty years before the French Revolution.

*

The geographical spread of the Enlightenment may to some extent be inferred from this sketch of its social diffusion. One can sense a rough kind of pattern within the boundaries of most states. The Court would normally be the centre of French taste, manners and ideas, and some of these attitudes would be imitated by the hangers-on and upper servants of the aristocracy. In the provinces, towns that were centres of lay or ecclesiastical administration, or the seats of important lawcourts, united within their walls considerable numbers of educated clergy and laity who tended increasingly to copy the *salons* of the capital and to establish local centres for the exchange of ideas. The most notable of such centres were the Academies, founded in many provincial towns of France during the century. Elsewhere they seem to have been mainly confined to capital cities, but there were a score in the French provinces by 1750 and twice that number twenty years later. Masonic lodges formed an alternative meeting-place for the local nobles, upper clergy, professional men and royal agents, and occasionally for men of humbler rank. Great sea-ports, such as Liverpool, Hamburg, Bordeaux and Marseilles, were also centres of cultural and intellectual activity. In the case of the French ports at least, this was less due to their commercial activity than to the fact that wealthy shipowners and bankers could afford to 'live nobly', as the French expression went, and to follow the example of the aristocracy. Arthur Young, travelling through Bordeaux in 1787, was mildly shocked by a theatre that had recently cost £270,000, Parisian actors paid twenty guineas a night or more and the 'highly luxurious' life of wealthy merchants, with their lavish entertainment, gambling and mistresses kept 'at salaries which ought to import no good to their credit'. Inland towns that lacked the wealth of the ports and the educated public provided by a lawcourt or cathedral chapter found it difficult to support any corporate cultural activity, although individuals might buy books, subscribe to learned periodicals and keep more or less in touch with the intellectual life of the capital. In the small market towns and country villages the circulation of new ideas probably depended mainly on the interests of the squire and the parson. Even at this level there may have been more individual activity than one might suppose: of the forty copies of the *Encyclopédie* known to have existed in Périgord, twenty-four belonged to parish priests.

Throughout most of Europe the second half of the century saw the rapid development of periodical literature of various kinds, the creation of provincial journals in the more advanced states and the beginning of national ones in the more backward. England, where the circulation of the *Spectator* had already reached the very high figure of 20–30,000, led the way, its newspaper sales almost doubling between 1753 and 1775. In France the *Mercure* was available in 26 towns in 1748 and in 55 by 1774. The French provincial press developed from practically nothing after 1770. In Russia, Poland and the Austrian Netherlands, periodical literature began about 1770. The political fragmentation of Germany led to the appearance of very great numbers of local newspapers, each town having its own by the end of the century. It would be absurd to regard these collections of local news and advertising as major vehicles of the Enlightenment, and the circulation of the more serious journals was often ludicrously small by English standards. The most important literary journal in Spain, the *Espíritu de los majores diarios*, had 765 subscribers in 1788 and the *Correo de Madrid* less than 300. It was nevertheless significant that the transmission of regular information was increasing in the west and had begun in the east. At its lowest level, the Enlightenment began with the substitution of information for an oral tradition of folk-memory, superstition and blind habit, and the mere practice of regular reading was at least a step along the road.

To investigate the special circumstances which gave the Enlightenment its particular colour in each European state would be far beyond the confines of the present book. In Spain, despite a reforming ruler, the new ideas made very little headway in the face of clerical opposition. Spain was also peculiar in that its cultural life was more vigorous in the great provincial towns than in the capital. Germany proved much more receptive, but issues here were complicated by the emergence of a new national literature, struggling to assert its independence of the French culture which maintained its hold over Court society. Frederick II (1740–86) in particular was a cultural Germanophobe who excluded Lessing from the Potsdam Academy to which he managed to attract, at one time or another, Maupertuis, Voltaire and La Mettrie. In the Habsburg dominions, the pious Maria Theresa (1740–80) and her son Joseph II (co-regent from 1765 and sole ruler 1780–90) had no sympathy with the religious scepticism of the Enlightenment, but were eager to rationalize the administration of their scattered territories, and their struggle against the conservative opposition of their nobility made them more receptive than Frederick to an attack on tradition in the name of scientific government. In Italy, reforming rulers, the exceptional strength of the Catholic Church and a lively native tradition in music and the theatre, created a complicated pattern of influences. The attraction of France was very strong; when men like Goldoni and the abbé Galiani came to Paris they either remained or tried to remain there, but French cultural domination in the peninsula was perhaps less oppressive – and therefore less violently resisted – than in western Germany. Eastern Europe was isolated by a linguistic barrier that excluded all but a tiny minority from works which were rarely translated into Russian or Polish. At the Courts of Catherine II (1763–96) and Stanislas Poniatowski in Poland (1763–95) French-speaking courtiers remained in very close contact with the fountain-head of the Enlightenment in Paris. Madame Geoffrin, whose *salon* was one of the most famous in Paris, visited Stanislas, and Diderot made the journey to St Petersburg. The reign of Stanislas saw an extraordinary cultural awakening, brutally arrested by the partitions that destroyed his country towards the end of the century. But in both Poland and Russia the Enlightenment remained an exotic importation, completely foreign to the

great majority of the inhabitants whose native culture perpetuated religious and folk legends in the vernacular. Nowhere
was the aristocratic character of the Enlightenment so pronounced as in eastern Europe. At the opposite end of the
continent, British society was also the furthest removed from
that of Russia. A relatively unimportant Court, an aristocracy
integrated with a large and well-educated community of
gentlemen, themselves linked to a thriving mercantile population, a vigorous national literary culture and a popular
tradition of hostility to France and, even more, to Roman
Catholicism; all these factors helped to create a unique
situation. Nevertheless, Englishmen shared in many of the
characteristics of the continental Enlightenment and the
English gentleman found himself very much at home in
Parisian society, but the English movement was spontaneous
and the direct influence of French literature was less marked
than elsewhere. It was England that pioneered the moral
weeklies and the sentimental novel, which catered for a wider
and less sophisticated public than the *salon*. It was perhaps
significant that British writers, with the most 'bourgeois'
public of any in Europe, should have been far less adventurous
and critical of the ordering of Church and State than those
across the Channel.

*

It will already have become apparent that the ideas of the
Enlightenment took time to travel. A movement that
reached its apogee in Paris between 1750 and 1765 spread
steadily throughout the French provinces during the generation before the Revolution. Its early progress in Germany was
checked and partially countered by the *Sturm und Drang*
movement of the 1770s. Farther east, it was the accession of
Catherine and Stanislas that launched its progress in Russia and
Poland. Together with the penetration of ideas, French
fashions and standards of social behaviour gradually shaped

the polite society of continental Europe and even to some extent that of England. The Italian, Caraccioli, with all the enthusiasm of the convert, published in 1776 a book with the self-explanatory title of *L'Europe française*, whose theme may be summarized in a couple of sentences: 'When the eighteenth century appeared, adorned with its grace and charm, there was more than one people in Europe which, where habits and learning were concerned, was still in the fifteenth century. The distance has shortened and, broadly speaking, every European is now a Frenchman.' Caraccioli was a superficial and rather silly man but he may not have been far from the mark when he wrote, 'The French fops [*petits-maîtres*] have contributed more than the savants to the metamorphosis of the Europeans. They have scarcely arrived in a town before they stir all families and all hearts, and people talk of nothing but their lively manners and sparkling vivacity.' Sensationalist psychology had its practical, as well as its theoretical side.

*

The Enlightenment was an attitude of mind rather than a course in science and philosophy. Few followed in detail the intellectual debate conducted by a handful of men in London and, more especially, in Paris, and even fewer accepted all the conclusions of the more radical thinkers. But despite local variations and individual self-contradictions, new values spread slowly through educated Europe. What was most significant was often what was most taken for granted, the 'common sense' of an age unaware of the extent to which the 'obvious' is an historical product that evolves in time. One cannot hope to do more than sketch an impressionistic picture of Enlightenment Man. Parts of his mental structure are probably inaccessible to us and every individual was a synthesis of special as well as common factors. Nevertheless, some attitudes were sufficiently general for us to regard them as typical of the majority. When men whose temperaments and beliefs differed as widely as those of Johnson and Voltaire shared a common way of looking at man and society, one may ascribe part of the reason to the influence of an international society in which each developed and to which each contributed. It is therefore legitimate to seek to determine a kind of lowest common denominator of attitudes which most of those who participated in the social and cultural world of the Enlightenment would have accepted as roughly representing their own opinions.

Like the seventeenth century, the eighteenth tended to regard itself as old in time. Only a few scientists and philosophers were beginning to think in terms of a time-scale so vast that the few millennia of recorded history became insignificant. But age now signified maturity rather than decay. Men compared their civilization with historical Greece and Rome, rather than with classical legend and the Old Testament and its uncompromising story of the Fall. In an age educated primarily in the classics, it was not surprising if conservatives like Johnson regarded Greek and Latin authors as incomparable and dismissed their own contemporaries as 'the moons of literature; they shine with the reflected light borrowed from the ancients'. But the fire had gone out of the controversy between 'ancients' and 'moderns'. Where civilizations, rather than individual authors, were concerned, most people – for the first time, perhaps, in modern history – preferred their own age to any that had gone before. Johnson himself could pontificate, in a different mood, 'I am always angry when I hear ancient times praised at the expense of modern times. There is now a great deal more learning in the world than there was formerly, for it is universally diffused.' Chastellux, in *De la félicité publique* (1772), was even more emphatic: 'All the long and brilliant career of the Roman Empire, so far as the philosopher is concerned, is not worth the latest period of English history, that is, the time which has elapsed from the revolution to the present day.'

But the hold of antiquity over men's imaginations was too deep and multiform to be easily shaken off. As the Roman Empire lost its prestige, Winckelmann launched a new classical revival, based on Greek and Roman sculpture: 'The only way for us to obtain greatness, even, if it be possible, to become inimitable, is by the imitation of the ancients.' At the same time, a shift of interest towards republican Rome, helped no doubt by Montesquieu's eulogies of republican virtue in general, brought the Romans back on to the stage in a new role, as both the embodiments of civic duty and the patrons of revolt. Cicero became the idol of the *philosophes* as the patron of a new cult of republican civic *vertu* and Brutus, rather than Augustus, came to personify the new Rome. This was a development that despots, however 'enlightened', were unlikely to appreciate. Voltaire wrote, in the *Mort de César*, in 1755:

> Fût-ce nos propres fils, nos frères ou nos pères,
> S'ils sont tyrans, Brutus, ils sont nos adversaires.
> Un vrai républicain n'a pour père et pour fils
> Que la vertu, les dieux, les lois et son pays.

Three years earlier, Barbier had recorded the comments of the Parisian crowd when the *Parlement* was engaged in one of its periodical skirmishes with the monarchy: 'There are true Romans for you.' This cult of Roman virtue was destined for a great future during the Revolution, when David could practise neo-classicism in both art and politics at the same time. To many men of the Enlightenment, however, it savoured too much of 'enthusiasm'. Both Fielding and Smollett introduced 'Romans' into their novels: the unpleasant Square in *Tom Jones* combines religious scepticism with the advocacy rather than the practice of republican virtue, until his death-bed repentance; Jolter, in *Peregrine Pickle*, an even more unpleasant character, 'looked upon particular friendship as a passion unworthy of his ample soul, and was a professed admirer of L. Manlius, Junius Brutus, and those later patriots of the same name, who shut their ears against the cries of nature and resisted all the dictates of gratitude and humanity.' Goethe seems to have shared the same outlook when he wrote in 1772, 'Roman patriotism! Heaven preserve me from anything so monstrous!'

However ambivalent their attitude towards Rome, the men of the Enlightenment were virtually unanimous in decrying the Middle Ages. The entire period from the collapse of the Roman Empire in the west to the sixteenth century tended to be dismissed as one of poverty, oppression, ignorance and obscurantism, 'centuries of monkish dullness, when the whole world seems to have been asleep', as Fielding put it. 'Gothic' was a term of abuse applied to every conceivable form of ignorance, prejudice, conservatism, or what we still call vandalism. Arthur Young exploded, on the subject of old Rouen – soon to become 'picturesque' – 'this great, ugly, stinking, close and ill-built town'. He much preferred the antiseptic geometry of Rennes, rebuilt after a great fire earlier in the century. Condorcet was to explain, in his *Esquisse d'un tableau historique des progrès de l'esprit humain* (1794), how technological progress, in the shape of gunpowder and the printing press, had put an end to the centuries of baronial oppression and ecclesiastical superstition and given birth to the modern world, which for most Frenchmen began with Henry IV (1589–1610). Opinions varied as to how one should regard the recent past. For Voltaire, the reign of Louis XIV was one of the world's great golden ages. The more constitutionally-minded preferred Henry IV and accused Louis XIV of having subverted the traditional French constitution. All were agreed, however, that where society and culture, as distinct from political liberty, were concerned, the entire modern age was incontestably superior to what had gone before.

When it came to contemplating the future, the French

writers at least were curiously pessimistic. Not until the last quarter of the century was there much confidence in progress in any field. Cyclical theories of history were common, and since the current age was regarded as a kind of culminating point, many were inclined to think that the way forward would also be the way down. The emphasis in Montesquieu's writing was on the difficulty of maintaining a satisfactory balance, on the causes of decline and the ways by which it could be postponed. Helvétius saw no means of reconciling economic equality with a high standard of living. His *De l'esprit* was permeated by the kind of nostalgia for primitive simplicity with which Rousseau is more commonly associated. The advocates of materialist determinism such as d'Holbach, and at times Diderot, seemed to envisage life as a perpetual flux rather than as evolution in any particular direction. The static short-term view of society of the majority made it difficult for them to think of future change, except as an educative process by which a greater proportion of the population might be elevated to the present level of the fortunate minority. In this respect also, the Enlightenment shows no indication of any awareness of social and economic forces fighting to break through traditional barriers and begin a period of revolutionary transformation. It was this assumption that, at best, the future would be a rectified version of the present, that most clearly differentiates the eighteenth century from the present day, despite their apparent similarity in so many respects.

*

However uncertain about the long-term future of humanity, educated men had no doubt that they were themselves living in what they described as a *siècle de lumières*, an *Aufklärung* or an enlightened age. It seemed to them, not without reason, that humanity was at last visibly freeing itself from the prejudices and superstitions that had produced so much blind

cruelty in the past. One way of charting the retreat of superstition is to see how witchcraft trials came to a spontaneous
end or were declared illegal in one country after another; in
France, England and Scotland to begin with, then in Prussia
and eventually in the Habsburg Empire and in Poland. As
was to be expected, popular prejudice did not keep pace with
educated opinion – a witch was put to death near Angers as
late as 1780. Belief in the miraculous raised more difficult
theological issues than belief in pacts with the Devil, but here
also one can see a change of attitude that at least relegated
them from everyday existence. Barbier reported in 1725 that
he had never seen such a procession, 'as regards the numbers,
including the highest bourgeois and their wives', as that
which accompanied the relics of Saint Geneviève, paraded
through the streets with prayers for an end to the rains that
threatened the harvest. He was uncertain as to the procession's
effectiveness: 'One must admit that the weather changed
completely after the procession. Admittedly, there was a
change of moon, but the rain had continued when the moon
had changed before.' But Barbier's scepticism, as recorded in
his diary, made almost annual progress, until six years later
he was writing, 'It is always by miracles and strange events
that religions have won favour in all ages and in every land . . .
the more one penetrates into religious matters, the more one
realizes how uncertain are the miracles accepted by the
Church.' A little later Goldoni adapted Molière's *Don Juan*
for the Italian stage in a way that he was to justify in his
autobiography: 'I thought I ought not to cut out the
lightning which blasts Don Juan, since the wicked have to be
punished, but I so arranged this that it could be either the
immediate effect of divine wrath, or that it could result from
a combination of secondary causes, which are always directed
by the laws of Providence.' Popular superstition was still
easily awakened, as a gentleman from St Omer discovered to
his cost in 1782 when he put up a lightning-conductor, and

superstitition was by no means confined to the peasantry. In 1777 the Elector, Maximilian of Bavaria, on his doctor's orders, swallowed a picture of the Virgin as a cure for small-pox. On the whole, however, the educated men of Europe were convinced by this time that natural phenomena were determined by natural laws, and many of them, like Barbier, extended their disbelief in contemporary miracles to those on which the Christian Church had based its claim to be the only true religion.

The men of the Enlightenment would probably have claimed that their emancipation from superstitious beliefs was merely one aspect of their general emancipation from social prejudices founded on local habit rather than on universal reason. One consequence of this, which appeared particularly offensive to many Christians, was a new attitude towards religious toleration. This may be illustrated by the Sussex landowner who wrote to his son in Amsterdam, advising him to attend different religious services in order to broaden his mind: 'Men of different opinions worship God in their own way; we are to respect them in their different manner of worship.' Lord Chesterfield put the same point of view with his usual charity and good sense, 'The object of all the public worships in the world is the same; it is that great eternal Being, who created everything. The different manners of worship are by no means subjects of ridicule; each sect thinks its own the best; and I know of no infallible judge, in this world, to decide which is the best.' The example of such *unchristian* charity gradually forced the Churches to give up religious persecution. By the end of the century royal governments were imposing toleration in Catholic states, in the Habsburg Empire during the reign of Joseph II and in France in 1787. Even the Inquisition, that old enemy of the *philosophes*, burned no more heretics in Europe after 1781.

Racial intolerance was virtually unknown, in western Europe at least, where the individual was considered, according to one's viewpoint, as a soul, a subject, or the possessor of universal and inalienable rights, none of which was affected by his racial origin. An exception must be made in the case of the Jews, whose persecution seemed to many Christians to carry a divine sanction – which could be a useful pretext for settling economic scores. Where non-European peoples were concerned, the question is more complicated. There was certainly no tendency to attribute peculiar virtues to the 'white' races. Most writers had their favourite civilization which could be held up to Europe as an example: the Chinese, the American Indians or the Polynesians. Nevertheless, this was the great century of the slave trade. American planters treated their Negroes as though they believed them to be racially inferior and their reluctance to grant civil rights to free mulattoes probably rested on racial prejudice as well as economic interest. There was, however, some significance in the fact that the movement for the abolition of the slave trade, which began towards the end of the century, was based not only on pity but also on the idea of the natural rights of man. Gibbon, at least, saw the distinction, when he wrote to Lord Sheffield in 1792 expressing his approval of the vote against the slave trade in the House of Commons. 'If it proceeded only from an impulse of humanity, I cannot be displeased. . . . But in this rage against slavery, in the numerous petitions against the slave trade, was there no leaven of new democratical principles? No wild ideas of the rights and natural equality of man? It is these I fear.' By this time the Revolutionary crisis had destroyed the unity of the Enlightenment, turning some towards political democracy and leading others to retreat from principles whose implications they could no longer accept. Thirty years earlier, when Sterne was writing *Tristram Shandy*, Uncle Toby was not faced by Gibbon's choice and his own attitude towards Negroes combined charity towards the unfortunate with acceptance of human equality. ''Tis the fortune of war which has put the whip into our hands *now* – where it may be hereafter, heaven knows!'

Not many were prepared to translate their theoretical belief in natural equality into practical terms when dealing with their social inferiors. Widespread fear of the *canaille*, the mob, could be rationalized by the argument that equality was only possible amongst those sufficiently educated to understand both their rights and their obligations. Even amongst the educated the barrier of noble birth retained much of its divisive power, especially in Germany. Where the poor were concerned, many shared the attitude that led the Duchess of Buckingham to disapprove of Methodism, even if they expressed it more tactfully. 'It is monstrous to be told that you have a heart as sinful as the common wretches that crawl on the earth. This is highly offensive and insulting.' Chesterfield, who thought himself in company as much above him, when he was with Addison and Pope, as if he had been with all the princes of Europe, was certainly not typical. Nevertheless his attitude merits attention as proof that there were some whose liberation from social prejudice had gone a long way.

Never be proud of your rank or birth, but be as proud as you please of your character. Nothing is so contrary to true dignity as the former kind of pride. You are, it is true, of a noble family, but whether a very ancient one or not I neither know nor care, nor need you, and I dare say there are twenty fools in the House of Lords who could out-descend you in pedigree. That sort of stately pride is the standing jest of all people who can make one.

When Chesterfield died he left two years' wages to servants who had been with him for five years or more, 'whom I consider as unfortunate friends, my equals by Nature, and my inferiors only by the difference of our fortunes'. There was more to Uncle Toby than Sterne's imagination.

We have already seen that the age had nothing but polite contempt for assertions of national superiority. The common people might easily be prevailed upon to hate the foreigners most of them did not know. Fielding, carried away by the sight of a three-decker in the Thames, could advocate ostentatious expenditure on the navy to 'preserve, among other nations, the notion of British superiority in naval affairs'. Statesmen took war and national competitiveness for granted. But the combined influences of the Enlightenment and the traditional values of an aristocratic society created a kind of freemasonry amongst the nobility of Europe and there were many who would have endorsed Montesquieu's view that he was 'human of necessity' but 'French by accident'.

*

Perhaps the most striking of the positive qualities and beliefs of Enlightenment Man was his conviction that a beneficent Providence regulated the course of nature and the promptings of his own heart. We have observed some of the implications of this attitude, which may be summarized in the words of the Jesuit, Hooke, in 1752: 'There is in all men a general benevolence and freely given goodness ... thus there is no duty that is not commended to us, not only by reason, but even by appetite.' Such a point of view encouraged humanitarianism, since it appeared only logical to attribute to others the natural qualities one claimed for one's self. In place of the repressive and disciplinary role which Christian pessimism had formerly attributed to public authority, there grew up a realization that the maintenance of order did not depend on savage punishments. The most striking example of this was the gradual abolition of torture throughout most of civilized Europe: in Prussia as early as 1742, in France, the Habsburg Empire, Sweden, Poland and much of Italy between 1772 and the outbreak of the French Revolution, and in Russia in 1801. In the Habsburg territories and in Prussia, the death penalty was increasingly reserved for the most serious crimes. Joseph II abolished it altogether, except for treason, in 1787.

Rather curiously, France and especially England failed to follow. In 1789 there were still over a hundred crimes which carried the death penalty in France, while across the Channel the number of capital crimes increased throughout the century until it stood at over 200 by 1815. Despite these important exceptions, the thesis expounded by Montesquieu and taken up by the Italian jurist Beccaria, whose treatise *On Crimes and Punishments* (1764) was a European best-seller, that punishment should be corrective and deterrent rather than vindictive, gradually permeated the penal law of Europe. For much of the century, however, the spectacle of criminal justice was brutal and degrading. Barbier records that in 1737 a Parisian crowd applauded the dexterity of an executioner who severed a criminal's head at one blow. Twenty years later his own attitude was changing more quickly than that of the public. Commenting on the public torture and execution of Damiens, who had stabbed Louis XV without doing him any serious harm, Barbier observed that the ladies of quality among the spectators 'supported the horror of the execution better than the men, which is no credit to them'. In 1769 Boswell mentioned quite casually to Johnson that he had just seen several convicts hanged at Tyburn. Diderot's claim that 'Social habits have been softened by the weakening of the prejudices that had maintained their [former] ferocity', can only be accepted with considerable reservations.

Despite this tenacity of barbaric attitudes where criminals were concerned, the men of the Enlightenment were becoming increasingly convinced that a society was judged less by its military prowess than by the standard of living of its humbler members. In this respect as in many others, Johnson, despite his Toryism, shared the views of the reformers. 'Where a great proportion of the people are suffered to languish in helpless misery, that country must be ill policed and wretchedly governed: a decent provision for the poor is the true test of civilization.' Gentlemen of education, he observed, were pretty much the same in all countries; the condition of the lower orders, the poor especially, was the true mark of national discrimination. A similar attitude under-lay the comments of the Spanish writer, Jovellanos, on the subject of European colonization, which would 'no longer seek nations to conquer, peoples to oppress, regions to cover with grief and poverty', but on the contrary would seek to bring to backward peoples 'the virtues of humanity, practical science and peaceful arts, all the gifts of abundance and peace'. Performance lagged a long way behind promise, especially where non-Europeans were concerned, but a new attitude made itself felt all the same, as the result of the Enlightenment and of the cult of sensibility that followed it. Rulers and wealthy subjects accepted a greater responsibility towards public welfare, with practical consequences that were to be seen everywhere in the provision of schools, hospitals and charities of various kinds. The *Institut de Bienfaisance* in Lyons raised several hundred pounds in a few weeks. The Parisian *Société Philanthropique* had over 600 members in 1787, when a subscription for hospitals raised over £100,000 in Paris alone. 'Benevolence' had its limitations, but it was not an idle word.

The age might more accurately be described as one of reasonableness than of reason. It valued good-natured socia-bility rather than the rigorous pursuit of logic to extreme conclusions. Convinced of the providential harmony of 'self-love and social', of truth and utility, its focal point was the *salon* where men and women enjoyed each other's company and combined intellectual speculation with *bienséance*. The tone was set early in the century, when the *Tatler* could review Swift's *Project for the Advancement of Religion* in language that may, but need not have been ironical. 'The real causes of the decay of the interest of religion are set forth in a clear and lively manner, without unseasonable passions ... the man writes much like a gentleman and goes to Heaven with a good mien.' Somewhat later, the same kind of attitude appears in Johnson's *Idler*: 'It is very difficult to determine the exact degree of enthusiasm that the arts of painting and poetry may admit. . . . An intimate knowledge of the passions, and good sense, but not common sense, must at least determine its limits.' Johnson's assumption that the arts were the subjects of reason rather than independent rulers in their own domain, had also been that of Hume, who wrote with elegant irony,

The *imagination* of man is naturally sublime, delighted with whatever is remote and extraordinary and running without control into the most distant parts of space and time in order to avoid the objects which custom has rendered too familiar to it. A correct *judgment* observes a contrary method and, avoiding all distant and high enquiries, confines itself to common life and to such subjects as fall under daily practice and experience, leaving the more sublime topics to the embellishment of poets and orators or to the arts of priests and politicians.

When one recalls the decorous sobriety of the eighteenth-century muses there is something comic – or prophetic – about the anxiety which their far from dionysiac evolutions raised in so many reasonable minds.

It was this very reasonableness that was soon to provoke the scorn of the *Sturm und Drang* movement in Germany, of Rousseau, and eventually of Romantics everywhere, as a denial of inspiration and of individual genius. The eighteenth century has still not recovered from the abuse which its successors have loaded upon it – not always without reason. Chesterfield's letters bring out both the dignity and the pettiness that reasonableness could imply. He seemed to regard social polish as an end in itself, and it is difficult not to be irritated by his careful defence of religion as 'a collateral security, at least, to virtue'. But it is arguable that Chesterfield's modest calculation of probabilities was preferable to the crusading certainties of an earlier period. 'Consult your reason betimes; I do not say it will always prove an unerring guide, for human reason is not infallible; but it will prove the best guide that you can follow.' 'Consult different authors upon the same facts and form your opinion upon the greater or lesser degree of probability arising from the whole, which, in my mind, is the utmost stretch of historical faith; certainty (I fear) not being to be found.' It is important to appreciate that the Enlightenment's tendency to suspect originality, since, as Chesterfield put it, 'The same matter occurs equally to everybody of common sense', implied no commendation of mediocrity. It was a consequence of the assumption of providential harmony, the perspective which made all lines converge. I hope it has already been shown clearly enough that the writers of the Enlightenment were uninhibited in their search for truth. If the results tended to stress the identity of virtue, nature and social utility, this was because of deeply held philosophical assumptions, not the product of a self-imposed censorship. To contemporaries, the new ideas appeared liberating, not constricting. 'Father', pleaded Goldoni, 'let me learn the philosophy of man, true morality, experimental physics.' However it has been subsequently discredited by misapplied Darwinism and misunderstood Freudian psychology, the Enlightenment's insistence that civilization is an artificial product of human rationality and sociability is not to be lightly dismissed. 'Pity', says Johnson, 'is not natural to man. Children are always cruel. Savages are always cruel. Pity is acquired and improved by the cultivation of reason.'

As the French Revolution was to demonstrate, the self-confidence of the educated, their readiness to engage in radical political and philosophical speculation and the willingness of a socially privileged aristocracy to mock religion and embrace principles implying the natural equality of man, all rested on the almost universal conviction that the social order was static. No one seems to have considered the possibility of an economic or social upheaval that might transform the shape of society. There was increasing talk of the probability of a revolution in France, but what the prophets seem to have had in mind was a *political* revolution and the example of 1688 in England suggested that this need have no far-reaching social consequences. Men of property were always uneasily aware of the potential threat from a hungry populace, uncontrolled by any effective police. Recurrent pillaging of grain stocks and the more serious riots in London in 1768-9 kept this fear alive. But no one seems to have believed there was, or could be, any connexion between such traditional eruptions of violence and the writings of men whom the rioters had certainly not read. Barbier, always quick to demand the stern repression of popular agitation, never linked it with the *philosophes*, to whom he was, on the whole, well-disposed.

The writers themselves took the existence of an unteachable majority for granted. Voltaire, in particular, liked to dwell on the subject. 'There is always, within a nation, a people that has no contact with polite society, which does not belong to the age, which is inaccessible to the progress of reason and over whom fanaticism maintains its atrocious hold.' 'It is expedient that the people should be directed, not that it should be educated; it is not worthy of teaching. . . . It is not the labourer one should educate, but the good bourgeois, the tradesman.' Similar opinions are to be found throughout his works. D'Holbach, an advocate of more radical ideas in politics and religion, also liked to emphasize that he wrote only for an élite. In the *Système de la nature* he asserted that 'Atheism, like philosophy and every profound and abstract science, is therefore by no means suited to the common people, nor even to the majority.' He emphasizes the same point in *Le Christianisme dévoilé* (1767). 'The people neither read nor reason. They have neither the leisure nor the capacity to do so. Books are made only for that portion of a nation which its circumstances, its education and its feelings raise above crime.' Such affirmations were not the monopoly of the well-born, nor were they merely designed to temper the winds of censorship. Diderot, who came of humble parents, justified his refusal to publish his more radical works in terms which suggested that he was not merely preoccupied by censorship. 'It would be to trample decency underfoot [from the author of the *Bijoux indiscrets*!], to draw the most odious suspicions upon one's self and to commit a crime of *lèse-société*.' He wrote privately to his publisher. 'I repeat, there are some readers whom I do not, and never shall desire. I write only for those with whom I should enjoy conversing. I address my works to the philosophers; so far as I am concerned, there is no one else in the world.' One can see the point of the remark in the *Spectator*, 'A philosopher, by which I mean a gentleman'.

Such attitudes implied neither contempt nor hostility towards those whose lot it was to perform socially useful work. The *philosophes* hoped that the slow progress of education would gradually raise up the more intelligent of the common people to participation in a polite society whose stability they took for granted. Whatever the actual consequences of their work, and whatever, after the death of almost all of them, they may have contributed to influence a revolutionary movement that had started for other reasons, the overthrow of the traditional social hierarchy was no part of their plan. On the contrary, their conviction of their own inability to do more than to spread enlightenment, tolerance and humanity amongst the educated seemed to them the guarantee that their beneficial teaching could do no harm to anyone.

PART TWO

Not Peace but a Sword

Chapter 5

THE SOCIAL AND POLITICAL ENVIRONMENT, 1740–89

THE historian is frequently led, without his being aware of it, to define his terms of reference in such a way that his enquiries will 'prove' a thesis which he began by assuming. So much happened in Europe between the outbreak of the War of the Austrian Succession in 1740 and the French Revolution that it is not difficult to assemble a substantial amount of evidence in support of various different and even conflicting theories. Where a large part of any synthesis must be subjective it is especially important to distinguish between what is known to be true, although not necessarily relevant, and what is merely a certain way of selecting, combining and interpreting events.

It is agreed that the population of Europe as a whole increased appreciably during the two generations before the French Revolution. While all contemporary statistics must be accepted with caution, it seems virtually certain that this rise occurred in all, or almost all states. The rate of increase, however, varied considerably, in a way that permits of no simple explanation. In Italy, numbers increased slowly, from $15\frac{1}{2}$ to 18 million between 1750 and 1800. Growth in France proceeded at a similar rate, the population passing from 22 to 27 million during the same period, and an increase of the same order occurred in Spain. At the opposite end of the scale the Russian population increased by about one half between 1762 and 1796 (from 19 to 29 million) and a very rapid rise was also to be found in parts of Prussia, in Hungary and in Ireland. The population of England and Wales appears to have expanded more than that of Europe as a whole, although not so quickly as that of Ireland. So complicated a pattern seems to indicate that several factors were at work. Internal colonization, planned or spontaneous, was probably the main explanation in Prussia and Hungary; Russia was still pushing her frontier eastwards into under-populated areas; in Ireland, the spread of potato-growing allowed the same area to support greater numbers. It is likely that agricultural productivity was slowly increasing, at least over much of western Europe, but taking the continent as a whole, the contemporary observer could not have detected anything strikingly new or irreversible in the general movement of population. There were famines during this period in parts of central Europe and, as Ireland was to prove so tragically in the nineteenth century, the peasant multitudes were still liable to decimation by crop failure. Population remained dependent on the productive capacity of a primitive agriculture and the growing pressure on the land suggested that the limit had almost been reached. Towns were often expanding, but mainly capital cities such as Berlin, Warsaw and St Petersburg, or a handful of trading towns such as Bordeaux and Hamburg, rather than centres of industry. Over the continent as a whole, the urban population was rising more slowly than that of the countryside.

To this general picture there is perhaps one exception. Reinhard and Armengaud in their *Histoire générale de la population mondiale* maintain that England was the scene of a 'demographic revolution'. This was perhaps less due to the rate of growth of the population, which did not become much higher than the European average until about 1790, than to the fact that in England the number of inhabitants was ceasing to be directly determined by good harvests and cheap food. The death rate in 1780 was not significantly lower than it had been at the beginning of the century. Thereafter it fell sharply, even when harvests were bad, and high food prices no longer brought near-famine and devastating epidemics.

But if one accepts that England was indeed showing the first signs of a wholly new demographic evolution, with population determined as much by industrial as by agricultural production, this was not recognized at the time. Malthus, writing his celebrated *Principle of Population* in 1798, ascribed the rise of the English population to the 'more rapid progress of commerce and agriculture'. He did not mention industry. He was well aware of the extraordinary growth of the manufacturing towns, but for him they were like any other towns, areas of high mortality, rather than sources of new wealth. Although his argument that size of population is determined by available resources could be adapted to an industrial society, Malthus himself thought in more traditional terms. His caution against projecting into the future past trends towards an increase of population is typical of his whole attitude. It seems reasonable to conclude, therefore, that there was nothing in the growth of European population that could lead the men of the eighteenth century to think that they were living at the beginning of a new age.

If we look at the development of the economy during the same period the position is somewhat similar. Decisive changes were beginning to take place in England and parts of Scotland, but these had not gone far enough by 1789 to transform the appearance of the country, while outside the British Isles only the first very tentative steps had been taken. The accelerated progress of the 'agrarian revolution' in England during the last quarter of the century led to the consolidation of many holdings. Enclosure brought the introduction of improved tools, better strains of animals and seed and more scientific crop rotation. As the new farming spread, the appearance of the countryside and the pattern of social relationships altered, but this was a very gradual process and one that had been going on for a very long time. From about the 1770s there also developed an industrial revolution that was eventually to transform the shape of much of the country.

The production of cotton goods increased tenfold, that of iron fourfold, between 1760 and 1787. Foreign trade, after a period of relative stagnation, began to expand very rapidly indeed just before the French Revolution. However much historians may disagree about the causes of these changes, the transformation itself is beyond question. It was, however, slower to acquire momentum and less dramatic in its early stages than used to be believed. If the production of cotton goods increased so quickly, this was partly because it began at a very low level; it was a long time before it challenged the importance of the old-established woollen industry. The new cotton-spinning machinery was small, relatively cheap and could often be worked by hand. Domestic industry was at first encouraged by the new inventions and the huge, power-operated mill that was to become the symbol of the cotton industry was still a rarity. The industrial revolution, as it had developed in England by 1789, was still in its early stages and not yet recognized as likely to determine the character of the country as a whole. The England of Dr Johnson was probably still more commercially than industrially conscious. The forces that were visibly changing it looked more like the acceleration of a familiar than the advent of a new experience.

Viewed from the Continent, the economic development of Britain must have seemed as exceptional as her political habits were eccentric. In France, admittedly, there was a movement in the third quarter of the century towards the consolidation of farms, but this soon lost momentum, although the social tensions which it generated survived until the Revolution. Otherwise, there seems to have been little that could be dignified with the name of an 'agrarian revolution'. Commerce prospered along traditional lines and here and there new industries were created, as often as not by nobles. Of the 601 forge-masters known in France between 1771 and 1788, 55 were clergy, 305 nobles and only 241 commoners. At about the same time one third of Russia's industrial enterprises were owned by nobles. The new English machines were slow to cross the Channel: France had at most 8 spinning mills using Arkwright's water-frame in 1790, as compared with 200 in England, and Germany acquired its first in 1794. Steam engines were few, and those mostly of the inefficient New-comen type, although Watt's greatly improved engine was in commercial use in England from 1776 onwards. Industrial production was certainly rising in much of Europe – although not everywhere, for Habsburg tariff policy led to an industrial decline in Hungary. But the advance was along familiar lines and production by machinery for a mass market was very rare indeed. Industrial capitalism, with its expensive fixed assets, was untypical and often dependent on nobles deciding to exploit the resources of their own estates. There was more economic advantage, for those with both capital and political influence, in the financial operations of the 'court capitalism' that had been familiar since the Renaissance: tax-farming, banking and various forms of speculation with borrowed capital. Industrial and commercial operations were developing in scale rather than changing in kind, and the middle-class entrepreneur aspiring to make his fortune by the sale of the products of his own expensive machinery was very rare.

If we turn to the way in which the states of Europe were governed, it is more difficult to separate fact from interpretation and administration from politics. It would, I think, be difficult to deny that, in terms of political organization if not of effective political power, the development of royal abso-lutism, already established in France, Prussia and Russia, made considerable progress in the Habsburg Empire under Maria Theresa (1740-80) and her son Joseph II (1765-90). A successful *coup d'état* by Gustavus III in 1772 restored to the Swedish king much of the authority that had been exercised by the nobility during the previous fifty years. In Spain, Portugal and Denmark, kings and their ministers tried to give a new effectiveness to autocratic monarchy. But, in the meantime, as the scale of the operations of government expanded and the machinery of administration grew in complexity, princes found themselves increasingly the prisoners of their own machines. It became impossible for them to exercise effective control in all departments – for example to know whom to promote to positions where zeal would have to supplement competence if the ruler's will were to be translated into action. Bureaucrats had to be allowed to function in accordance with the precedents that they created for themselves, in order to avoid administrative anarchy. The ineffectiveness of Joseph II was partly due to his overloading his administrators with a continual stream of new measures that they did not like. Frederick II in Prussia, despite his unquestioned personal authority, found himself unable to relieve the pressure of serfdom as he had intended. To check the growing *esprit de corps* of his civil servants he was even led to create local elective committees of the Junker nobility. Absolutism itself had to become bureaucratic in order to be effective.

Princes had had no reason to challenge aristocratic social values which they themselves shared. Where the natural inequality of man was concerned, Frederick II saw eye to eye with the Magyar or Breton squire. One result of the un-challenged survival of such values was that successful bureau-crats did not limit their ambition to promotion in the royal service. They were also concerned to acquire nobility if they did not already possess it, and to integrate themselves into the older aristocracy. The early rivalry between the new royal agents and the resentful nobility of robe and sword gave way to a more complicated pattern. In Prussia, the judges joined forces with their former enemies, the king's servants, in common opposition to the Frenchmen imported by Frederick II to collect indirect taxation. In France, robe and sword opposed a common resistance to those members of either group who gave way to the temptation of office and tried to give practical effect to the theoretical absolutism of the king, as his ministers or provincial agents. It was no longer practicable for the nobility to think of recovering the autonomy they had lost with the consolidation of the bureaucratic state. But they could and did strive to ensure that the new machinery was controlled by members of their own order and that it operated in ways of which they approved.

Conditions varied very greatly from one state to another, but almost everywhere the nobility were improving their general position, if not recovering anything that could be called political power. Frederick II, reversing his father's policy, restricted army commissions as far as possible to the Junkers, created a credit bank for their benefit and in every way increased the divisions within a society that was already one of the most hierarchical in Europe. The Prussian Code of 1794 even went so far as to deny legal recognition to the marriage of a commoner with a nobleman. In the Habsburg Empire the agents of royal absolutism themselves came from distinguished noble families and royal policy was for a long time applied only with the consent of local Diets dominated by the nobility. Maria Theresa, even when political necessity was driving her to assert the authority of the central government, still feared 'the destruction of the magnates on the specious pretext of protecting the majority, which seems to me even more unjust than unnecessary'. Joseph II, who eventually came to disregard these scruples, was soon in open conflict with many of his nobles, especially in the outlying parts of his scattered dominions. Their resistance to his policies was on the whole sufficient to frustrate the Emperor and to force his brother to undo a good deal of Joseph's work after his death. The French monarchy, in the inactive hands of Louis XV, entrusted the central government to noble ministers who encountered increasingly vigorous opposition from the *parlements*, the largely aristocratic representatives of an older conception of divided sovereignty. Royal *intendants*, themselves now usually nobles, became more sensitive to the attraction of their own social order as the gravitational pull of a divided Government weakened. Under Maupeou and Terray, in 1770, the monarchy made an attempt to reassert its theoretical absolutism, but the death of Louis XV four years later restored the old policy of vacillation and compromise which eroded royal initiative at the expense of traditional bodies, *parlements* and provincial Estates, which were almost always controlled by the nobility. In Russia the century saw the virtual creation of a noble class of the western kind. In the time of Peter the Great (1682–1725) noble status had involved the obligation of service to the state. Estates and the serfs who went with them, were the temporary rewards for such service. The nobles, unlike those of western Europe, did not base their claim to distinction from the rest of the community on military ancestry and did not claim to be ruled by a code of honour of the western kind. Nobles, in fact, were still liable to corporal punishment until 1785. Gradually the Russian nobility won the right to the permanent ownership of its estates while shaking off the burden of service. The charter which they received from Catherine II in 1785 settled every controversial issue in their favour. Freed from the obligation of state service, they were given a measure of local self-government through their own elected officials. All land not owned by the crown was assumed to belong to them and they were entitled to deport their serfs to Siberia at will. At the same time they were given ownership of the subsoil of their lands, mining rights, the right to engage in commerce and industry and to acquire property in the towns. The Semiramis of the North, as the *philosophes* liked to describe their Russian patron, was making sure of domestic support. It was a far cry from the serf-owner of the steppes to the English justice of the peace, but if one discounts the enormous difference in local conditions, a somewhat similar trend can be discerned in England. The gentry entrenched themselves more firmly and perhaps became somewhat more exclusive in the process. Ownership of land conferred local power, as justice of the peace and as officer in the militia. Promotion by influence and the conception of office as a form of property were common to England and continental Europe.

It is therefore clear that where population growth, economic development and administration were concerned, there was little structural change in the second half of the eighteenth century. England was beginning to evolve in a new direction but the process had not gone far and seemed an acceleration of familiar trends rather than a radically new departure. In Europe as a whole the structure of society was remarkably stable. The main element of change was the resurgence of the nobility as it established a new symbiosis with bureaucratic absolutism and, in one or two places, took advantage of new opportunities for the exploitation of its economic resources. On social and economic grounds one would have expected the period to be one of calm. The fact that it was marked by large-scale warfare and considerable social unrest means that the causes of tension must be sought in some other direction.

*

The main difference between the Europe of the first and second halves of the eighteenth century lay in the character of its rulers. Men who, for different reasons, were content to accept the *status quo*, gave way to others who were determined to overthrow it. 1740 saw the accession of Frederick II in Berlin and Maria Theresa in Vienna. Two years later came the resignation of Walpole who, to quote his biographer J. H. Plumb, 'had just held in check those aspirations natural to a society which was faced with enormous possibilities of commercial expansion'. Fleury, the pacific prime minister of Louis XV, died in the year after Walpole's resignation. Frederick II, young and ambitious, profited from the large army and well-filled treasury left by his father, to take advantage of the disputed Habsburg succession and seize Silesia. At about the same time England and France began a decisive struggle for colonial supremacy, in which the main prizes were Canada and India. As a result the main Powers of Europe were at war for 15 of the next 23 years. The War of the Austrian Succession (1740–8) failed to settle the colonial rivalry and left Maria Theresa determined to recover Silesia. The Seven Years War (1756–63) produced the triumph of England over France and the exhaustion of both Austria and Prussia. The maritime conflict perhaps arose from economic developments beyond the power of politicians in London or Versailles to control, but the continental conflict was largely due to the personal initiative of the King of Prussia. Having narrowly escaped disaster in the Seven Years War, Frederick, by 1763, was disinclined to risk further adventures and Europe might have expected a period of peace. But in 1762 Catherine II seized power in Russia and committed her country to a generation of expansion. Her wars against Turkey and encroachment in Poland, which was partitioned in 1772, 1793 and 1795, kept central and eastern Europe in continual tension. Joseph II, who reigned jointly with his mother from 1765 and alone, after her death, from 1780 to 1790, was determined to restore the Habsburg fortunes by war against Turkey and to acquire more territory in Germany itself. Finally, the revolt of the American colonies against England provided France with an opportunity to avenge her colonial defeat in the Seven Years War, and the two Powers fought each other once more from 1778 to 1783.

The wars of 1740–63 form a watershed within the eighteenth century. The Seven Years War was particularly destructive; Frederick II estimated the casualties directly caused by the war at 853,000 troops and 33,000 civilians and the devastation of crops probably led to more deaths from famine. It seems reasonable to assume a connexion – for which *Candide* provides specific justification – between this slaughter and the decline of belief in a beneficent Providence ordering all things for man's convenience. In more concrete terms, the war left the belligerents financially exhausted and the subsequent inflation of standing armies imposed a rate of government expenditure that could not be covered by traditional forms of taxation. The search for new sources of revenue drove some of the European monarchs to assert their right to tax the nobility, to use Church property for their own purposes and to abrogate traditional privileges that protected their wealthier subjects in certain areas. The inevitable resistance of those whose pockets were threatened took the form of an appeal to traditional rights which raised the whole question of the extent and nature of political sovereignty. Royal initative was countered by opposition – which sometimes went as far as open revolt – justified by the invocation of either traditional privilege or natural rights, or even both combined. Since privilege could shelter all or most of the inhabitants of a favoured area, opposition was not limited to the aristocracy, although they, as its main beneficiaries, generally took the lead.

The problem first arose in an acute form in the Habsburg Empire, because of the need to reorganize the ramshackle machinery of the state if Silesia were to be recovered. In 1740 the nobility were exempt from direct taxation: the Hungarian Diet, when it decided to raise troops on Maria Theresa's behalf, declared that the fiscal immunity of the nobility and clergy was an unchangeable fundamental law. The nobility of the Empire, through its local Diets, raised troops and collected the taxes that it did not pay itself. Although the annual tax burden per head in Austria itself was 21s, the Austrian Netherlands paid only 3s 6d (one tenth of the amount paid by their Dutch neighbours) and Lombardy 5s. Neither of these could be described as a poor area. The Empress and her son for fifty years waged a continual struggle to increase revenue and strengthen the central government. Joseph succeeded in increasing the yield of taxation by about 80 per cent. In the process the rulers were led to challenge one institution after another. Local Estates lost their right to collect taxes, the separate Chancery of Bohemia disappeared and the central government interfered more and more in Hungary and the Netherlands. Concern for revenue was one of the main motives behind the religious policy of Joseph II which involved the suppression of the contemplative orders and the secularization of much Church property, thereby adding a religious element to the opposition which his measures encountered. The government was led to intervene more and more within the manor itself, since the fisc could hope to gain what the lord lost. Feudal courts were restricted, the labour services due by the peasant to his lord curtailed, fees for marrying and leaving the manor limited and eventually, in 1789, Joseph decreed that the peasant was to pay $12\frac{2}{9}$ per cent of the value of his land to the state as taxation and $17\frac{5}{9}$ per cent to his lord. The result of this continual pressure was, in the first instance, a good deal of sabotage by the agents of the administration, since the bureaucracy relied on nobles to give local effect to its policies. Opposition finally broke out into open revolt: the Austrian Netherlands declared their independence in 1789 and only the death of the Emperor in the following year prevented the secession of Hungary.

Events in France took a somewhat similar course. The financing of a system of military roads, constructed to defend Brittany during the Seven Years War, set the central government against the Breton Estates and the *parlement* at Rennes. When the military commander had the leader of the *parlementaires* arrested, the other *parlements* of France joined in vociferous protest, which in turn led the king to an unusually blunt affirmation of the royal prerogative in 1766. Four years later an acute financial crisis was met by forced loans and a partial repudiation of the Debt. The opposition of the Paris *parlement* led to its complete reorganization, which involved suppressing the offices of its leaders without compensation. The government then proceeded to revise the assessment of taxes, although the nobility and the *Pays d'États*, which had retained their local Estates, were not entirely deprived of their privileged position. The accession of Louis XVI in 1774 brought the restoration of the *parlement* and a return to the conciliation of the nobility. But the War of American Independence revived in even more acute form the desperate need for new financial resources. Calonne, the finance minister, drafted proposals which included a universal land tax, to which clergy and nobility were liable, whose assessment was to be decided by new local assemblies representative of land ownership rather than social status. An assembly of notables, to whom Calonne submitted his proposals, adopted the parliamentary tactics of insisting on redress before supply and their opposition procured Calonne's dismissal. The Paris *parlement*, which opened proceedings against him and drove him to flee to England, raised the constitutional stakes by declaring that it was incompetent to approve of new taxation and demanded the summons of the Estates General – which had last met in 1614. Further resistance by the *parlement* drove the government once again to attempt in 1788 a far-reaching judicial reorganization that would have broken the power of the *parlements* to thwart the royal will. The ministerial *coup d'état* was answered by a wave of aristocratic opposition in the provinces which in places took the form of open revolt. The country was inundated by a flood of brochures, mostly supporting the *parlements*, which discussed the nature of sovereignty in terms that promised little future for divine right absolutism. The more conservative appealed to a 'traditional' French constitution which they had some difficulty in finding. Not having any document as convenient as Magna Charta had proved to seventeenth-century English lawyers, they fell back on Tacitus and the Germanic tribes.

Political antiquarianism was modernized by the endless repetition of the argument of *De l'esprit des lois* that monarchy required the moderating power of *corps intermédiaires* if it was not to degenerate into despotism. More radical protagonists, sometimes borrowing from Rousseau, took their stand on the natural rights of man, as embodied in a tacit social contract. The arguments, even the language, were soon to be taken up by the Revolution in a wider social context: 'We are all born citizens, we are all *enfants de la patrie* before we become subjects of the king. The king is merely the first subject of his kingdom.' The intention of most of the writers was probably less revolutionary than their words suggest. Many *parlementaires* were pressing contemporary slogans into the service of an old-fashioned local particularism: a Dauphiné lawyer rested the liberties of his province on those of the Allobroges; others claimed that the pact of association between Normandy and the French crown, or the marriage contract of Anne of Brittany were the 'social contracts' of their specific communities. A citizen of Toulouse went so far as to invoke the 'inalienable, imprescriptible, eternal' natural rights of municipal oligarchies. Much of the agitation was intended to prevent change rather than to promote it. Our concern here is with the fact that the outcry against royal policy had been determined not by social pressure from a rising class but by royal interference with the *status quo* in the search for new sources of revenue. Appropriately enough, it was the inability of the government to honour its short-term debts that brought about the resignation of Calonne's successor, Brienne, in August 1788. His replacement by Necker led to the second restoration of the *parlements*. With the Estates General due to meet in the following year, it seemed as though the French nobility was about to complete its triumph over royal autocracy.

Nothing on the European continent could provide a very close parallel to the difficulties which the British Government encountered in its relations with its North American colonies. The immensity of the intervening Atlantic transformed the nature of government; as Burke expressed it, 'Seas roll and months pass, between the order and the execution'. The innovating absolutist sovereign was not so much a king as a parliament, which based its authority on prescription, not divine right. The colonists themselves made curious conservatives. Their society was more egalitarian than any in Europe and the barrier of hereditary nobility did not exist. Most important of all, the extremely rapid growth of the American settlements in population, wealth and resources, introduced an element of automatic change into a relationship with England that was assumed to be more or less static. Nevertheless there were some parallels between the continents. The British Debt had roughly doubled as a result of the Seven Years War and while the level of taxation was higher in England than in any European country, the colonists paid very little. It was the attempt to make them contribute more towards a budget over which they had no control that first led them to protest. Unlike the French *parlements* or the Estates of Hungary or the Austrian Netherlands, they could not base their claims on medieval 'liberties'; any appeal to the past was liable to work to their disadvantage by invoking inconvenient memories of a period of dependence which they were now in a position to challenge. Perhaps for this reason they were driven to take their stand – though not without some conservative reservations – on the revolutionary principle of the natural rights of man. The preamble to the Declaration of Independence (1776), the most eloquent revolutionary manifesto in western history, proclaimed these universal principles, which it was difficult to applaud in America and deny in Europe. 'We hold these truths to be self-evident, that all men are created equal, that they are endowed by their Creator with certain unalienable rights. . . . That whenever any form of government becomes destructive of these ends it is the right of the people to alter or abolish it, and to institute new government, laying its foundation on such principles and organizing its powers in such form, as to them shall seem most likely to effect their safety and happiness.' We are no more concerned than was contemporary Europe with the question of how far the Americans succeeded in living up to their own difficult principles. The immediate lesson of the revolt was that a people had successfully deposed its ruler, created, by what could be made to appear a new social contract, a republican government, and justified itself in the kind of language that raised an immediate echo in eighteenth-century minds and hearts.

The Habsburg Empire, France and the American colonies offer the most striking but not the only examples of conflict arising from the determination of royal governments to provide themselves with new sources of revenue at the expense of the formerly privileged. Some states, such as Russia and Naples, limited the consequent social tension by confining themselves to the taxation of the clergy (Naples) or the expropriation of Church land (Russia). The combined onslaught on the Jesuits, which drove the Pope to dissolve the Order in 1773, with important effects on the entire educational system of Catholic Europe, was due in part to the temptation that the wealth of an unpopular Order dangled before secular-minded rulers. In the smaller German states the running fight between dukes, margraves, electors and their Diets continued as before. The intervention of Austria and Prussia in Württemberg in 1770 gave the victory to the Estates; in Bavaria the Elector Maximilian III had the better of the contest. Stanislas Poniatowski in Poland was in a particularly dangerous situation, with the monarchy weaker than any in Europe and Catherine II determined to perpetuate a situation which she found convenient. Even in Poland, however, the Four Year Diet (1788–92) brought about a peaceful revolution which, had it been allowed to continue, would have curtailed the authority of the great Polish magnates. When Gustavus III, by his *coup d'état* of 1772, ended fifty years of what he called 'insufferable aristocratic despotism' in Sweden, he began a new period of tension that was to lead to his own assassination in 1792. Over a considerable part of Europe, therefore, the latter part of the eighteenth century was a time of internal conflict which had often been precipitated by rulers looking for means of financing their past and present policies.

*

During the same period the social order was also disturbed, in one or two places, by a new kind of movement from below. This was quite distinct from peasant risings such as that in Bohemia in 1775 and Pugachev's revolt in Russia in 1773. It took the form of a protest by the educated against their exclusion from political power by privileged minorities who based their claim to govern on tradition and prescription. R. R. Palmer, in the first volume of his important work, *The Age of the Democratic Revolution*, opened a debate on the significance of these movements, which he saw as part of a ferment common to the Atlantic community, of which the American and French Revolutions were the most important outbreaks. If we confine our attention to Europe, the scope of these 'democratic' movements appears very restricted. France can scarcely be included before the autumn of 1788, for until then opposition had been almost entirely confined to the nobility and the legal circles which took their cue from the *parlements*. We are left with the protest movements in England, the Netherlands and Geneva, which were neither unreservedly democratic nor typical of western Europe as a whole. These movements shared several common factors. They represented the views of the educated but unprivileged, men who considered themselves unjustly barred from a share of political power. If one excepts the special case of the

Austrian Netherlands, all were directed, not against divine-right absolutism but against oligarchies whose claim to power rested on tradition alone. All were liable to be outbid by more extreme elements further down the social scale and each gave rise to a triangular conflict of considerable complexity.

In Geneva the ancient rivalry between the ruling patricians and the 'citizens' flared up in a new conflict that enlisted Voltaire and Rousseau as partisans of magnates and bourgeois respectively. The citizens, defeated when they appealed to tradition, began to invoke the support of the 'natives' – three quarters of the population – with arguments based on natural rights. The patricians gave some ground in 1768, but the natives suspected the citizens of being mainly concerned for their own interests, and French intervention in 1782 allowed the city fathers to recover the ground that they had lost. A somewhat similar situation arose in the Netherlands where the oligarchy of Regents found themselves opposed by a new party of 'patriots' composed for the most part of gentlemen of town and country. The situation was complicated by the existence of a monarchist party of opposition, whose leader was the stadtholder, William V, and whose support came partly from the peasantry and the urban poor. The Regents broke their alliance with the patriots, rather than concede the latter's political demands, and in 1787 a virtual civil war between the patriots on the one hand and the combined forces of the Regents and the House of Orange was decided by British and Prussian intervention in favour of William V. The situation in the Austrian Netherlands was different in that the local magnates, under the leadership of Van der Noot, themselves began the revolt against the Austrian Emperor. They were soon challenged by a more radical party, led by Vonck, which demanded not merely independence, but municipal reform. The conservatives prevailed in 1790, with clerical and peasant support, and unleashed a White Terror against the Vonckists, which was only suppressed when Austrian troops regained control of the country. The situation in England, though less violent, was not wholly dissimilar. A moderate movement began about 1779 to demand the reform of a parliament whose franchise was defended in the name of traditional rights, what Burke called 'a constitution made by what is ten thousand times better than choice: it is made by peculiar circumstances, occasions, tempers, dispositions, and moral, civil and social habitudes of the people, which disclose themselves only in a long space of time.' Montesquieu's conception of an *esprit général* was becoming an argument for immobility rather than a possible criterion of change. Perhaps discredited by the savage Gordon riots in London in 1780, the reformers made no progress in England and little headway in Ireland.

*

The result of these different policies, movements, resistances and revolts was to create a pattern of quite extraordinary complexity and confusion. In one respect royal authority was going farther than ever before and in its desperate search for revenue beginning to challenge the hierarchical conception of society that it had hitherto respected. On the other hand, members of the nobility in some European states were acquiring a measure of control over the machinery of political absolutism. The British parliament, which was regarded on the Continent as the embodiment of the rights of the citizen, was defended at home as the untouchable legacy of traditional privileges. Chastellux might almost have been replying to Burke when he wrote in *De la félicité publique*, 'You speak of prescription. That applies, no doubt, between individuals, but can it exist between one class of citizens and another? Can it exist against the public interest?' Conservatives were already warning against the limitless possibilities of *salus populi suprema lex*. There was not so much a European debate as a general pandemonium, for principles that seemed reassuring in one context proved highly inconvenient in another. Rousseau might be assumed from *Du contrat social* to be an extreme advocate of popular sovereignty, but in Genevan politics his sympathies did not extend as far as the natives, and his support for Stanislas Poniatowski appeared reactionary to *philosophes* who applauded the partition of Poland as a blow struck by the enlightened Catherine against the fanaticism of Polish Catholics. French *parlementaires* provided the later revolutionaries with an anthology of demagogic hyperbole that they declaimed in support of aristocratic reaction. Prescription, natural rights and public utility appeared in every possible combination of agreement and antithesis.

Amongst this general confusion it is perhaps possible to glimpse one or two general characteristics. The struggle was on the whole concerned with political power and the fruits of office or with the defence of traditional privileges. Inevitably, it assumed a certain social colouring, but this tended to differ from one region to another. There is no good reason for interpreting the conflict in any country, except, just possibly, in England, as having anything to do with the struggle of an emerging social class to win political recognition. More important was the rivalry between 'ins' and 'outs' which frequently corresponded to the hostility of 'country' to 'court'. Whether one thinks of the hatred of the French provincial merchant for the Versailles speculator, the contempt of the Magyar squire for the Hungarian magnate who had been ensnared by the pensions and marriage alliances he could obtain at Vienna, the country gentry and Dissenters in England, or the Dutch patriots held at bay by municipal oligarchs, in all these cases there was either growing resentment against traditional practice or, more often, an appeal to the good old days against the way things were developing. Local circumstances determined whether the agitation was for or against change. Opposition was probably more articulate than in the past and in the heat of controversy the arguments that were soon to serve both revolution and counter-revolution were already being forged. There were a few signs that hitherto dormant sections of the population might respond to ideas filtering down from above in unexpected and unwelcome ways. In the Habsburg territories agrarian revolt and urban atheism had already begun to appear. In the face of such phenomena the first hints of a general reaction against the Enlightenment were also to be found. The Austrian police began using secret agents in 1785 and the Elector of Bavaria took action against the *Illuminati*, a mystical freemasonry, in the same year. The death of Frederick II in 1786 was followed by a return to severe religious censorship in Prussia. Some parts of Europe, notably the Iberian peninsula and Prussia, were comparatively free from open unrest, but over most of the continent the generation that separated the end of the Seven Years War from the beginning of the French Revolution was one of tension and discontent that contrasted sharply with the stability of the early part of the century.

Chapter 6

THE INNER VOICE

By the 1760s the scientific and philosophical speculation of the Enlightenment seemed to have ended in an impasse. Chance, or the blind determinism˙ of matter in regular but aimless motion, appeared to regulate the operation of the universe and the destiny of man. If metaphysical speculation had any meaning at all – which the sceptics denied – it served merely to open a window on to the blank wall of necessity. A brilliant and inquisitive age was not likely to be content for long with such a prospect, and in response to the challenge new attitudes were evolved that transformed the terms in which men thought of themselves and of the order of the universe. One of the most significant of these attitudes, which forms the subject of the present chapter, was the acceptance of the heart as legitimate consort of the head. It is important, from the outset, to realize what this new assumption did *not* imply. To present it as a revolt against an age of arid intellectualism seems to me to betray extraordinary insensitivity towards the vigour of eighteenth-century life and the excitement of its speculative thought. What happened was not that the artist usurped the position formerly occupied by the scholar, but that both turned to the emotions for the guidance they had previously expected of their reason. Sentiment came to be accepted as the source of a kind of knowledge to which intelligence could not aspire, and as the arbiter of action. But if feeling became pilot, reason remained in command, except for a few extremists whose shipwreck discouraged imitation. The definition of their respective roles could never be established with finality but there was no question of the elimination of reason. However dramatically this new attitude may have seemed to challenge the urbanity of the Enlightenment, both grew from a common stock and both were rooted in the same intellectual soil. Sensationalist psychology had always insisted that knowledge came from the senses, that the passions were the winds which alone could drive the ship forward, even if their excess might overwhelm it. Conversely, the new cult of sensibility, though it emphasized conflict and apparent disharmony in man and nature, remained true to the belief in a providential order within which all 'natural' aspirations could be reconciled.

In so far as one can ascribe a definite starting point to a change in attitude, the most appropriate date would be 1749, when Rousseau wrote his prize essay on the subject set by the Dijon Academy: *Whether the restoration of the arts and sciences has contributed to the refinement of morals*. In other words, the 'reaction' against the Enlightenment preceded most of the major works of the Enlightenment itself! In fact, the next twenty years saw a dialogue between Rousseau and his opponents in France, with hints of a new outlook in England, such as Burke's *Philosophical Enquiry into the Origin of our Ideas of the Sublime and the Beautiful* (1756) and Sterne's *Sentimental Journey* (1768). The torch was then passed to Germany where a national literary revival at first invoked the authority of French rebels, such as Diderot and Rousseau, in the struggle to free itself from the domination of French classicism. The social and political climate across the Rhine may have contributed to give the ensuing *Sturm und Drang* movement a shrill note of anarchic protest which was unique to Germany and soon led Goethe and Schiller to break away. By the time of the French Revolution the cult of sensibility had spread over much of western Europe. In France alone there were seventy editions of Rousseau's *Nouvelle Héloïse* between 1761 and 1789. The new emphasis on simplicity, feeling and the rural virtues appeared in all kinds of places, from Court fashions at Versailles to the *Lyrical Ballads* of Wordsworth and

Coleridge in 1798. Its philosophical implications were the subject of Kant's three *Critiques* (1781–90).

It is impossible in a general survey of this kind even to try to convey the scope and brilliance of what is sometimes referred to as *pre-romanticism*. Feeling is individual and each of the writers with whom we are now concerned was intensely aware of his own individuality. As he himself would have been the first to agree, Rousseau demands a place of his own. There is something absurd about any attempt to imprison within a 'trend' the man whose autobiography begins: 'I feel my own heart and I know men. I am differently made from any of those I have seen. I dare to believe that I am different from any man who exists. If I am no better, at least I am not the same.' We cannot linger over what was most individual, and perhaps most valuable about the men of the period. Nor is it my intention to write literary history that would bring out the ways in which they influenced each other. My aim is to re-create the intellectual climate in which they lived and to which they contributed by their manner of living and writing. Inevitably, this implies concentration on what was common rather than on what was unique and risks reducing them all to a universal mediocrity.

A second difficulty is to communicate through reasonable prose the fierce insights of passionate intuition. Emotional writing was characteristic of all the men with whom we are here concerned, whatever their subject. An earnest, somewhat bombastic tone and a penchant for prophetic denunciation appear in Helvétius's *De l'esprit* (1758). D'Holbach's *Système de la nature* (1770) ends, somewhat incongruously for a work of materialist determinism, with what one can only describe as a hymn in praise of nature: 'Come back, runaway child, come back to nature. She will console you, she will drive from your heart the fears that confound you, the anxiety that torments you, the passions that unsettle you, the hatred that keeps you from the men you should love. Restored to nature, to humanity, to yourself, scatter flowers along the road of life. . . .' If the rationalists could use language of this kind, more passionate – and more moving – eloquence was only to be expected from the devotees of feeling. Rousseau described himself as 'intoxicated with virtue' and Byron wrote of him:

> His love was passion's essence: – as a tree
> On fire by lightning, with ethereal flame
> Kindled he was, and blasted.

One cannot analyse writers of this kind without analysing much of the life out of them. As Wordsworth wrote in the *Lyrical Ballads*:

> We murder to dissect.

Of Rousseau in particular, but also of the Goethe of *Werther* and the Schiller of the *Robbers*, one can only say that the reader who does not *feel* the point can never hope to understand it. This may be true of all art, but it is true of the *Nouvelle Héloïse* in a way that does not apply to *Tom Jones*. My ambition, in this chapter, is not to imitate the resonance of these silenced voices but to tempt the reader to seek it for himself.

*

In one sense, the new trend of ideas arose directly from the disillusionment of the Enlightenment about the providential order of nature which provided for the wants of man and, as Pope expressed it, 'bade Self-love and Social be the same'. There was a turning back towards an older Christian view of nature as a battlefield and of man as a creature torn between duty and self-interest. In Hume's *Dialogues Concerning Natural Religion*, published in 1779 after his death, it is the Christian, Demea, who affirms, 'The whole earth . . . is cursed and polluted. A perpetual war is kindled against all living creatures.

Necessity, hunger, want, stimulate the strong and courageous; fear, anxiety, terror, agitate the weak and infirm.' Goethe took up the same note in *Werther* (1774): 'There is not a moment in which one is not a destroyer and has to be a destroyer. A harmless walk kills a thousand poor crawling things, one footstep smashes a laboriously built anthill and stamps a whole little world into an ignominious grave. . . . I can see nothing but an eternally devouring, eternally regurgitating monster.' From the conflict in nature the transition was easy to the inevitable disharmony between the individual and society. This was one of the main themes of Diderot's *Neveu de Rameau*, probably written between 1761 and 1774, in which the question is argued in Diderot's favourite dialogue form, Rameau's nephew maintaining 'In nature, all species devour each other; all ranks devour each other in society.' In the *Entretien d'un père avec ses enfants* (1770) Diderot again investigated the conflict between law and natural morality. His conclusion is worth quoting as an example of his ability to live amicably with problems which he did not know how to solve.

'The point is, father, that in the last resort the wise man is subject to no law. . . .'

'Don't speak so loudly.'

'Since all laws are subject to exceptions, the wise man must judge for himself when to submit and when to free himself from them.'

'I should not be too worried if there were one or two people like you in the town, but if they all thought that way I should go and live somewhere else.'

Such moral agnosticism was completely alien to the temper of Rousseau, whose revolt against his literary colleagues began when he dissociated 'the restoration of the arts and sciences' from moral progress. He was led on to postulate a new kind of conflict, between the demands of an increasingly unequal and sophisticated society and the natural instincts of its members. As the gap between the two widened, the chances of the individual finding his own fulfilment in what the community regarded as its collective interest became more and more remote. Even if theoretically possible, such a hypothetical coincidence seemed to him too flimsy a foundation for human morality. At the turning point in the *Nouvelle Héloïse*, when Julie announces to her lover, Saint Preux, that she has married the Baron de Wolmar in deference to her father's wishes, and intends to be faithful to her husband, Rousseau makes her challenge, head-on, the belief of the Enlightenment that recognition of the long-term identity of personal and collective interest would suffice to guarantee the right action of the reasonable man.

I infer the beauty of virtue from a conception of order, and its merit from the general utility. But of what weight is that against my personal interest, and, at bottom, which concerns me more, that I should achieve happiness at the expense of the rest of mankind or that the rest of mankind should achieve its happiness at my expense? If fear of shame or punishment prevents my acting badly for my personal gain, I have only to conceal my evil deeds. Virtue will have nothing with which to reproach me, and if I am caught in the act, they will punish, as they used to do in Sparta, not the crime but the carelessness.

Rousseau must have been moved indeed if even the standards of Sparta were to be rejected.

Whether social utility was an inadequate guarantee of moral action, or whether the long-term self-interest of the individual was not necessarily identical with the welfare of the community and with civil law, in either case the rationalistic ethic of the *philosophes* whom Julie denounced as 'dangerous reasoners' seemed to have fallen apart in their hands. If they were not to return, shamefaced and hypocritical, to a Church in whose dogma and revelation they could not believe, they had to provide themselves with an alternative guide to action and a new means of grappling with problems which empiricism seemed merely to have explained away.

★

There was a surprising consensus, for an age which is generally regarded as one of 'reason', that the intellect was a blunt and fallible instrument for the exploration of human experience and a treacherous guide to the solution of moral problems. This attitude was clearly defined by Marivaux in his novel, *La Vie de Marianne* (1736–41),

There is no way of communicating a complete impression of people; at least, it does not seem possible to me. I know the people with whom I live much better than I could define them ... they are sentient beings so complicated and so precisely defined that my thought confuses their image as soon as it fastens on them; I don't know how to approach them to express what they are. They are in me, but not accessible to me. ... There seem to me a thousand occasions when my soul knows more than it can tell, and has a spirit of its own which is far superior to my everyday one. It seems to me too that men are far superior to all the books they write.

Marivaux's doubts as to the omniscience of reason were to be taken up, in one way or another, by writers of very different schools. Marianne herself set the tone: 'So far as I am concerned, I believe that only feeling can give us reliable information about ourselves and that we must not put too much trust in what our minds twist to their own convenience, for they seem to me great dreamers.' This attitude became the theme of many a moral sermon. Diderot claimed, 'It is wrong to attribute the crimes of men to their passions: it is their false judgements that are at fault. The passions always inspire us rightly, for they inspire us only with the desire for happiness. It is the mind that misleads us and makes us take false roads.' The Christian, Burke, concurred: 'Men often act right from their feelings, who afterwards reason but ill on them from principle.' Parson Sterne applied the same judgement to himself. 'I can safely say for myself, I was never able to conquer any one single bad sensation in my heart so decisively, as by beating up as fast as I could for some kindly and gentle sensation to fight it upon its own ground.' The French moralist, Chamfort, towards the end of the century, expressed his similar viewpoint in the pseudo-anthropological terms that Rousseau had popularized. 'In the present state of society, man seems to me to be more corrupted by his reason than by his passions. His passions (I mean those which appertain to primitive man) have preserved, within the social order, whatever fragments of nature still remain.' Madame Roland, in the autobiography which she wrote while awaiting execution in 1793, drew a parallel with the physical sciences. 'The human mind is not called to perceive [difficult questions] in the clear light of demonstrable proof, but what does proof matter to the sensitive soul? Is feeling not enough? . . . Feeling plays the same part in ethics that motion does in physics.'

This superiority of the intuitive power was not confined to ethics. Even as a source of ideas, the imagination was felt to be quicker and bolder in perception than plodding reason. One would scarcely expect to find its praises sung, and lyrically too, in *L'Homme machine*, but La Mettrie claimed that it was superior to reason as a source of ideas in both the sciences and the arts. 'By its flattering brush the cold skeleton of Reason takes on pink and living flesh.' Burke hammered home the same message in his essay on the Sublime and the Beautiful.

Whatever turns the soul inward on itself, tends to concenter its forces and to fit it for greater and stronger flights of science.

Whenever the wisdom of our Creator intended that we should be affected with any thing, he did not confine the exercise of his design to the languid and precarious operation of our reason; but he endued it with powers and properties that prevent [i.e. anticipate] the understanding, and even the will, which seizing upon the senses and imagination, captivate the soul before the understanding is ready either to join with them or to oppose them.

From Germany, Hamann, the 'Magus of the North', gave his cryptic assent: 'Thinking, feeling and understanding all depend on the heart, and a little enthusiasm and superstition not merely claim some indulgence but are a yeast necessary to set the soul fermenting towards the heroism of philosophy.' Rivarol brought the question down to earth again with the precise economy of classical French prose. 'If there existed on earth a species superior to man, he would sometimes admire our instinct but often scorn our reason.'

When Rousseau made himself the most fervent and eloquent spokesman of this inner voice of conscience or imagination, as opposed to what Keats was later to describe as 'consecutive reasoning', his was therefore neither an original nor an isolated voice. What distinguished him was not merely the passion of his advocacy or the persuasiveness of his lyrical prose, but the insistent vigour with which he examined the problem from every angle. Far from being the prophet of blind emotionalism, it was his concern to accommodate both heart and head that made it difficult for him to arrive at any fixed conclusion. In the *Nouvelle Héloïse* in particular, he was writing as a novelist rather than as a philosopher, and the conflicting views of his characters probably reflect states of his own mind which he was under no obligation to reduce to a single system. Part of the difficulty arises from a double confusion, with the 'heart' referring sometimes to the conscience and sometimes to physical passion, and 'reason' representing either mechanical empiricism or a kind of disinterested 'super-ego'. Rousseau's starting point was a blunt denial of Condillac's claim that reflection was itself a form of sensation. 'Perception is feeling; comparison is judgement. Judgement and feeling are not the same thing.' Rousseau, like Kant, also saw that perception alone could confer no sense of obligation towards action that was not directed to personal advantage. On this issue, the two main characters of the *Nouvelle Héloïse*, Saint Preux and Julie, are in agreement. God 'has given us reason to know the good, conscience to love it and freedom to choose it'. 'Conscience does not tell us the truth about objects but the rule of our duties; it does not tell us what we must think but what we must do; it does not teach us right reasoning but right action.' The problem was the correct identification of the goal which conscience would provide the force to pursue. Sometimes Rousseau made conscience the arbiter, as well as the main-spring of action: 'Whatever I feel to be right is right. What-ever I feel to be wrong is wrong. The conscience is the best of all casuists. . . . Reason deceives us only too often and we have acquired the right to reject it only too well, but conscience never deceives.' Just as often, however, he insisted on the need to control the wayward promptings of the heart by the cool judgement of reason. 'Our heart deceives us in a thousand ways and its motives of action are always suspect, but reason pursues only what is good; its rules are sure, clear, easy in execution, and it never loses itself except in the kind of useless speculation for which it is not designed.' One could multiply examples of either attitude *ad nauseam* and Rousseau's own attempts to reconcile the two are not very helpful: 'My rule to trust sentiment rather than reason is confirmed by reason itself.'

Despite these obscurities of Rousseau's thought – or feeling – his general position emerges fairly clearly. Empirical observa-tion of existing society and utilitarian arithmetic provide neither the solution to moral problems nor a sense of obliga-tion sufficient to drive us to discharge unwelcome duties. To know what we should do we must 'consult the inner light', *rentrer en soi-même*, seek the innate principle of justice and virtue *au fond de nos âmes*. Moral judgement, in other words, depends not on education and an appreciation of the identity of self-interest and the common welfare, but on an inner voice which speaks at least as clearly to the peasant as to the philosopher. At the same time, Rousseau insisted that this inner voice was morally autonomous, that its independence could never be alienated to any external authority. He was as prompt and vehement as Voltaire in denouncing the claim of any Church to dictate to him what he ought to believe. Priests of different religions 'can say to me as much as they like: submit your reason. A priest who is misleading me could say just the same. I must have reason for submitting my reason.' Through all, or almost all, of Rousseau's work ran the constant theme that the individual must be taught and must teach himself to follow his own conscience, irrespective of the conventions of a society which could only be reformed by the moral initiative of its members. If he preached the gospel of the heart, it was with the conviction that beneath the self-interested sophistication of social man lay natural feelings that were an infallible guide to moral action. His concern was not with the liberation of the emotions as an end in itself, but with the 'virtue' to which he believed them to hold the only key.

Kant is often considered as the philosopher who summed up the achievement of the Enlightenment, defined the frontiers of empirical knowledge and established for pure reason and for ethics realms of their own beyond the mere appearances of the world of phenomena. But the full Kantian philosophy, in all the majesty of its architectonic unity, was known to very few men in the eighteenth century. It is legitimate, within a survey of this kind, to treat the philosopher of Koenigsberg as a man who brought the opinions of his age into philosophical focus, instead of considering his work in purely philosophical terms or as a starting point for new ways of thought. The close similarity between the attitudes of Kant and Rousseau has been brilliantly analysed by Cassirer in his *Rousseau, Kant, Goethe*. Kant himself was well aware of his debt to the man whose portrait was the only picture in his study. It was perhaps with Rousseau in mind that he wrote in an early essay of 1764, 'It is in our days for the first time that people have begun to see that while the power of representing truth is *knowledge*, that of perceiving the good is *feeling*, and that these two must not be confused with one another.' For Kant, as for Rousseau, judgement must be dissociated from perception. 'By means of sense, objects are *given* to us and sense alone provides us with *perceptions*; by means of the understanding objects are *thought* and from it there arise *concepts*.' In his *Critique of Pure Reason* (1781) Kant argued that empirical knowledge could convey information, not about things as they really existed (*noumena*) but only as they were perceived as *phenomena* by a human observer who imposed on them dimensions of space and time which belong to the observer, not to the object. By reducing the external world to measurable phenomena, Kant reserved for science a region within which its objective laws could operate freely and without impediment. By breaking the link between matter – which was observed only as phenomena – and mind, which was capable not merely of forming concepts but of thinking about the concepts themselves, Kant claimed to have exposed the false logic behind materialist determinism.

In the *Critique of Practical Reason* (1788), he followed Rousseau in placing the responsibility for moral action within an inner faculty, the mind's intuitive awareness of itself as *noumenon*, and of its obligations. Moral duty was thereby withdrawn from possible determination by the material world of perceived phenomena. 'However many natural causes, however many sensory stimuli there may be, which drive me to *will* something, they cannot produce [my state of] *being under obligation*.' Since, for Kant, this sense of duty arose directly from the self as *noumenon*, it took precedence over any conclusions that the mind might draw from the external world of phenomena. The conflict between duty and desire imposed a choice on the mind. The mind's own nature presented duty as an imperative, what Kant called a 'categorical imperative' since the order was absolute and unconditional. When he declared that 'reason and not the experience of impressions and objects, is the source of moral obligation' he was in substantial agreement with Rousseau's statement that 'reason alone teaches us to know good and evil. Conscience, which makes us love one and hate the other, although independent of reason, can therefore not develop without it.' Kant's 'reason', as the inner voice of *noumenal* man, corresponded to the moral legislator whom Rousseau sometimes described as conscience and sometimes as reason.

For both men, the individual existed primarily as a morally autonomous unit whose obligations were self-imposed and owed nothing to the external authority of a religious creed or the determinist pressure of a material environment. The moral sense of the uneducated was as precise and urgent as that of the philosopher. Delight in self-surrender to this inner voice was of value, not for itself, but as recognition of the sanctity of the moral law. Emotional self-identification with the good, said Kant, 'gives rise to a windy, extravagant and fantastic habit of mind' whereas, in the case of the truly moral man, 'the soul believes itself to be exalted, just in the measure in which it recognizes the elevation of the holy law above itself and the frailty of its own nature.' This was exactly the point of the *Nouvelle Héloïse*. In the early part of the novel, the confusion of passion with virtue, by Julie and Saint Preux, was described by Rousseau himself as 'full of wordy padding'. The later books, for which their author had a much higher regard, exemplify the self-surrender of passion to what all the characters recognize as the moral law, in such a way as to turn the novel into a veritable Kantian epic.

*

This preoccupation with the individual conscience, common to both Rousseau and Kant, was partly the cause and partly the consequence of a whole mental climate. It would be misleading to suppose that it was directly responsible for the emergence of new attitudes towards individual genius, religious and aesthetic experience and the rights of man in society. To some extent, all of these developed autonomously at about the same time and interacted with each other in the process. It is therefore impossible to understand any one of them in isolation and impracticable to consider them all simultaneously. All rested, in one way or another, on a new awareness of individual uniqueness – although not necessarily as this was understood by Rousseau and Kant. What has been said above may therefore help to set what follows in some kind of intellectual context, but it would be unwise to look for close logical connexions where the people concerned were more aware of their differences. Individualism, after all, cannot be pressed too far as a collective attitude.

One of the most striking changes concerned men's attitude to individuality itself. The followers of Locke had tended to regard minds as computers, processing sense-data in accordance with universal laws. A given environment, physical or social, would therefore produce relatively homogeneous values. In this way, classical insistence on the absolute rules of the objective world, rather than on the idiosyncrasies of the individual observer, was prolonged into the mid-eighteenth century. We have already seen this attitude reflected in Chesterfield's belief that 'The same matter occurs equally to everybody of common sense, upon the same question.' The contrary view, with its implications fully developed, appears rather surprisingly in the book that was regarded as the very embodiment of the Enlightenment: Helvétius's *De l'esprit* (1758). Helvétius, in fact, offers the clearest and most comprehensive statement of the nature and quality of 'genius'.

Although the greatest good of the greatest number was the only criterion of social action left open to the materialist, Helvétius had nothing but contempt for the values of the majority. Time and again he castigated 'sensible people, those idols of the mediocre', who are 'made to follow the beaten track'. Their reasonable judgements are not merely un-exciting but actually false. 'The nature of sound judgement is to draw accurate conclusions from accepted opinions. But these opinions are mostly wrong, and sound judgement, in the majority of cases, is therefore the art of methodically false reasoning.' From this position it was only a small step to the justification of revolt for its own sake, as a manifestation of personal nonconformity. The opposite of the ordinary man is the man of genius, who is distinguished from the multitude by the intensity of his passions – and hence, for the sensational psychologist, the quality of his perceptions. Helvétius, it is true, affirms that all men are born with potentially equal faculties and that genius is entirely a product of education. 'The only advantage which the man of genius enjoys over other men is his habit of concentration and his method of study.' Nevertheless, once he had graduated, so to speak, the genius was different in kind from his fellow-men. Since his values were not those of the majority, he must expect to be an object of ridicule during his lifetime. He was compensated, however, by exemption from the rules that restrict ordinary men. The passion that constituted his genius was equally likely to drive him to glorious virtues or to sensational crimes. But the latter were justified by their necessity and Helvétius rounds angrily on mediocrities who claim to offset their lack of distinction by their blameless lives. 'Are you any better? What does the moral or immoral conduct of the individual matter to the community? A genius is still a worthier man than you, even if he has his vices.'

There was a good deal in *De l'esprit* to set Rousseau's teeth on edge and Helvétius was one of the *raisonneurs* who most irritated him. Nevertheless, there was much in common between their conception of the characteristics and prerogatives, if not the origins of genius. This appears clearly enough in Rousseau's account of his own life. Where they differed – and the distinction was capital – was over the exemption of genius from the moral law that governed ordinary people. The Baron de Wolmar maintained that 'Cold reason never produced anything distinguished and the only way to overcome one passion is by setting another against it. When the passion of virtue arises, it rules absolutely and holds all the rest in equilibrium. That is what makes the real sage, who is no more sheltered from the passions than anyone else, but who alone knows how to conquer them by themselves, as a pilot holds his course though the winds be contrary.' For Rousseau, the pilot was not free to decide which was the right course.

It was in Germany that the revolt of the individual against conventional values and restraint of every kind reached its paroxysm in the *Sturm und Drang*. The title of the movement was taken from a play by Klinger, one of its more violent members. Goethe, looking back in the early nineteenth century on a part of his career that he could now afford to view with detachment, said of the period about 1775, 'The time was yet far distant when it could be affirmed that genius is the power of man which, by its actions, gives laws and rules. At this time it was thought to manifest itself only by overstepping existing laws, breaking established rules and declaring itself above all restraint.' Even Goethe and Schiller, who were both to return to classical canons of order and universality, were for a time swept away by the tide of emotional revolt. Goethe's *Götz von Berlichingen* (1773) and even more Schiller's *Robbers* (1781) glorified the anarchic liberty of the individual who made his own rules. In *The Sorrows of Young Werther* (1774), a novel that carried much of educated Europe off its feet, Goethe wrote, 'All exceptional people who created something great, something that seemed impossible, have to be decried as drunkards or madmen.' It was perhaps only natural that everyone should want to be exceptional, and a contemporary supplied the following description of the first night of the *Robbers*. 'The theatre was like a lunatic asylum, with rolling eyes, clenched fists, hoarse uproar among the audience. Strangers fell sobbing into each other's arms, women tottered, half-fainting, to the door. It was a universal disruption into chaos, out of whose mists a new creation is emerging.'

When all established values were under fire, it was inevitable that some of the universal criticism should appear to have a political bias. As Goethe later wrote, rather condescendingly, 'There were no external enemies to fight, so people fashioned tyrants for themselves, and to this purpose princes and their servants were made to lend their characters. . . . It is remarkable how many poems of that time are imbued with a spirit destructive of every class distinction, whether monarchic or aristocratic.' This political protest was to prove a fire of straw and Goethe was perhaps right in regarding it as merely a pretext for striking attitudes of revolt. The writers of the *Sturm und Drang* were young men and one of the many meanings of *bourgeois* is 'father'.

Possibly more significant was a kind of destructive fury that manifested itself on occasion, as in the *Robbers*. Klinger wrote, 'I am torn asunder by passions which would overwhelm anyone else . . . every moment I should like to fling humanity and all that lives and breathes to the chaos to devour and to hurl myself after them.' Goethe closes his autobiography, around the year 1775, with a discussion of the *demonic*, as a natural force running contrary to the moral order in nature. Men possessed by this demonic power have power over others. 'All the moral forces combined are of no avail against them; in vain does the more enlightened portion of mankind attempt to throw suspicion on them as dupes or deceivers – the masses are attracted by them. . . . Nothing can overcome them but the universe itself, with which they have begun the fight.' Although the cases are perhaps not really parallel, it is tempting to associate with Goethe's speculations on evil as a positive force, independent of honest error or mere self-interest, the extraordinary novel which Choderlos de Laclos published in 1782, *Les Liaisons dangereuses*. In this book human sexuality, which the century was accustomed to regard with the easy-going acceptance of Tom Jones or the innocent carnality of Fanny Hill, becomes a monstrous instrument for the exercise of human destruction as an end in itself, and its chief manipulator, the Marquise de Merteuil, is one of the most terrifying characters in all fiction. The moral autonomy of genius had unforeseen implications that would have horrified the gentle Helvétius.

★

Closely allied to the new conception of genius was a changed attitude to artistic creation and the emergence of aesthetics as a subject in its own right – the word itself was created by the German philosopher, Baumgarten, in 1735. Traditional classicism had held that nature was ruled by fixed laws which prescribed the different literary and artistic genres appropriate to different kinds of experience. The artist 'copied nature' in the sense that he distilled from a situation its essential, universal content; his concern was with the situation, rather than with his own reaction to it. Stylistic rules, such as the dramatic unities, were merely a superficial aspect of a whole attitude. This 'Cartesian' classicism, assuming an innate response to absolute standards, had little to commend it to the empiricist of the school of Locke and it was Locke's sometime pupil, the Earl of Shaftesbury, who transferred the centre of aesthetic enquiry from the object to the creative process by which it came into being. Imitation of nature thus came to be conceived in a dynamic rather than a static sense – to use Picasso's definition, not expressing nature, but working like nature. This creative power Shaftesbury described as 'genius'. Since English writers tended to draw on Shakespeare for their examples, genius came to be associated, in England and later in Germany, after the discovery of

Shakespeare by German writers, with the transcendence of classical rules.

Burke, in his *Philosophical Enquiry into the Origin of our Ideas of the Sublime and the Beautiful* (1756), adopted a somewhat similar viewpoint. 'Besides the ideas, with their annexed pains and pleasures, which are presented by the sense, the mind of man possesses a sort of creative power of its own.' Burke's argument had particular reference to literature: 'The influence of most things on our passions is not so much from the things themselves, as from our opinions concerning them; and these again depend very much on the opinions of other men, conveyed for the most part by words only.' One may therefore be affected by a description of something of which one has no personal experience, and words may be combined to create associations that do not exist in nature. 'The truth is, all verbal description, merely as naked description, though never so exact, conveys so poor and insufficient an idea of the thing described, that it could scarcely have the smallest effect, if the speaker did not call in to his aid those modes of speech that mark a strong and lively feeling in himself. Then, by the contagion of our passions, we catch a fire already kindled in another, which probably might never have been struck out by the object described.'

Lessing's *Laocoön* (1766) also reaffirmed the privileged status of poetry, as compared with painting and sculpture, and Lessing, like Burke, stressed the evocative character of poetry, which left room for the creative imagination of the reader to develop its own response. The demand for a new approach to poetry, and hence for a new kind of poetry, was first satisfied in Germany, especially by the lyrical poetry of Goethe. Its triumph in England may perhaps be dated from the appearance of the *Rime of the Ancyent Marinere* in 1798. It was left to Kant to draw philosophical conclusions from the change in attitude towards aesthetic experience. In his *Critique of Judgement* (1790) he suggested that the aesthetic sense offered a kind of bridge between the world of phenomena and the *noumenal* self. Its material was finite, but aesthetic judgement itself was of a different order from ordinary sense impressions, referring to a higher order of being. 'Imagination, as a productive faculty, is powerful to create, as it were, another nature out of the matter which actual nature supplies. By its aid, when ordinary experience becomes commonplace, we frame to ourselves a new world which, though subjected to laws analogous to those of the natural world, yet is constructed on principles that occupy a higher place in our reason.'

The changed conception of the nature of aesthetic experience made it possible to discriminate sharply between the sublime and the beautiful. The latter was what was harmonious, a source of immediate pleasure. The sublime, however, while also giving pleasure, defied rules of proportion and invariably carried with it an element of terror. Burke linked the sublime with the sense of self-preservation, arising from the *idea* of pain and danger. For him, in consequence, it was 'the strongest emotion which the mind is capable of feeling'. Helvétius emphasized the universality of the sublime, its appeal to humanity as a whole, whereas harmony of proportion, on which beauty relied, was a matter of local convention. But Helvétius too, when he came to give a specific illustration of the sublime, described sea, night, tempest and lightning in a massive accumulation of what he called 'secret terror'.

The pursuit of the sublime in nature is not one theme but the key to many attitudes. At its simplest, it points merely to a preference for a different kind of scenery. Rousseau's taste was to become so general that it is difficult to remember how revolutionary it was at the time. 'No flat country, however beautiful it may be, ever appeared so to me. I need torrents, rocks, firs, dark woods, mountains, rough tracks to climb up and down, precipices by my side to give me a nice fright.'

Behind this change of taste lay a new attitude, which saw in nature not a demonstration of order but an invitation to reverence. 'From the *forbidding* mountain range,' wrote Goethe's Werther, 'across the *barren* plain untrodden by the foot of man, to the ends of the *unknown* seas, the spirit of the Eternal Creator can be felt rejoicing over every grain of dust.' In other words, the gratification of a sense of the sublime involved both solitude, and the kind of country that was untouched by man, if not actually hostile to him. The Alps, in fact, were anti-social. This seems to have been one of the symptoms, if not the causes, of the breach between Diderot and Rousseau, two men who had so much in common. For Diderot, a picture of high mountains, ancient forests and immense ruins evoked episodes of classical or religious history. The roar of an invisible torrent led him to speculate on human calamities. Everything in nature was referred to man in society: 'Man is born for society . . . put a man in a forest and he will become ferocious.' For Rousseau, man only reached his highest insights when alone and humbled by the savage force of nature. Both were alike in their search for natural spontaneity, but what turned the one towards society drove the other into solitude.

Communion with the sublime in nature led also to a new conception of religion, which again separated Rousseau and his followers from the materialists and the philosophical Deists. Rousseau was not inclined to pantheism and it would be difficult to define the connexion which he thought to exist between nature and God. To some extent it was a negative one: nature implied the absence of human society and of books, both of which Rousseau associated with artificiality, pretence and mere cleverness. Alone, in congenial natural surroundings, he was most aware of his own individuality and of that inner voice which he believed to be attuned to God. This emotional communion with a deity who was formless but felt, who spoke in terms of feelings of guilt and virtue rather than through awareness of logic and order, set Rousseau apart in France, though his own writings were to make converts all over France and Europe after his death. Although prepared to conform to the religious observance of the country in which he found himself, he was sceptical of all dogma, much of which he regarded with contempt, as contrary to reason. Emotional Deism of this kind took root more easily in Germany than in France, where Roman Catholic dogma and the entrenched position of the Church encouraged more extreme attitudes on either side. Rousseau's religion, with its anti-Catholic bias and vaguely Protestant overtones, had much to commend it to German Protestants, brought up on Leibniz and Wolff. Although his psychological approach was altogether different, Kant, as usual, took up a position very close to that of Rousseau: the whole purpose of religion was moral action and man was a wholly free moral agent – which implied the rejection of original sin. For Kant, as for Rousseau, Christianity had a primarily symbolic value as the messenger of divine truths which were unrelated to the veracity of the Gospels, which neither could accept. Natural religion conveyed to each man all that he needed to know in order to perform his moral duty. Church membership might help to reinforce the religious instinct, but learned theology and superstitious ritual diverted men from their basic duty to observe the moral law, which they would find in their own hearts if they were ever to find it at all.

*

Another consequence of the change in the climate of opinion was a more critical and passionate approach towards political problems. In terms of political theory, the tendency to see man as being in conflict with his environment implied that the actual relationship between the individual and his society was one of disharmony. The primacy accorded to the inner voice suggested that society must be changed to make it worthy of the individual, and not *vice versa*. At the same time belief in an underlying natural or providential harmony encouraged all to regard such a restoration of former concord as theoretically possible. Theory could appear to be blowing the trumpets of revolution, but in practice, none of the writers with whom we are concerned considered himself to be much of a radical. All accepted the *status quo* as a political fact, and in the last resort, all were more concerned to help the individual find his inner freedom, irrespective of the kind of society in which he had to live, than to preach social or political change.

Belief in the alienation of the individual from contemporary society was inseparable from the cult of primitivism. The best-known example of this is Rousseau's lament for the lost virtues of 'natural' society and his long search for the way back – an anticipation, in terms of humanity as a whole, of what Wordsworth was later to feel about his own life:

> O joy! that in our embers
> Is something that doth live,
> That Nature yet remembers
> What was so fugitive!

In this instance at least, Rousseau was merely emphasizing a point of view shared by most of his contemporaries. At one time or another, most of the political writers of the century agreed that human society had degenerated from the bracing discomfort of primitive natural liberty to a state of sophisticated enslavement to political authority and social convention. As early as 1721, in his *Lettres persanes*, the urbane Montesquieu observed of the barbarian tribes who overthrew the Roman Empire: 'These peoples cannot accurately be called barbarians, since they were free. They have become so, since for the most part subject to absolute rulers, they have lost that mild liberty which is so much in conformity with reason, humanity and nature.' Helvétius, as usual, proved a sensitive barometer to the climate of opinion, however contrary this may have been to his own way of life and to his formal philosophical beliefs. In *De l'esprit* he developed a thoroughly Rousseauist defence of the austere, democratic and belligerent virtues of the Spartan republic. 'As they become more civilized, nations imperceptibly lose their courage, their *vertu* and even their love of liberty . . .* Immediately after its formation every society, according to the particular situation in which it finds itself, advances more or less quickly towards slavery.' Despotism leads to depopulation, a reversion to barbarism and a new revolution of the eternal cycle. Although d'Holbach did not adopt this historical argument in his *Système de la nature*, his repudiation of contemporary society was as violent as that of Rousseau: 'The state of society is a war of the sovereign against the community and of each member against the rest. Man is wicked, not because he is born wicked, but because he is made so. Almost everywhere he is enslaved.' As a materialist, d'Holbach's values were utilitarian: '*Vertu* is what is really and consistently useful to human beings living in society.' Logically, the communal interest should therefore have determined the values of the individual. But d'Holbach was too much the man of his age to subscribe to so totalitarian a sentiment. His conception of nature gave him a standard of values external to society, so that he could complain that in contemporary society 'the majority finds itself *nécessairement déterminé au mal*.' Diderot's *Supplément au Voyage de Bougainville*, written in 1772 although not published before his death, was a philosophical fairy-tale based on the reaction of the explorer, Bougainville, to his discovery of Tahitian society. Bougainville himself had qualified his first impression of Tahiti as a new Garden of Eden, although his companions agreed in regarding the local customs of sexual hospitality as 'the gentle impulses of an instinct that

* The word *vertu*, when used by eighteenth-century writers in a political context, is virtually untranslatable. It implies simplicity, self-government and, above all, the citizen's willing subordination of his personal interest to the communal good.

is infallible because it has not yet degenerated into reason'. Like them, Diderot presented Tahiti as an earthly paradise precisely because it was closer to nature than contemporary Europe, in the sense that social practice reflected basic human instincts rather than artificial conventions. For him, as for Morelly and Rousseau, such 'natural' society implied primitive communism and the absence of private ownership of land. The negative side of this state of mind is to be seen in the feeling that polite society in Europe had refined itself into an emotional vacuum. As Werther put it, 'We cultured ones – cultured until there is nothing left. . . .' 'Love, loyalty and passion' were to be found only in the uncultured. Chamfort gave powerful expression to the same feeling. 'Genuine sentiments are so rare that I sometimes stop in the street to watch a dog gnaw a bone. It is when I am returning from Versailles, Marly and Fontainebleau, said M. de R, that I am most intrigued by this spectacle.'

Rousseau's awareness of conflict between the individual and society, his championship of the former and his belief that primitive society was better adapted to human happiness, freedom and dignity, were therefore attitudes that he shared with many contemporary writers. His prize essay of 1749 presented civilization as an inevitable source of moral corruption. He developed this argument at greater length in his *Discours sur l'origine et les fondements de l'inégalité parmi les hommes* (1754) which described the slow process of degeneration and included his famous *boutade*: 'The man who first had the idea of enclosing a field and saying *this is mine*, and found people simple enough to believe him, was the real founder of civil society.' With the self-delusion of the *émigré*, Rousseau found his Tahiti in his native city-state, Geneva, and much of his subsequent political writing was a defence, in general terms, of his idealized view of Genevan democracy. His *Lettre à d'Alembert sur les spectacles* (1758), which marked his breach with the *philosophes*, used d'Alembert's suggestion that Genevan culture would benefit from the establishment of a theatre, as the pretext for a eulogy of Swiss simplicity in which Sparta was held up as an example for Geneva, although Rousseau was realistic enough to admit that his fellow-countrymen had perhaps not *vertu* enough for their girls to dance naked at public festivals. In his subsequent works he continued to develop the same themes: the inevitable conflict between the natural instincts of the individual and a society as artificial as that of France, and the possibility of at least reducing this tension in the case of a small and relatively uncorrupted society which would take Sparta for its model.

The conflict which Rousseau and his contemporaries deplored was a conflict of moral values, not primarily one of material interests. Helvétius, it is true, referred to 'an eternal seed of hatred between the great and the small' and Rousseau denounced the dangers of great wealth and great poverty, which he believed to be inseparable. But for all of them, what mattered most was not so much the standard of living as the moral quality of a society, as determined by the moral values of its individual members. Rousseau insisted that the essential difference between men and animals was man's free will as expressed in positive choice. Julie, at the end of the *Nouvelle Héloïse*, 'does not study any more, she does not read any more, she acts'. In this respect, the contrast between Rousseau and the young Goethe is particularly striking. Werther's only positive act is self-destruction, whereas the entire training of Émile has the making of rational moral choices as its essential object. All the writers at present under consideration applied to politics what Burke wrote about learning, 'The elevation of the mind ought to be the principal end of all our studies, which if they do not in some measure effect, they are of very little service to us.' Their criterion of political morality was the interest of the community as a whole but, like d'Holbach, they meant what was 'really' useful, not what was merely of material advantage. From this point of view, the individual found his free-dom in purposive moral action and the moral welfare of the society as a whole was the criterion by which subjective individual standards could be judged. This moral utilitarianism was what Rousseau intended to be the lesson of his treatise on government, *Du contrat social* (1762), whatever else subsequent generations may have read into it. Rousseau found in his dream of the ideal society compensation for the perfect communion which so conspicuously eluded him in his personal life. His citizens entered into a social contract as tight as the sacrament of marriage. 'With all my worldly goods I thee endow' was translated as 'the total alienation of each member, with all his rights, to the community as a whole'. Society now possessed one flesh, in the form of a *moi commun*. When called upon to express a political choice, each citizen should think only in terms of what he conceived to be the welfare of the community as a whole. In the ideal state, where enlightenment and disinterestedness went hand in hand, the man who found himself in a minority would know that he had been mistaken in his estimate of this communal interest and would at once accept the majority opinion as the expression of his own will. Rousseau, it need scarcely be said, was not suggesting that this was how existing political assemblies operated or could be made to operate. He was trying, for the edification of the citizens of Geneva, to establish the terms on which a political community could strengthen and give effect to the fallible moral inclinations of its citizens, instead of frustrating and perverting them, as seemed to him to be almost universally the case. Kant's views on politics seem to have been very similar. For him too, the essential objective was moral action by the individual. The categorical imperative was an order to *do* something. The criterion of morality was conformity to the general will. As Kant put it, my action is only moral if 'I can also will that my maxim should become a universal law'. For both, the individual found his freedom from the tyranny of the self in the sacrifice of his particular interest to the moral welfare of the community. Kant reformulated Rousseau's theory of the general will in his own terms. 'When we abstract from all the personal differences of rational beings, and likewise from all the content of their private ends, we get an idea of a complete and systematically connected whole of all ends (a whole of rational beings as ends in themselves, as well as of the special end which each of them may set up for himself), i.e. a kingdom of ends. ... To this kingdom of ends every rational being belongs as a *member*, who, though universally legislative, is yet submitted to the laws he enacts. At the same time, he belongs to it also as *sovereign*, because as legislative he is submitted to no will but his own.'

Where Rousseau and Kant parted company with many of their contemporaries was in the explicitly democratic implication given to their theories by their emphasis on the sanctity of the individual conscience. As early as his prize essay of 1749, Rousseau wrote, 'O *vertu*, sublime science of the simple soul, does it then take so much trouble and complexity to know you? Are your principles not engraved in every heart? To discover your laws, does it not suffice to commune with one's self?' It was an essential element of the belief in an inner voice that this conscience should not depend on acquired knowledge. Indeed, in so far as the knowledge that went with wealth and education implied conditioning by an artificial and vicious society, the conscience of the peasant was exposed to fewer temptations than that of the lord. Rationalists who had based social morality on the reasonable man's awareness of the identity of 'self-love and social' had, willy-nilly, made it a somewhat mandarin virtue, accessible only to the educated. Voltaire had at times conveyed this impression when he denounced the 'ignoble masses who respect only force and never think', or when he denounced Rousseau as 'a tramp who would like to see the rich robbed by the poor, the better to establish the fraternal unity of man'. D'Holbach also had asserted that only a very small number of men could 'really' be described as reasonable. By making the untutored conscience, rather than the educated intellect, the source of moral action, Rousseau outflanked all such objections. Within his terms of reference all men had to be treated as equal. This was also true for Kant, whose assertion that rights appertained only to rational beings demolished all claims founded on hereditary rank, on status or on office. In practice, Rousseau at least had almost as many reservations about the 'populace' as Voltaire, but it was largely thanks to him that the theory of the social and political equality of men as sovereign moral units entered modern European thought.

The emergence of a new conception of patriotism in the late eighteenth century will be discussed in the next chapter. For Rousseau, this followed logically from his conception of the state. Patriotism was almost synonymous with *vertu* in the sense of implying the subordination of personal to social objectives. In time of national danger it signified the readiness of all men to bear arms in defence of their state. Rousseau, like Helvétius, went further than this in his insistence that luxury and sophistication were the enemies of healthy morals and sound policies, so that patriotism took on many of the trappings of an idealized antiquity: frugality, the segregation of the sexes, public ceremonial and military exercises. The main outlines of the France of 1794 had already been sketched in long before the outbreak of the Revolution.

So much in the attitude of Rousseau and his contemporaries anticipates Romanticism and the nineteenth century that it is as well to conclude this brief survey by emphasizing the extent to which they belonged to their own age. They looked resolutely backwards, not merely to a hypothetical Golden Age, but more specifically towards the beginning of the century. Rousseau, the man who denied Voltaire's assertion that the Lisbon earthquake had excluded the possibility of a benevolent providence, went back to Leibniz and even, at times, to the abbé Pluche. His insistence on the freedom of the will confronted him, as it had confronted them, with the problem of explaining moral and physical evil. In both *Émile* and the *Nouvelle Héloïse* he insisted that such evil as existed was largely the product of human folly. 'O man, look no further for the author of evil. That author is yourself. There is no evil apart from that which you inflict or endure, and both come from yourself. . . . Do away with our fatal progress, do away with our errors and vices, do away with the work of man, and all is well.' His awareness of conflict in the world about him would not have allowed him to accept Pope's 'whatever is, is right', but with the fundamental buoyancy of his age, he persisted in his belief that it could become, at least, less wrong. Since, for Rousseau, society became progressively more unnatural – and hence more vicious – as one ascended the social scale, his repudiation of the values of aristocratic society implied not social revolution but its opposite, the preservation of the poor in a situation where their natural virtues were at least partially shielded from the perversions of civilization. This theme runs throughout his work. He wrote in his prize essay, 'What are we to think of these compilers who have rashly broken open the door of the sciences and introduced into their sanctuary a populace unworthy to approach it?' In his letter to d'Alembert he wrote, 'In a state as small as Geneva, all innovations are dangerous.' The *vicaire savoyard* explained in *Émile*, 'To be discontented with my lot is to wish that things were not as they are, it is to wish for disorder and evil.' The beneficent Julie refused to encourage her villagers to better themselves, since the cultivation of their talents was of less importance to themselves and to the community than their preservation in a state of simplicity and relative innocence. Since this view is unlikely to commend itself to a meritocratic age, it is perhaps worth reminding the reader that an opinion which might have sounded suspect in the mouth of a wealthy man like Helvétius or d'Holbach could scarcely be a product of unconscious hypocrisy on the part of Rousseau. It was the expression of a philosophy that had led Rousseau himself to sacrifice the career of comfort and social success which his talents had made accessible to him. Rousseau was more concerned with the moral reformation of the individual than with what would nowadays be considered social reform, and he was inclined towards a form of political quietism which could imply a lack of interest in political action. 'Liberty', said Rousseau, 'is not inherent in any form of government, it is in the heart of the free man.'

The apparent contradiction between Rousseau's roles as moral revolutionary and individualist on the one hand, and social quietist and extreme advocate of the moral sovereignty of the community on the other, can only be reconciled in terms of the assumptions of his own age. A pre-Darwinian, pre-Marxist society conceived of nature as harmony and of human society as part of the natural order. Without this providential harmony, the inner voice would have announced the same unpalatable choice between moral anarchy and social determinism that had distressed the rationalists. Scylla was represented by Helvétius' 'genius', a moral law unto himself; Charybdis by Rousseau's conception of the sovereign will of a community: 'By the mere fact of its existence, it is always what it ought to be.' Only the identification of the individual conscience with the will of God made it possible to steer between anarchy and totalitarianism. Nature embodied providence and human society was demonstrably unnatural. Revolt was therefore not merely permissible but a sacred duty, but revolt not in the interest of an oppressed class, but on behalf of outraged nature. Its ultimate object was to restore, as far as that was still possible, a natural harmony which would be expressed not in terms of economic equality or material prosperity, but of moral purpose. As Herder summed it up, 'Man must seek above all to follow the guidance of nature and make his institutions and laws conform to nature. That is how he will find peace, for a sovereign goodness presides over the destinies of the human race.'

Rousseau and his followers parted company with the rationalists because of their awareness of discord and disharmony. Unlike Pope, they felt that 'self-love and social' were generally in opposition and the lot of the man who aspired to virtue in contemporary society was one of strife and tension. However, they shared with the optimists of the early part of the century a basic faith in the existence of a beneficent Providence, by whose agency all might yet be made harmonious. Where they differed was in their insistence that reform must begin within individual hearts, before it could transform society – a message sometimes obscured by Rousseau's shrill attacks on that society. He and his followers therefore occupied a place of their own in the intellectual history of the eighteenth century, but their underlying optimism and belief in a form of providential harmony aligns them with the Enlightenment rather than with the Romantic revolt.

Chapter 7

TIME AS A NEW DIMENSION

A. SCIENTIFIC TIME

THERE is a natural tendency for historians of science to treat eighteenth-century biologists as 'fore-runners of Darwin'. This is, of course, a perfectly legitimate and meaningful way of looking at them, but it was obviously not how their contemporaries saw them. Our own concern is with the general intellectual atmosphere which resulted from the dissemination of new scientific hypotheses. From this viewpoint, what matter most are the discoveries rather than the omissions and the spread of relativist and transformist assumptions rather than the failure to arrive at a satisfactory theory of organic evolution by a continuing process of natural selection.

Until about the middle of the century, those who wished to dispute the view that the earth, as we know it, was a special creation of the Christian God, or of some more abstract Providence, had no effective reply to Sganarelle's argument in Molière's *Don Juan*: 'I understand perfectly well that this world which we see is no mushroom that came all by itself in a single night. I should like to ask you who made these trees, these rocks, this earth, this sky up above, and if all that created itself. ... Can you see all the inventiveness with which the machinery of man is assembled, without wondering at the way in which everything is organized and interrelated?' If one accepted the limited time-scale of the Old Testament and its apparent evidence that from the Fall onwards the natural world was very much as it is today, this static and self-regulating order could not plausibly be ascribed to chance.

Within a century of the appearance of *Don Juan*, however, it was generally accepted that the history of the earth had included great physical changes.★ Such views were not confined to scientists. The French explorer, Bougainville, described in his *Voyage autour du monde* (1771) one of the more striking aspects of the Straits of Magellan. 'This cape, which rises to more than 150 feet above sea-level, is entirely composed of horizontal beds of petrified shellfish. I took soundings at the foot of this monument which testifies to the great changes that have happened to our globe.' Biological evidence was less easy to interpret but enough was known to show the former existence of creatures that were now extinct. It was increasingly recognized that geography, geology and biology were historical subjects, and Buffon's great work, whose first volume appeared in 1749, was called a *Natural History*.

The immediate question, if nature had a history, was to know how much time was available. A biblical chronology automatically excluded any gradual process of transformation over immense periods of time. The issue was both clear and imprecise: if the Bible was literally correct, scientists disposed of rather less than 6,000 years; if not, they had no means of even guessing the real age of the earth and were free to dispose of as many vague aeons as their theories might seem to require. The revolutionary widening of mental horizons implied by this latter perspective seems to have encountered surprisingly little psychological resistance. In 1721 Montesquieu wrote in the *Lettres persanes*, 'Is it possible for those who understand nature and have a reasonable idea of God to believe that matter and created things are only 6,000 years old?' He went on to postulate that Adam might have been the Noah of an earlier and unrecorded Flood. In a much later edition he added at this point, 'But such destructions are not all violent. We see several parts of the earth grow weary of providing subsistence for men. What do we know as to

★ See above, pp. 90–91.

whether the entire earth has not general causes of exhaustion, slow and imperceptible?'

By mid-century the great antiquity of the earth was generally admitted as a reasonable hypothesis, if not actually taken for granted. Hume wrote in his *Dialogues Concerning Natural Religion*, 'Many worlds might have been botched and bungled, throughout an eternity, ere this system was struck out; much labour lost; many fruitless trials made, and a slow but continual improvement carried on during infinite ages in the art of world-making.' Diderot thought in terms of 'millions of years', Helvétius of 'an infinity of centuries'. Rousseau started from the same scientific basis as the others. In his *Discourse on Inequality* he insisted that the most primitive extant society was far different from the state of 'natural' man. 'One may judge how many thousands of centuries it would have taken to develop successively all the operations of which the human mind is capable.' D'Holbach, a little later, when writing his *Système de la nature*, has a striking passage that recalls the earlier cosmic visions of the *Lettres persanes* and Voltaire's *Zadig* but expresses them in dynamic terms.* 'Suns are extinguished or become corrupted, planets perish and scatter across the wastes of the sky; other suns are kindled, new planets formed to make their revolutions or describe new orbits, and man, an infinitely minute part of a globe which itself is only an imperceptible point in the immense whole, believes that the universe is made for himself.' Buffon, when preparing his *Époques de la nature*, published in 1778, privately estimated that the first stages in the cooling of the earth would have required a million years. He was more cautious in print, but from the theological point of view his account of the appearance of man 70,000 years after the creation of the earth was just as scandalous. The English geologist, Hutton, wrote in his *Theory of the Earth* (1788), 'We find no vestige of a beginning – no prospect of

* See above, p. 83.

an end.' Six years later, Erasmus, the grandfather of Charles Darwin, referred in *Zoonomia* to 'the great length of time since the earth began to exist, perhaps millions of ages before the commencement of the history of mankind'.

Granted an awareness of great changes and of sufficient time for these to have been produced by gradual forces that might still be imperceptibly at work, the intellectual Columbuses of a new scientific age were quick to head for uncharted waters. Buffon, in 1749, suggested that the sizes and orbits of the planets were consistent with their having been torn from the sun by the gravitational pull of a passing star. Laplace and Kant each speculated on the nebular origin of the solar system. Rousseau considered that some existing islands might have become detached from the continents to which they originally belonged, and Diderot, in his *Supplément aux voyages de Bougainville*, written in 1772, almost hinted at the theory of continental drift. 'Who knows the early history of our globe? How many stretches of land, which are now cut off from each other, were once joined together?' In the same year Chastellux suggested that the Grecian archipelago had been formed by the breaking of a barrier separating the Black Sea from the Mediterranean. From the scientific point of view much of this intellectual exploring was mere speculation that it was impossible to verify or refute. This does not necessarily make it less significant in terms of the general intellectual history of the period. Two aspects are particularly worthy of note. The suspicion of 'systems' and 'hypotheses' which had characterized scientific thinking earlier in the century had now given way to the search for syntheses and explanations – one is sometimes tempted to think that, for Diderot, *philosopher* consisted primarily in this kind of free speculation that was more concerned with formulating theories than with trying to prove them. Secondly, men were becoming accustomed to regard even the most familiar and elemental aspects of their world as being in a state of continual change. The new mental habit of considering the present, not as a standard by which the past might be known or inferred, but as something like a 'still' whose meaning was inseparable from the motion picture to which it belonged, was obviously capable of more than scientific application and was notably to revolutionize men's conception of history.

It was in biology that the idea of change was perhaps of most immediate relevance to men's picture of the universe. The issue which it seemed to raise was not so much the descent of man from earlier forms of life as the existence of a Providential order, and hence of God. To appreciate the problems of these eighteenth-century biologists and to understand their tentative and unsatisfactory solutions to them, it is necessary to look rather more closely at the presuppositions with which they started. The first question was whether systems of classification, like that of Linnaeus, could hope to approximate to an arrangement which actually existed in nature, or whether they were merely a convenient human way of sorting out a mass of undifferentiated evidence. True to the Newtonian distrust of hypotheses, Buffon, in his first volume, adopted the latter view. 'Individuals alone exist in nature, while genera, orders, classes, exist only in our imagination.' But by the time he wrote his second volume – published, like the first, in 1749 – he had completely reversed his position, maintaining that the sterility of hybrids proved that species had a real existence in nature, an attitude he was to maintain for the rest of his life. Unfortunately, in the very act of defining species, Buffon implied their fixity, and this barrier to evolutionary thought was to prove singularly effective.

Ignorance of the very complicated processes involved in sexual reproduction was a no less formidable obstacle. 'Ovists' who accepted the theory of *emboîtement* or pre-formation, with the seed of all future generations contained in the wombs of their present parents, were inevitably committed to the fixity of species, whose pattern had been decided, once and for all, at their creation. This theory was challenged by Needham's 'proof' of spontaneous generation. If Needham was correct, biologists were faced with the prospect of an infinite flux, in which inanimate matter could come alive and the fixity of species was replaced by the endless possibility of new creations with no necessary similarity to anything that had preceded them – a theory which appealed irresistibly to the adventurous mind of Diderot. When Spallanzani, by a series of brilliant experiments in 1765, claimed to have disproved Needham, despite his own observation that spermatozoa were living organisms, he reverted to the ovist theory and the fixity of species that it implied.

The hypothesis of natural selection, in the sense that 'monsters' were incapable of survival, had been examined – and rejected – by Aristotle. 'In cases where coincidence brought about such a combination as might have been brought about by purpose, creatures . . . having been suitably formed by the operation of chance, survived; otherwise they perished and still perish.' Such a theory was obviously incompatible, not merely with Genesis, but with any belief in Providential order. It did not, however, necessarily imply continuing organic evolution. If 'suitability' were conceived in terms of a static environment, the elimination of 'monsters' might have been a once-for-all process, leaving the viable species to go on perpetuating themselves unchanged. This was the view advanced in La Mettrie's *Système d'Epicure* (1750), whose very title is perhaps an indication of its classical inspiration. 'The first generations must have been very imperfect. . . . It is obvious that the only animals which could live, preserve themselves and perpetuate their species will have been those which happened to be provided with all the parts needed for procreation.' Even if one believed that new forms of life were being continually created, the generally accepted idea of a Great Chain of Being implied that anything which did not form part of an existing species would find no room for itself on a ladder of nature, all of whose rungs were already occupied, and would therefore prove unviable.

A less tangible, but none the less effective impediment to evolutionist thinking was the assumption – derived from both Christian and classical sources – that natural history was a story of degeneration. As so often happened, genuine scientific evidence could be quoted in support of an untenable theory. Thus Chastellux wrote, in *De la félicité publique* (1772), 'The enormous size of the bones of [extinct] land animals proves the antiquity of their race and reveals a slow degeneration of species.' In so far as the evolution of species was admitted at all, it seemed more plausible to think in terms of the transmission of hereditary defects, gradually weakening an original creation, rather than to postulate the evolving of more complex from simpler forms, for which no clear scientific evidence was yet available.

Finally, men's accessibility to new theories was influenced, if not actually determined, by their philosophical presuppositions. This is clearly demonstrated by the case of Voltaire, whose denial of plain geological evidence would have provoked his own devastating scorn if it had come from some unfortunate abbé intent on vindicating the literal truth of the Old Testament. Voltaire was, and always remained, a Newtonian, wedded to a Providential explanation of the universe and the fixity which that implied. In 1749 he attacked those who would make the earth two million years old, to find room for the explanation of biological changes that he himself refused to accept. 'Nothing which grows and lives has changed; all species have remained always the same.' As was so often the case, Voltaire invoked the comforting authority of Newton. 'A taste for marvels engenders systems; but nature seems to take pleasure in uniformity and constancy, just as our own imagination likes great changes, and as the great Newton says, *Natura est sibi consona.*' Towards the end of his life he was still repeating the same lesson: 'What then is the true system? That of the great Being who has created all, who has given to each element, each species, each genus, its eternal form, its place and function.' Voltaire's dogmatism had possibly disastrous consequences if it was his savage attack on Maupertuis, the most dangerous enemy to his peace of mind, which relegated to oblivion the most original biologist of the eighteenth century.

In the opposite camp to Voltaire, materialists of the school of Diderot and d'Holbach were perhaps reluctant to envisage any theory of progressive evolution which might seem to imply a directing Providence, if not a divine order. They might have been happy to accept a theory of natural selection operating through chance mutations, which they could have interpreted as a dynamic version of their own conception of the universe as matter in random motion, but such an option was not yet open to them. Any evolutionary theory that implied improvement rather than degeneration would suggest the operation of some purposive force, and Deism would come in by the back window while they drove out Christianity through the front door. Just as Voltaire clung to fixity to preserve his faith in Providence, they upheld the idea of a universal flux as the only apparent means of denying it.

*

It was perhaps a combination of the obstacles considered in the previous section that prevented eighteenth-century biologists from arriving at a satisfactory theory of evolution, which was not beyond their grasp, as a hypothesis, even though they would not have been able to establish it on sound scientific foundations. Where species were concerned, opinions – even the opinions of the same man – tended to oscillate between fixity and an eternal flux. Some, like Leibniz, made the best of both worlds by relegating the time when change was possible to a region that was certainly dim and presumably distant. 'Perhaps, at some time, or somewhere in the universe, the species of animals are, or were, or will be, more subject to change than they are at present in ours; and several animals which possess something of the cat, like the lion, tiger and lynx, could have been of the same race and could be now like new subdivisions of the ancient species of cats.' De Maillet's *Telliamed*, published after his death, in 1748, reads more like science fiction than biology, though it may have helped to stimulate more serious works by the accidental felicity of some of its author's speculations. De Maillet affirmed that life had originated in the sea, each present land-animal being descended from its appropriate aquatic opposite, men, for example, being derived from mermen. This metamorphosis was still continuing, wrapped in the convenient mists of inaccessible northern regions. New species were produced by seed drifting in from other planets. Much of this was an easy target for Voltaire's irony, but de Maillet's conception of a process of gradual and continuous change that was still at work was an important contribution to scientific thinking and his picturesque detail at least helped to ensure a wide circulation for his book. Rousseau treated transformism seriously and even though he rejected it in favour of a static Providential order, he did so on scientific grounds, quoting Buffon's argument that the sterility of hybrids proved the fixity of species. Diderot, who had found the idea of an eternal flux unacceptable in 1753, embraced it in 1769 in his fascinating *Rêve de d'Alembert*, which is alive with his own intellectual excitement, Taking up d'Holbach's idea that all life is relative to its material environment, he accepted that this implied change, but his assumption of spontaneous generation prevented him from attaining to any conception of evolution as a continuous, if not a purposive process.

Buffon wrestled all his long life with the problem of the fixity of species, once he had recognized their real existence in nature. His changing views have been skilfully unravelled by A. O. Lovejoy in one of his contributions to *The Fore-runners of Darwin*, edited by B. Glass. It seems improbable that Buffon disguised his real thoughts to evade a censorship that never proved very dangerous to him. In 1753, much impressed by similarities in the anatomical structure of vertebrates, he acknowledged that this could admit of an evolutionary explanation. 'One could equally well say that the ape is of the family of man, that he is a degenerate man, that man and ape have a common origin; that, in fact, all the families, among plants as well as animals, have come from a single animal.' This Buffon rejected, partly on biblical grounds, but also because the sterility of inter-specific hybrids and the absence of 'missing links' suggested to him that 'the number of probabilities against it is so enormous that even on philosophical grounds one can scarcely have any doubt upon the point.' Any hypothesis that implied degeneration rather than improvement raised very difficult problems about the nature of the initial creation. By 1765 Buffon's belief in the fixity of species had hardened: 'Species are the only entities of nature, perduring entities, as ancient, as permanent as nature herself.' In later years his doubts revived. His volumes on birds, published in 1770 with the significant title of *Ornithologie historique*, conceded that some species of birds were 'so close to one another that they may be regarded as collateral branches of a common stock or of stocks so close to one another that they may be supposed to have a common ancestry.... These related species have probably been separated from one another only through the influences of climate and food and by the lapse of time, which bring about all possible combinations and give play to all the agencies which make for variation, for improvement, for alteration and for degeneration.' This was coming very close indeed to an evolutionary theory, but, as Lovejoy observes, Buffon's assumption that the natural environment remained static prevented his seeing the struggle for existence as leading to an evolving process of natural selection. By 1776 he was even sceptical about the total sterility of hybrids – the basis of his belief in the fixity of species – and could pose the question: 'Were all the species of animals formerly what they are today? Has their number not increased, or rather diminished?' Once again, his preference for a diminishing number of species suggests that he was thinking more of degeneration than of improvement.

Where natural selection was concerned, the same assumption of a static environment prevented Diderot and Maupertuis from progressing further than Buffon and La Mettrie, or, for that matter, than Aristotle. The clearest and fullest statement of a point of view common to them all is perhaps that in Maupertuis's *Essai de cosmologie*, written in 1741. 'Could one not say that since, in the accidental combination of Nature's productions, only those could survive which found themselves provided with certain appropriate relationships, it is no wonder that these relationships are present in all the species that actually exist? These species which we see today are only the smallest part of those which a blind destiny produced.' In the *Critique of Judgement*, Kant, like Leibniz and the French *philosophes*, situated this experimental period in the beginning of time, 'until this womb [of the earth] becoming rigid and ossified, restricted its birth to definite species incapable of further modification.' He did however envisage natural selection as once having not merely eliminated the unviable but favoured those creatures which 'adapted themselves more perfectly to their native surroundings and their relations to each other' – i.e. as a process of improvement rather than of degeneration.

Since the emphasis was in general on the elimination of the unfit, within the context of an unchanging environment, it is not surprising that little was said of adaptation, for which, in any case, evidence was hard to find. The assumption of the inheritability of acquired characteristics, combined with the idea of adaptation to environment, offered the kind of short cut to a theory of evolution that Lamarck was to take in the early years of the nineteenth century. Diderot had anticipated him in 1769, in a tantalizingly brief passage in the *Rêve de d'Alembert*. D'Alembert cries out in his dream, 'The more senses one has, the greater one's needs.' This is taken up by Dr Bordeu, one of the three characters in the dialogue: 'He's right. Organs produce needs and reciprocally, needs produce organs.' Bordeu then produces a fanciful story of generations of armless men acquiring new arms from the development of their shoulder-blades and the passage ends, on a typical Diderot note, with Mademoiselle de Lespinasse speculating on the probable evolutionary consequences of *la galanterie effrénée*! Once again, the century approached the very threshold of a theory of evolution, only to turn back.

One biologist did not turn back, but went on to form genetic theories which anticipated Mendel's, and to verify them by observation. Since our concern is not so much with eighteenth-century science in itself as with its contribution to a general intellectual climate, and since Maupertuis's discoveries were little known or heeded, it would be inappropriate to describe them in the detail which they would merit on scientific grounds alone. Ironically enough, his first contribution to the Enlightenment was to introduce Newtonian thought to France, and more particularly, to Voltaire, who was subsequently to use the ideas which he had learned through Maupertuis, to destroy the reputation of his mentor. Maupertuis's genetic theories are to be found in the *Essai de cosmologie*, written in 1741 but not published until 1750, the *Dissertation sur le Nègre blanc* of 1744, the *Vénus physique* of the following year and the *Système de la nature* of 1751. He began by recognizing that, since offspring revealed characteristics present in both parents, their genetic structure could not be explained purely by ovist theories. This was presumably common knowledge amongst stock-breeders, but it ran counter to orthodox scientific opinion and it offered possibilities of scientific investigation which Maupertuis was quick to seize. Using cases of albinism in Negroes, and the periodical recurrence of six-fingered hands in the members of a Berlin family, by the application of the mathematics of probability, he evolved a theory of genetic transmission which hinted at the existence of dominant and recessive characteristics. He realized that 'monsters' corresponded very closely to normal types – the sixth finger in his Berlin family, for example, was always on the hand – which would be difficult to explain if life consisted merely of the random association of living material. He therefore postulated a theory of *monstres par défaut et par excès* which could be regarded as an anticipation of the relatively recent discovery of supernumerary or missing chromosomes. In the *Système de la nature*, Maupertuis saw that his ideas made a theory of organic evolution possible.

Could one not explain in this way how from two individuals only, the multiplication of the most dissimilar species might ensue? They would have owed their origin merely to some accidental formation in which the basic parts would not have preserved the arrangement present in their parents. Each degree of error would have created a new species, and from these repeated variations would have arisen the infinite diversity of animals that we see at the present day.

Glass, in the symposium to which reference has already been made, sums up Maupertuis's achievement. 'Virtually every idea of Mendelian mechanism, of heredity and the classical Darwinian reasoning from natural selection and geographic isolation is here combined, together with De Vries's theory of mutations as the origin of species, in a synthesis of such genius that it is not surprising that no contemporary of its author had a true appreciation of it.'

*

Leaving aside the unfortunate Maupertuis, the eighteenth century failed to discover a theory of evolution when such a theory might have won easy acceptance. The century was less inhibited than the Darwinian age by the fulminations of ecclesiastical authority. The whole temper of the period was different, and although the reception of new ideas by polite society was often superficial and frivolous, the scientist who could evade the slow-footed censorship and express himself in elegant prose was sure of an appreciative audience, however bold his speculations. Maupertuis's suggestion that there might well exist 'a species intermediate between monkeys and ourselves' does not seem to have aroused any widespread indignation, although it appeared in his most popular work, the *Vénus physique*. Biologists, however inconclusive and misleading their theories, had at least discovered, or rediscovered, some of the processes that were to form the elements of the later Darwinian synthesis. The antiquity of the earth was generally accepted and new evidence was continually being accumulated on the nature of the similarities and differences between extant and vanished species. The idea of natural selection was widely accepted, even if it was, as yet, relegated to the first chapter of natural history. Geologists were familiar with the evidence for almost unimaginable changes in the earth's surface, which some of them at least attributed to the continuous operation of natural forces over an immense period of time. More and more branches of science were taking on a historical dimension. The twentieth-century reader is inevitably most acutely aware of the limitations of eighteenth-century science, of its ignorance of basic processes and of the presuppositions of earlier ages which led it still to think in terms of the Fall, of the original creation of species as they now exist and of degeneration from a distant Golden Age. What was more significant at the time was men's emancipation from an Old Testament chronology that made human and natural prehistory unintelligible. With this went the partial rejection of a static conception of the universe, according to which all life had been created more or less in the contemporary pattern, so that any generalization about man or nature was equally applicable to the whole of recorded time – which was all the time there was. This immense widening of men's intellectual horizons was bound to influence the way in which they now began to consider their own past.

B. HISTORICAL TIME

To compare Bossuet's *Histoire universelle* of the seventeenth century with Chastellux's *De la félicité publique* of 1772 or the *Esquisse d'un tableau historique des progrès de l'esprit humain* which Condorcet wrote in 1793 is to perceive at a glance how men's attitude to their past had been transformed in the course of the eighteenth century. The rejection of the Old Testament as a literal account of what happened not merely extended the time-scale as far as the historian wished, it left him free to decide for himself what had been the forces of historical change and their manner of operating. The philosophy of the historian determined the divisions which he introduced into his narrative. For Bossuet, the periods of history were perforce those of the Bible: from the Fall to the Flood, from the Flood to Abraham and the emergence of a Chosen People, from Abraham to Moses and the appearance of a written law. For both Chastellux and Condorcet the decisive changes were technological. Condorcet's four main periods of history were the pre-linguistic, the pre-literate, the historical past and the future. Within a given period what mattered most was the transition from a nomadic to a pastoral society, or inventions such as gunpowder and printing. Both broke away from the cyclical pessimism of the earlier part of the century and saw recent history, at least, as a linear progress towards a future that would be morally better in proportion to its technological improvement. The proscribed Condorcet, hiding from the Revolutionary dictatorship and knowing that his own death was probably imminent, could write with an optimism as superb as it was disinterested, that 'no limit has been set to the improvement of human faculties, that the perfectibility of man is really boundless, that the progress of this perfectibility, henceforth independent of any power that would arrest it, has no other limit than the duration of the globe where nature has set us. No doubt this progress may be more or less rapid, but there will never be any retrogression.' In a similar vein, Chastellux in a brilliant and entertaining chapter ridiculed those who regretted 'the good old days' (*le bon vieux temps*). 'In conclusion, let us say that to regret *the good old days* one must not know what they were like.' It is perhaps significant that these anti-clerical heralds of a dynamic future were not representatives of a 'rising middle class', but nobles.

It is fashionable, in our own guilt-ridden age, to mock the rationalist optimism of men such as these, and it is, of course, undeniable that they would have been horrified and incredulous if anyone had predicted to them the monstrous unreason that was to degrade the twentieth century. But the peculiar animosity with which the Enlightenment is often treated is perhaps less due to its own shortcomings than to our guilty consciences. When they considered the slow decline of religious persecution, judicial torture and murderous popular superstitition, the humanizing of the laws of war and the growing outcry against the slave trade, the writers of the Enlightenment had some justification for exclaiming with Diderot, 'I love that philosophy which raises up humanity', and they could well claim that it was not their principles, but the denial of them that was to darken the future. The rationalist history of Chastellux and Condorcet has a validity of its own and within its limitations it represents a way of looking at the past that is of perennial value as a means of interpretation and a guide to present action. From another point of view, however, it was already obsolete when it was written. Both writers considered history as the slow unfolding of a universal and unchanging 'reason'. Chastellux contrasted the history of the earth, very long and full of immense changes, with the brief and, by implication, linear history of man. Condorcet, though he recognized at one point that the invention of the alphabet had modified the nature of human change itself, on the whole maintained a similar outlook. 'We have seen human reason gradually take shape by the natural progress of civilization.' Reason, in other words, was a constant factor that came slowly to its full maturity, rather than a variable product of society itself. Their attitude offered an embarrassing parallel to that of the Roman Catholic Church. As R. R. Palmer has shown in his *Catholics and Unbelievers in Eighteenth-century France*, the Church believed in a continuous and unchanging religious tradition which enabled the *corpus* of contemporary belief to be applied to any period of the past. Its position was essentially static: the fundamentals had never varied, at least since the Crucifixion, and the pageant of history was the continual re-enactment of the same drama in different costumes. For the writers of the Enlightenment the things that changed were of much more significance since they regulated man's life in this world, which constituted the whole field of their enquiries. Nevertheless, for them as for the clergy, the theme of history was a dogmatic constant. The vehicle of change, human reason, was itself unchanging, and progress consisted of the extension of reason's empire rather than in the evolution of 'reason' itself. This view had already been challenged by writers for whom history was a process of intellectual evolution in which every aspect of human thought and action was subject to time.

*

The Neapolitan writer, Vico, who lived from 1668 to 1744, might be regarded as the historical equivalent to Maupertuis, in the sense that his revolutionary anticipation of subsequent attitudes was so much at variance with contemporary ways of thought that his writings were neglected until long after his death. Vico's *New Science*, published in 1725, was known to both Montesquieu and Goethe, but neither seems to have been much influenced by it, and Vico remained in obscurity until the nineteenth century. The present-day reader can find a brilliant exposition of his ideas, by Sir Isaiah Berlin, in a collection of lectures given at the Italian Institute in 1957-8 and published under the title of *Art and Ideas in Eighteenth-century Italy*. Vico's starting point was a conception of knowledge that seems to foreshadow Kant. Mathematical knowledge is absolutely true, but only because mathematics is a human invention. Scientific knowledge deals only with the external appearance of things. Historical knowledge, however, is what Kant would have called *noumenal* in the sense that man has a direct perception of his own ideas. By inference, he can use this self-knowledge to understand the motives which lie behind the actions of his fellow-men. The historian, unlike the scientist, can at least try to explain not merely *how* but *why*.

Vico's approach to history involved the projection of this basic attitude from the individual to the society of which he formed an integral part. The historical process consisted of the developing self-knowledge of societies, which became increasingly aware of their ability to control their material environment and to influence the complex of assumptions and attitudes which is misleadingly described as 'human nature'. For him, human nature was therefore a social creation, in continuous evolution. It could be inferred, not merely from the conventional objects of historical study in Vico's day, but from all the multifarious and organically related aspects of a society, such as its language, myths, folk-lore and the nature of its economy. The values of a given society were therefore explicable only in terms of that society and such abstractions as the idea of a social contract between primitive men were absurdities. The 'reason' of the Enlightenment was one example of such meaningless abstractions. It followed from Vico's assumptions that the present was only intelligible if one knew how its traditions, beliefs and way of thinking had evolved from the past. The story of the past, instead of being an educative manual, in which reason struggled with ignorance and superstition – from the viewpoint of the Enlightenment – or righteousness with sin – from that of the Church – was an account whose meaning lay within itself, in which any period was as significant as any other.

Vico paid particular attention to language, which he saw not merely as the embodiment of the whole complex spirit of a period, but as a creative force in its own right. 'Minds are formed by the character of language, not language by the minds of those who speak it.' In the early stages of the history of a people its language is metaphorical and its habits of thought consequently poetic rather than analytical. Early myths were to be regarded neither as accounts of actual events nor as mere literary inventions, but as a way of looking at history. Vico described them as 'the civil histories of the first peoples, who were poets'. His historical approach implied a more sympathetic attitude to such early societies and the recognition that increasing social sophistication implied loss as well as gain, but it did not necessarily involve any nostalgia for the lost simplicities. In a sense, one could describe Chastellux as an unconscious follower of Vico when he insisted that, in the eighteenth century, language must be concrete. 'The problem is that nothing is more difficult to the mind than abstraction, which has to support itself by reference to physical objects; that is why arguments are always tending to drift away towards descriptive images, a vicious and incorrect style whose worst abuse is allegory.' Burke, in his essay on the sublime and the beautiful, similarly regarded delight in poetic imagery as typical of 'children and primitive peoples'. It was not until Herder that the figurative language of popular tradition was held to be inherently superior to clear and abstract prose, and in Herder's case there were particular social and political reasons for this preference.

Vico, one should perhaps mention in conclusion, like many writers of his day, believed that history observed a cyclical pattern – the result, perhaps, of his inevitably limited knowledge, which gave a disproportionate importance to the rise and fall of classical European civilization and the rebirth of classical culture in western Europe at the Renaissance. This view proved singularly tenacious. Rationalist historians grafted on to it the idea of linear progression from a specific point in time, generally assumed to coincide, more or less, with the advent of secular absolutism and the scientific revolution of the seventeenth century, while later Romantic historians were inclined to commend the Middle Ages precisely because they saw them as a period of primitive freshness at the beginning of a new age.

From the admirers of Vico and Herder, Montesquieu generally gets short shrift, presumably because he is identified with the rationalist arrogance attributed to the Enlightenment as a whole – what Sir Isaiah Berlin has dismissed as 'the fallacious belief in a fixed, ultimate, unchanging human nature'. R. G. Collingwood, in his *Idea of History*, while conceding Montesquieu's importance, maintained that 'instead of explaining . . . history by reference to human reason, he thought of it as due to differences in climate and geography.' This is to do less than justice to the author of *De l'esprit des lois*, although one must recognize that Montesquieu was at times almost obsessed by the effects of climate, and that his concern to write a book of practical statecraft led him to pay comparatively little attention to historical influences of which he was aware, since these were outside the sphere of action of the legislator. It is, however, no fanciful interpretation to read into Montesquieu's work an awareness that human values are an evolving creation of society itself. His own enumeration of the factors governing society included 'climate, religion, laws, the principles of government, the example of the past, social practices, manners. From these a consequent general spirit is formed.' This conception of an *esprit général* is basic to Montesquieu's thought. All laws and institutions are relative to it. The *esprit général* is the resultant of a multitude of conditioning factors, but since some of these – such as religious beliefs and the economic organization of a society – are the products of human volition, Montesquieu had arrived at Vico's concept of human nature as at least partially a social product. No one saw more clearly than he did that society was an integrated whole which it was fatal to try to regulate by the precepts of any universal principle of 'reason'.

Moreover, the *esprit général* was both the effect of environmental conditioning in the widest sense and also the cause of reactions to that environment. As an active force it implied that different societies would respond differently to similar material pressures. There is far more than a crude theory of climate behind Montesquieu's penetrating observation that 'The customs of an enslaved people are part of its servitude, those of a free people are part of its liberty.' Since he was writing about government rather than about history he was more concerned with establishing a balance between the forces in operation at a given moment than with tracing their development in time. In this sense his analysis is static, but he was quite well aware that some of the forces that he was trying to bring into equilibrium changed in direction and power with the passage of time, so that the desired balance required continual adjustment. He did, indeed, regard liberty as a universal good – but he insisted at the same time that the idea of liberty was subjective and socially determined. In the concluding section of the book, which the modern reader is understandably tempted to omit, Montesquieu applied his theories to the beginnings of Frankish law. Here there is no trace of geographical determinism. The development of society is seen as socially conditioned. The most 'organic' historian could scarcely fault the image – and Vico and Herder at least would have found his use of metaphor significant – which

Montesquieu applies to the study of feudal institutions. 'Feudal law makes a fine spectacle. An ancient oak rises up. From afar the eye perceives its foliage; on a closer approach it makes out the trunk, but it gets no glimpse of the roots. One must dig down into the earth to find them.' Unlike Vico's *New Science*, *De l'esprit des lois* was a best-seller, but Montesquieu's enthusiasm for the history of the Dark Ages as a subject interesting in its own right, as the study of the evolution of a particular society whose institutions both reflected and conditioned its special values, seems to have attracted few disciples.

With Herder the study of history moved a decisive step forward, not merely by reason of the intrinsic importance of what he wrote, but because he began a school of German historical thought which took up, developed, and in some cases distorted his ideas, so that a new conception of history became an essential part of man's way of looking at himself and his relations with his environment. Herder drew his own inspiration not from Vico and Montesquieu but from trends in German philosophy which led back to Leibniz, trends which emphasized *becoming* rather than *being* and envisaged the present as a continual transition towards something new. Herder stands at the last crossroads of the Enlightenment. Behind him lay the traditions of German philosophy and increasingly rationalist interpretations of a somewhat vague Lutheran theology. In some respects the development of his thought recalls Rousseau, and the general temper of his optimism was that of the Enlightenment. At the same time he points forward to the growth of new attitudes, at first in Germany, and later, to some extent in England, which were breaking up the cosmopolitan unity of the Enlightenment, before the whole movement was engulfed in the turmoil of the French Revolution and the Napoleonic wars.

Like Rousseau and Kant, Herder began by denying that human experience could be equated with the sum of sense-impressions. His belief in an interaction between mind and the sense-data which it received avoided materialist determinism and left room for moral choice. Again like Rousseau and Kant, Herder was also attracted by a teleological explanation of phenomena. In this respect all three returned to the assumption of the early Enlightenment that the meaning of an event was deducible from its end or purpose, rather than something to be inferred from the causal sequence that preceded it. True to the Leibnizian tradition, Herder was more concerned to discover the laws regulating change than to investigate the present relationships between phenomena conceived as existing in a timeless present.

In his historical method, Herder attached particular importance to language. For him, as for Vico, language was an active force rather than a mere social product. 'Each nation speaks in the manner it thinks and thinks in the manner it speaks.' He believed the different families of languages to go back to the beginning of human history. This implied the separate creation of distinct human groups (the term 'races' is only permissible if one continually remembers that, for Herder, it implied linguistic, not genetic community) which corresponded to the contemporary biological theories of the separate creation of different fixed species. This correspondence may have been more than accidental for Herder took a lively interest in biology and was fond of using biological language. The vehicle of a particular language – the social equivalent to the species – was the *Volk*, united by its common language and not necessarily by race. Any political unit that did not correspond to a *Volk* – the polyglot Habsburg Empire was an obvious example – was an artificial creation. What bound the *Volk* together was not merely the convenience of a shared language, but a much deeper community of ways of thought, shared traditions and the kind of collective memory enshrined in folk-lore and fable. It was therefore both a partnership between contemporaries and a continuing dialogue between the generations. The individual could not realize himself in isolation, since his values were neither innate, nor the mere reflection of his immediate environment, but arose from a relationship between himself and his people. The circumstances in which he lived induced Herder to exclude from the *Volk*, in his native Germany, both the aristocracy (French in language and culture) and the lowest orders of society. His identification of *Volk* with *Bürger* looks at first sight like an anticipation of ideas of a class struggle, or at least the translation into philosophical terms of the impatient demands of a frustrated middle class. Herder's own resentment at the social obstacles in his way may have influenced his thinking, but in fact his *Bürger* were even further removed from an economic class than the *peuple* of Rousseau. The *Bürger* were the people of German tradition: farmers (whether landowners or labourers), merchants or artisans. For Herder the criterion was cultural, just as it was political for Rousseau. Neither showed any awareness of class conflict as such, despite Rousseau's dislike – on paper at least – of the rich. But if Herder's conception of the nature of the *Volk* was somewhat restricted, he was emphatic that all peoples had equal rights. 'There must be no order of rank ... the Negro is as much entitled to think the white man degenerate as the white man is to think of the Negro as a black beast.' He explicitly rejected the idea of a *Favoritvolk* and maintained that 'No nation ought to be allowed to wield the sceptre over other nations by virtue of its "innate superiority".' Despite superficial similarities of language, it was a far cry from Herder to the conception of a master-race.

For Herder, history was therefore the story of the development of the *Volk* as exemplified by the study of its language, folklore and institutions. His conception of the historian's art was similar to the new attitude towards art in general. The historian, like the painter, was less concerned to reproduce an external reality than to enter into a relationship with it. Only by sympathetic acceptance of his subject could he hope to make it meaningful. The whole bent of Herder's thought inclined him away from mechanical determinism. But for him, as for Rousseau, escape from determinism threatened a return to belief in Providential guidance. He believed, like Hamann, whose obscure profundities exercised a great influence on his contemporaries, that 'The future determines the present and the present determines the past, as the purpose determines the constitution of the means to be used.' But in that case, either the purpose is itself the inevitable product of what has gone before – in which case the argument is circular – or it is some force which can never be known at the time of its operation, except by an act of faith. Herder, who believed the world to be progressing towards an ideal society of polycentric *Volk* units, each living in harmony with the others and ordering its own affairs by custom rather than authority, was never quite sure whether this was a purely human objective, which might or might not be achieved, or the inevitable fulfilment of the will of Providence.

Herder, like Rousseau, believed that progress could come only by slow and evolutionary methods – although Herder was to welcome the French Revolution. Both conceived of progress in primarily moral terms, as the education of the individual to fit him for self-government in a free society where each would freely subordinate his private desires to the welfare of the community as a whole. Both were spurred on by what F. M. Barnard, in *Herder's Social and Political Thought*, describes as 'faith in a secular redemption'. Unlike many writers of the Enlightenment, notably Voltaire, but also Diderot, they believed in civic virtue spreading upwards from below, by the education of the majority to the self-control that came with self-knowledge, rather than in the limited dissemination of a mandarin culture amongst a favoured minority. As a result, although the two men themselves were anything but revolutionaries, revolutionary implications could be read into their doctrines, which were absent from the earlier writings of the Enlightenment.

*

Looked at from a different perspective, the growth of a more organic conception of society was merely one aspect of a more general breakdown of cosmopolitanism. With very few exceptions the men of the Enlightenment had been cosmopolitan in both theory and practice. Voltaire, in 1768, made the universe as a whole, not the interest any particular society, the criterion by which the morality of an action could be judged. A similar feeling prevailed in Germany. Herder, despite his preoccupation with the *Volk*, insisted that the terms of reference of morality were universal, not national, and Schiller wrote in 1789, 'The patriotic interest is important only for immature nations, for the youth of the world; it is a narrow, trivial ideal to write for but one nation; this limitation is, for the philosophic spirit, simply unbearable.' Such attitudes corresponded, more or less, to the existence of a European nobility, united by French classical culture, by the French language and by a shared code of honour. They did not so much condemn war as ignore it, perhaps considering it as an extension of the duel, carefully organized, with its rules of *bienséance*, as a gentlemanlike way of dealing with a situation where honour had been compromised. Towards the end of the century the cosmopolitans became less socially exclusive and more pacific. The emphasis, in the case of Chastellux and Condorcet, for example, shifted from an international aristocratic society to the peaceful coexistence of peoples. Condorcet, in particular, emphasized the importance of the social levelling which he expected the future to bring, and he was one of the very few men to advocate the equality of the sexes. Chastellux, a vigorous economic liberal, maintained that war was not merely loathsome in itself, but an economic absurdity. 'Let us hope that, wearying at last of so many useless distractions and dangerous misunderstandings, we shall begin to feel that the interests of all nations are the same and can be mutually reconciled. Let us hope that wars will become rarer and less bitter.' His condemnation of war is an eloquent example of the way in which the principles of the Enlightenment could triumph over the most cherished aristocratic conception of honour. 'The first of all advantages which a people should demand is peace. Peace is the source of all order and of all merit. . . . War inspires ferocity; it offers prospects of glory and ambition which the coarsest minds can easily grasp and that is how it perverts our useful sentiments by ennobling our vices and everywhere setting force in the place of justice.' The serene Condorcet, writing when the Revolutionary wars had already begun, attacked the prosecution of an alleged national interest at the expense of one's neighbours, insisted that Europe formed a single society, vituperated against the iniquity of the slave trade and maintained that in the future war would come to be regarded as the greatest of all crimes.

Such enlightened – and Enlightened – attitudes did not reach down to the bottom of the social scale. Chastellux conceded that national hatreds still aroused the passions of the *canaille*. The German Swiss, Zimmermann, whose *Essay on National Pride* appeared in 1758, claimed that in England, 'a foreigner, if not dressed like an Englishman, is in great danger of being assailed with dirt for being thought a Frenchman.' Even the educated found unconscious bias difficult to eliminate. Zimmermann's attack on the national pride of other nations offers a delightful example of this, one of his main objectives being to reassure the Germans that they were at least as good as other nations, if only their excessive self-deprecation would allow them to recognize the fact. 'Could the nations of the North . . . avoid that noble esteem of themselves which their laws, their religion and their bards so forcibly inspired? If they have not inherited from their forefathers a fondness for softer and more civilized renown, yet they have inherited the noblest examples of manliness of soul, which have been deeply impressed on their ardently emulative minds.'

More important than the occasional self-deception of people like Zimmermann was the fact that, as Hazard described in his book translated as *European Thought in the Eighteenth Century*, the ideal of a cosmopolitan society was already breaking up before the outbreak of the French Revolution. To some extent the eclipse of Latin as an international language had curtailed the European exchange of ideas. If one compares the books reviewed by two of the most influential French journals, the *Journal des Savants* and the Jesuits' *Mémoires de Trévoux*, in 1715–19 and in 1750–54, the percentage of those written in Latin declined from 36 to 10 and the percentage of those published outside France, from 44 to 20. In the case of books published in German-speaking countries, the fall was even sharper, from 21 per cent to 3 per cent of the whole. Rebuffed and humiliated by the frequently tactless French tendency to equate culture with French classicism, some Germans turned to brooding over their soil and ancestors. 'Even now,' wrote Zimmermann, long before Herder, 'every patriotic German treads with inward emotions of reverence the ground where the solemn remains of his illustrious ancestors repose in silence, and approaches with awe the forest where their fame still hovers round the ancient oaks.' Belloy, in the *Siege of Calais* (1765), perhaps exasperated by the conspicuous lack of patriotism shown by many French intellectuals during the Seven Years War, wrote:

> Je haïs ces coeurs glacés et morts pour leur pays
> Qui, voyant ses malheurs dans un paix profonde
> S'honorent du grand nom de citoyen du monde.

Helvétius, on a more philosophical level, had already asserted that a universal morality would have to await the creation of an international society in the remote future, and that in the meantime patriotic feeling was 'absolutely exclusive of the love of humanity as a whole'.

More significantly, the writings of Rousseau and Herder formed the starting point for two new conceptions of patriotism, of which Rousseau's was the more immediately dangerous, although Herder's was soon to be perverted in an even more sinister direction. Rousseau's patriotism was essentially civic. For him, a people was a political unit, bound by the free acceptance of a common constitution. His ideas stemmed from classical roots and might not unfairly be summarized as an attempt to re-vitalize the Genevan city-state by injecting into it the virtues of ancient Sparta. His preference of Sparta to Athens was ominous and emphatic. Civic *vertu* included, as one of its major attributes, not merely the readiness of the citizen to defend his state against attack, but the aggressive assertion of its interests against all outsiders. He summed up his attitudes with brutal clarity at the beginning of *Émile*:

Every restricted society, when it is small and closely unified, alienates itself from the greater whole. Every patriot is severe with strangers: they are merely men, they are nothing in his eyes. Abroad, the Spartan was ambitious, avaricious, unjust; but disinterestedness, equity and peace reigned within his own walls. Beware of those cosmopolitans who go on distant bookish quests for the duties which they disdain to fulfil in their own surroundings.

In *Du contrat social* Rousseau carried the theoretical implications of this attitude to their logical conclusion. The social contract itself took the form of 'the total alienation of each member, with all his rights, to the community as a whole'. Since obligation did not exist in the state of nature, but was created with society, the community was therefore the source, not merely of law, but of moral values also. There could be no appeal, in the name of the individual conscience, to any standard beyond the collective interest of the society of which he was a member. 'The sovereign [i.e. the general will], by the mere fact of existing, is always what it ought to be.' Rousseau was probably unaware of all the totalitarian implications which future generations were to read into his thought, and the men of his own century tended to use his concept of the general will in the limited sense that what the majority regards as its interest must take precedence over prescription and all sectional interests. Nevertheless, the general trend of Rousseau's thought, and not merely the more abstract passages of a theoretical work, stressed the primacy of the political unit over the international community as a whole, and interpreted this in frankly belligerent terms.

Herder, as we have seen, viewed the cosmopolitan values of the Enlightenment as the reflection of an aristocratic French culture which he found personally antipathetic. His conception of the *Volk* implied separateness, based on the sharing of local traditions and a culture whose vitality was a function of its regional roots and language. His view was somewhat similar to that of Burke, who wrote in 1784, 'A nation is not an idea only of local extent and individual momentary aggregation. . . . [Its choice] is a deliberate choice of ages and generations; it is a constitution made by what is ten thousand times better than choice; it is made by peculiar circumstances, occasions, tempers, dispositions and moral, civil and social habitudes of the people, which disclose themselves only in a long space of time.' The future was to show that this organic conception of society lent itself to the identification of the *Volk* with race and to the assumption that one's own folk-values, the subject of so much veneration, must be superior to those of outsiders. If Herder were to be judged in accordance with his own belief that the explanation of anything is only to be inferred from the end to which it contributes, his works should perhaps have been put in the dock at the time of the Nuremberg trials, but viewed by the more pragmatic standards of the Enlightenment, his own vigorous assertion of the equal rights of every *Volk* to go its own separate way in peace and harmony acquits him of the xenophobic conclusions that others were to draw from his theories.

It would not, perhaps, be wholly fanciful to see in the growing cultural self-consciousness of Germany towards the end of the eighteenth century hints of a revolt of Teuton against Roman. There are obvious dangers in taking such an idea too far. Frederick II, the German national hero, was an aggressive cultural Germanophobe who remained true to French classicism all his life. Goethe and Schiller both returned to classicism, symbolized in Goethe's case by his voyage to Rome in 1786. Nevertheless, there is perhaps enough in the idea for it to merit a very brief examination.

Rome stood for classical values that were universal, rational and timeless. To some extent at least, this was true both of the centre of Christendom and of the Rome of antiquity. In the eighteenth century the legacy of secular classicism had been appropriated by France, whose king, moreover, was His Most Christian Majesty. To some extent, therefore, a revolt against French classical culture was liable to take the form of a repudiation of the Roman heritage. Protestant Germany had been cut off from Rome by the Reformation. The revival of German letters involved a form of cultural self-assertion against both the French language and the classical taste with which it had become identified. It was perhaps not accidental that the renaissance of German literature coincided with a new interest in German mythology and in particular with Arminius, or Hermann, the leader of a Germanic revolt against the Roman legions. Klopstock, the first great German poet of the century, was the author not merely of the *Messiah* but of the *Hermannschlacht*. Kleist's popular 'Ode to the Prussian Army' included the significant passage: 'The heroes of the future will narrate your glory; they will prefer you to the Roman legions and your king, Frederick, to Caesar.' Goethe, in his autobiography, described how his tutor, amused by Goethe's passion for a particular woodland retreat, 'playfully assured me that I showed myself a true German. He related to me circumstantially, out of Tacitus, how our ancestors delighted in the feelings which nature awakens in us in such solitudes.' Since Teutonic legend was as emphatically rural as Roman civilization had been urban, the growing passion for the countryside was so much grist to the mills of mythology. Goethe's subsequent reaction to Strasbourg Cathedral involved a complex reorientation, by no means limited to architecture. 'The fact that this building had been founded in an old German town and had prospered thus far in genuine German times, and that the name of the builder, on his modest gravestone, was also of native sound and origin, induced me, in my admiration of this work of art, to change the hitherto decried appellation of "Gothic architecture" for that of "German architecture", thereby laying claim to it as a national product.' When he came to write his essay on 'German' architecture in 1771, Goethe emphasized 'that it should not be considered foreign but native . . . that it could not be compared with the architecture of the Greeks and Romans because it sprang from an entirely different principle.' It would be easy to read too much into evidence of this kind, but subsequent history is a warning against ignoring altogether such hints of a revolt against the Christian and classical heritage of western Europe.

If such a division of cultural loyalties could be traced, Britain stood uneasily poised between two worlds, classical in taste, but opposed to France by religion and political rivalry. The rising tide of folk-poetry, as exemplified by the success of Bishop Percy's *Reliques of Ancient English Poetry* (1765) and the bogus Ossian, led to a cult of the primitive, to the neglect, for example, of the Romanized Arthur. But British history did not offer very much scope for an *anti*-Roman mythology and no one made a successful national epic out of Boadicea's revolt.

Whatever the possible significance for European culture as a whole of this partial revolt against classical values, and it would be easy to exaggerate its importance in the eighteenth century, the generation before 1789 certainly saw the decline of cosmopolitanism and a new insistence on the uniqueness of nations, based on a new awareness of them as entities evolving in time. In this respect, as in others, the Enlightenment was already a declining force when the impact of the French Revolution threw everything into confusion.

Chapter 8

THE REVOLUTIONARY CLIMACTERIC

To ask what relationship, if any, linked the Enlightenment and the French Revolution, is a legitimate question – provided one does not expect the answer to be either scientific or simple. The difficulty is not merely that we predetermine the result by the terms in which we define the two movements. Each was extremely complex and composed of apparently self-contradictory elements. The relationship between them appears to vary as we concentrate on different aspects of either. The more nuances we introduce into our awareness of these movements the more difficult it becomes to think in terms of any simple causal relationship between them. As always in history, cause and effect are to some extent reversible: what some men did as a result of ideas they had received from the Enlightenment influenced the picture of the Enlightenment which they and others transmitted to posterity. Stumbling amidst this *embarras de richesses*, the historian is in permanent danger of being buried beneath his own treasure trove. As facts, ideas and shadowy intuitions cascade about him, he is overwhelmed, like Prince Andrew in *War and Peace*, when he listens to Natasha singing, by the contrast between the splendour of which he has at least a dim perception and the little that he can hope to define for himself or communicate to others. His most rewarding insights are liable to be the most elusive and the most easily misunderstood. This chapter does not, therefore, aspire to offer any 'objective' solution to the question it began by posing. It is rather a kind of historical telescope which, by the isolation, magnification and foreshortening of certain aspects of the subject, may perhaps give them an artificial clarity and coherence.

Without trying to define the content of the Enlightenment, one may say that in its earlier, rationalist phase it challenged the claim of Christian theology to have explained the nature of man and his relationship to his natural environment, and in particular rejected the idea of religious persecution. It assumed that men enjoyed inalienable natural rights, such as unrestricted access to information, freedom of speech and freedom from arbitrary arrest; many of its spokesmen included economic liberalism as one of these natural rights. In a general sort of way, all this amounted to the belief that men would live with greater happiness and dignity if their social institutions were determined by what was considered reasonable or scientific rather than regulated by prescription – the assumption that attitudes, privileges and social arrangements acquired legitimacy, if not indeed divine sanction, by the mere fact of having existed for a long time. The Rousseauist revolution, which partly contradicted these attitudes and partly supplemented them, insisted that 'reason' must accommodate itself to an inner moral sense, which in turn implied the duty of the individual to sacrifice his personal advantage to the moral welfare of the living community on which he depended. Although this community was the source of his own existence as a moral being, its legitimacy was, in the last resort, dependent on its satisfying the moral and material needs of the individuals who composed it.

We have seen that these ideas, in France, were most widely diffused amongst the nobility of Paris and Versailles, the agents of the royal bureaucracy and the professional classes. They made less impression on the business community and their impact on the anonymous mass of town artisans and peasants was indirect, if not insignificant. The Enlightenment, in both its rationalist and emotional aspects, was not primarily a political movement, except in the sense in which anti-clericalism was a political programme of a kind. The letters to Sophie Volland, in which Diderot describes in great detail the events of his everyday life and in particular the discussions *chez* d'Holbach, show very clearly that it was disinterested intellectual speculation rather than possible political action which really excited these people. This was equally true of their readers. Madame Roland found *Du contrat social* difficult and not very rewarding, whereas the *Nouvelle Héloïse* swept her off her feet. In England, the Whig leader, Fox, said of *Du contrat social* that he 'believed it was one of the most extravagant of that author's works. So much so that he had only read the beginning.' An obscure Arras lawyer, who still called himself *de* Robespierre, shared the general enthusiasm of the educated for the author of the *Nouvelle Héloïse*. A law case in the spring of 1789 allowed Robespierre to speculate on the Brave New World that seemed to be in the making.

You, generous nation, which alone among the peoples of the world, without a fatal revolution, without any bloody catastrophe, by your own magnanimity and the virtuous character of your king, have resumed the exercise of the sacred and imprescriptible rights that have been violated in every age. . . . Here is the basis of that social contract of which people talk so much, which is far from being an agreement produced by human volition; its fundamental conditions, written in heaven, were determined for all time by that supreme legislator who is the only source of all order, of all happiness and of all justice.

Just as the Enlightenment was not primarily political, the origins of the French Revolution were not primarily ideological. As explained in Chapter 5, the crisis opened in 1787 when Calonne, making a virtue of financial necessity, tried to commit the French monarchy to the policies of reforming bureaucratic absolutism that Joseph II was struggling to implement in the Habsburg Empire. The Notables and the *Parlements* hoped to exploit the financial weakness of the crown in order to restore organs of collective aristocratic power – notably the provincial Estates – that had been destroyed or emasculated by Bourbon absolutism. Like the

English parliamentarians of the previous century, they insisted that their objective was a return to an ancient constitution. During the pamphlet war that reached its climax in 1788 the majority seem to have based their claim on this appeal to prescription. Modern writers were pressed into service and a contemporary complained that 'They put on show and repeat everything that Montesquieu and Rousseau have so well deduced against despotism.' Montesquieu, himself a former member of the Bordeaux *parlement*, seemed to provide a theoretical justification for what might otherwise have seemed mere antiquarianism. But the conflict would probably have taken much the same course if *De l'esprit des lois* had never been written, and it does not seem to have spread far beyond the legal and aristocratic circles immediately concerned. Faced with an unsatisfactory choice between reforming absolutism and reactionary constitutionalism, the majority of the educated commoners remained aloof.

What transformed the debate and for the first time gave it a truly national resonance was the campaign for the election of deputies to the Estates General, in the winter of 1788–9. This campaign was dominated by an assertion of the natural equality of man that was accompanied by a bitter outburst of hatred, directed against the nobility as a social order. The abbé Siéyès, in the most famous pamphlet of the time, so far forgot his Christian charity as to describe the nobility as 'some horrible disease eating the living flesh on the body of some unfortunate man'. The intensity of this passionate assertion of human equality, similar in some respects to the depth of feeling about racial equality at the present day, was the key to the first phase of the Revolution proper. It made an immediate impact on most of Europe, not merely in those countries where the nobility still formed a privileged caste, but also in England. It was this which led Wordsworth to write, long after his principles had changed:

Bliss was it in that dawn to be alive.

He expressed himself more prosaically, but to the same effect, in 1794. 'Hereditary distinctions and privileged orders of every species, I think, must necessarily counteract the progress of human improvement.' This new faith in human equality did not arise directly from the Enlightenment. However implicit in the argument of *Du contrat social* it may appear to the modern reader, Rousseau's own life and the idealized society portrayed in the *Nouvelle Héloïse* indicate a revolt against Parisian salon society rather than a specific protest against what the perceptive royalist journalist, Rivarol, defined in 1789 as *le préjugé de la noblesse* – which Rivarol identified as the essential cause of the Revolution. In a sense the new revolt was anti-Rousseauist, since its partisans aimed not to overthrow an artificial society but to open it to those who were gentlemen in the British sense without being *gentilhommes* in the French one.

Social equality in this limited sense of the equality of gentlemen and nobles raised very difficult problems in both practice and theory. The objective was a society roughly similar to that in Britain but whereas, in Britain, such social attitudes could be defended in the name of tradition, in France they could only be created by the rejection of tradition in the name of abstract principle. The principle involved, being of universal application, was bound to excite the whole of western Europe, whereas the British society that embodied it, however imperfectly, had appeared to be an insular anomaly of little relevance to the Continent. Since, in France, the conception of the natural inequality of man was the theoretical basis of a whole complex system of law, taxation and local government, its overthrow implied a complete reorganization of the country's institutions. The appeal to principle rather than to precedent also opened up a further problem: it was difficult to justify the equality of gentlemen and nobles without conceding that artisans and peasants were equal to gentlemen, however remote such 'democratical principles' might seem from the social realities of 1789. Behind the principle that commended itself to the educated commoners of the Third Estate – and to an important minority of the nobles themselves – lay the shadow of political democracy which, it was generally assumed, would lead to an assault by the enfranchised poor against the unequal distribution of property.

On 23 June 1789 Louis XVI, to break the deadlock between the privileged orders and the Third Estate, promulgated a royal programme of reform to which he was to adhere for the rest of his life. On every issue which could be considered directly related to the Enlightenment – parliamentary control of taxation, the abolition of *lettres de cachet*, the freedom of the press, internal free trade and the reform of the law – the king offered substantial concessions. Had French society resembled that of England, he gave enough ground for a settlement like that of 1688 to have been possible. On the issue of social equality, however, he returned a blunt negative. The first clause of his Charter declared, 'The king wills that the ancient distinction between the three Orders of the state shall be maintained in its entirety as essentially bound up with the constitution of his kingdom.' It was this which produced the crisis of July, the revolt of Paris and most of the towns of France, and it had very little indeed to do with the Enlightenment.

If the first phase of the Revolution, from 1789 to 1791, was not directly caused by the Enlightenment, it nevertheless transferred political power in France to the men who had been most influenced by the Enlightenment. As the moderate royalist leader of 1789, Mounier, wrote long afterwards, 'It was not the influence of those principles which created the Revolution, it was on the contrary the Revolution which created their influence.' The real rulers of France at the time of the Constituent Assembly came from those sections of society most influenced by the writing of the *philosophes*:

members of the Court nobility such as Lafayette, Noailles and La Rochefoucauld, intellectuals like the astronomer, Bailly, now mayor of Paris, Duport from the Paris *parlement*, Barnave, a lawyer from Grenoble. The Assembly reorganized the entire political shape of the country on principles of secularism, rationality, uniformity and election to office – even to such 'offices' as those of bishop, parish priest and judge. With the abolition of *parlements* and manorial courts went an attempt to reform French law along the lines advocated by Beccaria. Duport and his political opponent, Robespierre, fought side by side in an unsuccessful attempt to obtain the abolition of the death penalty, but even though capital punishment was retained, the instrument invented by one of the deputies, Dr Guillotin, was very different from the former barbarity of breaking on the wheel. As was to be expected with such men in control, the social consequences of the Revolution were somewhat limited. Economic privileges that depended exclusively on birth were abolished, together with such relics of personal servitude as had existed in 1789, but traditional payments connected with the occupancy of land were put in the sacrosanct class of 'property'. The sale of the enormous estates of the Church on the whole benefited the well-to-do rather than the poorer peasants. Where the laity were concerned there was no expropriation of land and the abolition of the purely personal dues owed to manorial lords was of very limited scope. The Assembly defeated the advocates of both political and economic democracy. It curtailed the very broad franchise on which the Third Estate had been elected in 1789 and when a member asked why the new naval penal code provided corporal punishment for seamen but not their officers, he was told that the loss of honour which an officer incurred by the mere fact of punishment made any comparison of penalties irrelevant.

The combined effect of the Assembly's moderation in practice and the Rousseauist enthusiasm of its moral principles

– such as open diplomacy and the renunciation of aggressive war – excited the admiration of most of the people in Europe who did not feel personally threatened in their privileges. This was particularly marked in Germany, where even men who had reacted against French classicism and corruption acknowledged with regret that the regenerated France had won the moral leadership of Europe. The aged Klopstock, in a poem on the Estates General, begged his pardon of the French people if 'formerly turned towards the Germans, I called on them to shun what I now invite them to imitate'. Herder, who had also reacted against French cultural imperialism in the past, preached in favour of the Revolution at Weimar even when his own prince had joined the Prussian army that was intended to suppress it. In Britain, the initial enthusiasm of Blake, Wordsworth, Coleridge, Southey and Burns expressed a new feeling of sympathy which in many cases overcame the tradition of political enmity.

This situation was radically, if not immediately, transformed by the outbreak of war between France and Austria and Prussia in 1792, extended to Britain, Holland and Spain in the following year. R. R. Palmer has shown, in the second volume of his penetrating *Age of the Democratic Revolution*, that although the war did not begin as an ideological crusade it gradually became one. Beleaguered France, attacked on all sides and invaded across every land frontier, was the scene of a 'second' revolution which overthrew the king in 1792, executed him in the following year and subordinated every principle to national survival. Driven to depend on the support of those who were not gentlemen, the Republic introduced a democratic franchise, abolished the remaining manorial rights without compensation, imposed price controls in the interest of the poorer urban consumer and unleashed the Terror against its presumed enemies. Responding to the desperate enthusiasm of 1793-4, one or two members of the Committee of Public Safety, notably Robespierre and Saint-

Just, devotees of Rousseau, seemed to see France as the embattled Sparta/Geneva of Rousseau's dreams. By terror and extermination they hoped to create the kind of ideal moral community that had increasingly haunted the thinkers of the later Enlightenment. The actual struggling republic became the Ideal City, engaged in an inevitable war to the death against an old order in which moral corruption and political despotism were two faces of the same coin. 'Monarchy', said Saint-Just, 'is not a king, it is crime; the republic is not a senate, it is virtue.' Robespierre, in his speech of 7 May 1794 on 'The relations between religious and moral ideas and republican principles' at last avenged Rousseau against the sophisticated *philosophes* who were alleged to have persecuted him. Contrasting the technical progress of the previous two thousand years with its moral stagnation, and castigating the Encyclopedists in passing, Robespierre aspired to regenerate France by dedicating the republic to a Supreme Being whose principles were those of the *vicaire savoyard* and whose worship was to fill the void described in the last chapter of *Du contrat social. Vertu* was to be the criterion of every aspect of public life. *If faut moraliser le commerce.* Saint-Just, taking up Rousseau's conception of society as a means for reinforcing the morality of its members, wrote that it was for the legislator to shape men into what he wanted them to be. The final objective, for both of them, was a moral utopia in which the state as a repressive institution would have 'withered away', leaving a community of St Preux and Wolmars to live in peace with itself and with its neighbours. Others, both in France and elsewhere, were more impressed by the fact that between April and June 1794 the revolutionary tribunal in Paris sent over 1,100 people to the guillotine.

Just as the war drove France to one extreme it pushed the allied nations, reluctantly or not, in the opposite direction. Pitt, although he had been unwilling to go to war, used methods against the Revolution, such as the printing of forged

French currency, which he would probably have considered dishonourable if employed against a 'legitimate' government. Francis II, who ruled over the Habsburg Empire from 1792, found it impossible to continue the struggle against his own aristocracy while waging an unpopular war against revolutionary France. Catherine II, whose 'enlightenment' had always been something of an export commodity, pursued an increasingly repressive policy at home and she and Frederick William II overthrew the new Polish constitution in the name of the 'Most Holy and Invisible Trinity' and of counter-revolutionary principle. Many of the European intellectuals – Kant being a striking exception – were repelled by the violence of the Revolution and its increasingly belligerent nationalism. Europe was less impressed by the offer of help to peoples striving to recover their liberty, towards the end of 1792, than by the renunciation of aggressive war two years earlier. Nevertheless, an important minority of discontented townsmen in Holland, Italy and the Rhineland saw in French military success the means to their own social and political emancipation. When the Terror gave way to relatively moderate government in France in 1794, the Revolution appeared to the frightened governments of Europe to become more rather than less of a menace to their own authority.

Men of moderate opinions outside France saw the danger that military and political opposition to the French Republic might be accompanied by a blind repudiation of the Enlightenment as a whole, and fought against it as well as they could. One of them, Mallet du Pan, wrote in 1796, 'There has been formed in Europe a league of fools and fanatics who, if they could, would forbid man the faculty to think or see. The sight of a book makes them shudder; because the Enlightenment has been abused they would exterminate all those they suppose enlightened. ... Persuaded that without men of intelligence there would have been no revolution, they hope to reverse it with imbeciles.' The moderates were to be disappointed, for the long war hardened attitudes all the time. French constitutional monarchists could make no peace with a Pretender who in 1797 declared his intention to bring back the French 'to the holy religion of their fathers and the paternal government that was so long the glory and happiness of France'. As early as 1793, the abbé Maury, who had been a member of the Constituent Assembly, advised the Pope that when the counter-revolution should have triumphed it would no longer be necessary to tolerate French Protestants. Religious toleration had been introduced by Louis XVI before the Revolution – but the paladins of reaction prided themselves on being *plus royalistes que le roi*. Even in England, where the threat from France was least immediate, the poets – with the exception of Blake – soon migrated to the Establishment and the Government began dismantling those safeguards of individual liberty that had appealed so much to Voltaire and Montesquieu, with the Treasonable Practices Act, the Seditious Meetings Act and the suspension of *Habeas Corpus*.

Palmer has shown how the military conflict took the form of a struggle between the Enlightenment and an increasingly reactionary defence of a supposedly traditional order. As a direct consequence of the success of French arms, urban revolutionaries created 'sister republics' in Holland, Switzerland, northern Italy, the Papal States and Naples. In so far as time permitted, these were reorganized on French lines, clerical and seigneurial privilege and local particularism giving way to unitary republican government, secular, egalitarian and 'reasonable'. It was symbolic of the ideological clash that when the Second Coalition launched its attack against France in 1799 the decisive military contribution was made by Russia and the cause of throne and altar also benefited from the support of a Turkish contingent. The French won, but in the process Bonaparte seized power in Paris and his rule was to transform the nature of the confrontation.

As Revolutionary France became Imperial France in 1804 its impact on Europe became less ideological and more military. Napoleon himself, like his namesake in George Orwell's parable about another revolution, became increasingly indistinguishable from the kings and emperors whom he was fighting. He was, of course, by birth a noble, even if only a Corsican one. Once established in power he encouraged the French exiles to return, and not merely the more moderate, but men like Chateaubriand who considered themselves the sworn enemies of the Revolution. Napoleon's own rule became increasingly autocratic and monarchical. After his Habsburg marriage the servility and ceremonial of the Imperial Court rivalled any in Europe. Even after his overthrow the Powers treated the defeated Emperor as something more than a successful revolutionary. Within France Napoleon on the whole maintained the civil equality won during the Revolution, at least in the restricted sense in which birth conferred no formal privilege. Such of the legacy of the Enlightenment as related merely to national efficiency, for example internal free trade and advanced technical education, became a permanent part of French society. But much that the Enlightenment regarded as essential disappeared, notably freedom of the press and freedom from arbitrary arrest. In many respects Napoleonic France was closer than the France of Louis XV to Montesquieu's conception of despotism.

The almost continual warfare of the Napoleonic period at first led to an extension of the Revolution, when most of Germany was reorganized after the collapse of Prussia in 1806. But French rule became increasingly associated with conscription, economic discrimination, censorship and police repression. More and more it came to reflect efficient bureaucratic absolutism rather than the Enlightenment of Chastellux and Condorcet. For a short period it seemed as if France's enemies might turn against her the ideological weapons that had made her so formidable. Stadion, from Vienna, called for a national revolt of Germany; the young Czar, Alexander I, fell fleetingly under the influence of his reforming minister, Speransky; Stein, taking French experiments as his model, set about the reform of Prussia. But where the Habsburg Empire and Russia were concerned, this was a mere passing phase and the great crisis of 1812–13 saw both intent on the restoration of the old order. The case of Prussia is more complicated. Not merely did the Government continue rebuilding on more modern lines the state that had collapsed after the battle of Jena in 1806; the war of liberation of 1813 made Prussia for a time the focus of German hopes for some kind of a new order. The Enlightenment, as we have seen, was not primarily a political movement. Voltaire in particular, more concerned with what was done than with who did it, would have had no objection to reform being imposed from above by the descendant of his sometime friend, Frederick II. But, as I hope to show at the end of this chapter, the reshaping of Prussia corresponded to a new conception of the relationship between the individual and the state, whose theorists were at pains to stress their dissociation from what they considered to be the anarchic individualism of the Enlightenment.

It is impossible to regard the conflict that enveloped the whole of Europe in 1814 as corresponding in any meaningful sense to a struggle for the survival or extension of the principles of the Enlightenment. Napoleon was an autocrat without a pedigree, opposed by governments intent on restoring the *ancien régime* as far as this was still practicable. The latter considered themselves to be fighting against the Enlightenment which they had come to identify with the Revolution and the upstart Emperor. Napoleon was its defender only to the extent that its more practical aspects proved useful to efficient absolutism. With his defeat and the restoration of the Bourbons in Paris in 1814 the last sparks of the Enlightenment as a political force sputtered out.

*

In conclusion, it remains for us to consider the movement of ideas which coincided with the revolutionary and Napoleonic struggle, contributing to it and in turn being influenced by it. It was perhaps significant of an increasing polarization of European thought along national lines that this study falls naturally into three groups: the French-speaking authors (as exemplified by the abbé Barruel, Chateaubriand and the Savoyard, de Maistre), who repudiated the Enlightenment *en bloc* and advocated a return to faith and obedience; Germans such as Fichte, who tried to advance beyond the Enlightenment to a new era of human civilization, and the British, who for the most part conducted a separate debate with each other.

The three *Francophones* were men of very different character and ability. Barruel, who had already attacked the Enlightenment in a work published in 1781, achieved a certain notoriety by his *Mémoires pour servir à l'histoire du Jacobinisme* (1797). This lengthy work purported to prove that the Enlightenment and the Revolution were both aspects of a carefully organized plot to overthrow altar and throne and eventually attack property. Almost everyone of any importance in the eighteenth century had played some part in the plot – the *philosophes*, including Rousseau, Frederick II, Joseph II, Catherine II, a good many of the German princes, all the reforming French Ministers – although the majority were dupes who were to be exterminated after their particular part of the conspiracy had achieved its objectives. What is striking, in the case of Barruel, is not so much the fertility of his own imagination as the extent to which others listened to him. His identification of a Masonic plot behind the French Revolution still has sufficient currency for modern French historians to think it worth their time refuting it. If Barruel was the Peeping Tom of the Counter-Revolution, de Maistre was certainly its Grand Inquisitor. It is difficult to treat this Piedmontese ambassador to St Petersburg with the attention that his intelligence deserves since one cannot help suspecting that he was mentally ill. His insistence on the importance of punishment and sacrifice seems to have been an unconscious pretext for indulging his obsession with the infliction of pain, and especially with bloodshed, which he describes as frequently as possible and with obvious enjoyment. In this respect he is closer to the Marquis de Sade than to the other writers of the Counter-Revolution, and his religion was that of the Aztec rather than anything that would nowadays be recognized as Christianity. It would be both nauseating and wearisome to reproduce at length all de Maistre's variations on the theme that 'blood is the fertilizer of the plant called genius'. The following quotation from his *Soirées de Saint-Pétersbourg*, written during the Napoleonic wars, will be quite sufficient:

Do you not hear the earth which cries out, demanding blood? The blood of animals does not suffice, nor even that of criminals who fall beneath the law's axe. . . . The earth has not cried out in vain: war blazes out. . . . The whole earth, drenched with blood, is merely an immense altar on which all that lives must be immolated without end, without restraint, without respite, until the consummation of things, until the death of death itself.

De Maistre, despite his obsession, was both able and influential through his life and his writings. Sir Isaiah Berlin, in his typically vigorous essay, *The Hedgehog and the Fox*, has shown the extent of his influence on Tolstoy. Chateaubriand, the last of these three writers, is relevant to our present enquiry as the man who in 1802 published the *Génie du Christianisme*, a work which enjoyed enormous popularity and commended him, as he perhaps intended it should, to Napoleon. Chateaubriand's subsequent career showed him to be a man of distinguished literary and some political talent. One can only assume that the *Génie du Christianisme*, as embarrassing in its style as it is frequently infantile in argument, was intended primarily as propaganda. Chateaubriand himself explained his plan: 'In considering the proofs of the existence of God and the immortality of the soul, we shall eliminate abstract ideas and employ only the reasons of poetry and sentiment.' The result was something very different from both the sublimities of Blake in the same cause and the *haute vulgarization* that Voltaire had applied to Newton. Instead of presenting technical arguments in a way that would impress the general reader, Chateaubriand ignored them altogether, to produce a kind of soporific reassurance that would confirm his audience in habits of obedience. His book has much more in common with present-day exploitation of mass media than with the genuinely educational preoccupations of the Enlightenment.

De Maistre and Barruel assumed that the Revolution was the natural product of the Enlightenment and totally repudiated both. As not infrequently happened, what de Maistre called 'a kind of holy fury' got the better of his good taste and he referred to the movement as a 'river of slime'. Locke came in for particular censure as the sower of the evil seed. 'These germs . . . quickened in the warm mud of Paris . . . have produced the revolutionary monster that has devoured Europe.' But Locke was merely the rather unintelligent vehicle of a principle that went back to the Reformation. 'It is that which has unhappily dominated Europe for three centuries; it is that which denies everything, which shakes everything, which *protests* against everything; on its brazen forehead is written NO.' It followed logically that 'The philosophy of the eighteenth century is completely null (at least as regards the good) because it is purely negative.'

With this attitude went a blank denial of the scientific progress of the century, which was not refuted, but merely rejected *a priori*. De Maistre, in his long *Examen de la philosophie de Bacon*, written about 1815, could quite legitimately attack the use of the inductive method on philosophical grounds, but, unlike Kant, he made no attempt to distinguish between different kinds of knowledge and fell back on the old habit of throwing the Old Testament at the *philosophes*. They 'have told us: *we are not short of time.* You are indeed short of time, for the epoch of the Flood is there to stifle all the fictions of the imagination.' He insisted that science must be subordinate to religion, for the benefit of both. 'The more theology is cultivated, honoured, dominant, the more – other things being equal – the science of man will be perfected.' This inevitably raised the inconvenient spectre of Galileo, and the contortions in which de Maistre involved himself in order to prove that the Italian astronomer had not been condemned by the Church are a reminder that the historical past to which he and others appealed was a past that they amended to suit their own convenience.

Barruel denounced in passing those who challenged the chronology of the Old Testament and condemned Buffon for trying to explain 'mysteries reserved for Revelation alone', but the most picturesque biology was that of Chateaubriand. Like de Maistre, he included Newton on the side of the angels, but he made no attempt to deal with the problems that Newtonian physics had raised. For the most part, his account of Creation was a wild fantasy in which his imagination was buttressed by folk-lore and old wives' tales. The snake, for example, 'charms birds from the sky and beneath the bracken crib the ewe abandons her milk to it.' Fossils were all deposited by the Flood – a theory which Réaumur had disproved as long ago as 1720. Geological evidence in general was dismissed by an argument which, if not original, had not been heard for a long time. 'God must have created, and no doubt did create the world with all the signs of age and fulfilment that we perceive in it ... The oaks when they pierced the fertilized soil without a doubt bore at one and the same time old crows' nests and a new posterity of doves.' Even the abbé Pluche, who had not had the benefit of reading Buffon, might have hesitated at that – but Pluche was making an honest, if naïve, attempt to explain, where Chateaubriand was merely trying to reassure. The general level of his argument may be illustrated by the following passage. 'Religion uses only general proofs; it judges by the order of the heavens, the laws of the universe; it sees only the graces of nature, the charming instincts of the animals and their convenience to man. Atheism brings you only the shameful exceptions; it sees only disorder, swamps, volcanoes, harmful beasts, and, as though trying to hide itself in the mud, it interrogates reptiles and insects to provide it with proofs against God.'

Both Chateaubriand and de Maistre were naturally eager to preserve youth from the contamination of the scientists. The former expressed it in this way:

Should we not fear that this mania for referring all knowledge to physical signs and seeing in creation only fingers, teeth and beaks, may insensibly lead youth to materialism? ... It is by a happy combination of physical and moral knowledge, and above all through the concordance of religious ideas that we will succeed in giving back to our youth that education which once formed so many great men.

De Maistre linked science with both religious scepticism and political reform.

Nowadays one sees nothing but *savants*. ... In all directions they have usurped a boundless influence, and nevertheless, if one thing is certain in this world it is, in my opinion, that it is certainly not for science to conduct men. ... It is for prelates [he did not say 'priests'], for nobles, for the great officers of state to be the depositories and custodians of the conservative truths, to teach the nations what is evil and what is good, what is true and what false in the moral and spiritual order. The others have no right to discuss matters of this kind; they have the natural sciences to keep them amused, so what ground for complaint have they? As for anyone who speaks and writes in such a way as to steal a natural dogma from the people, he should be hanged like a common thief.

De Maistre was not content with the perfectly defensible point that their technical knowledge does not confer on scientists any privileged insight into questions of ethics. His real concern was that science should be subordinated to religion and the 'people' delivered from intellectual temptation. 'History, chronology, astronomy and geology, etc. have all been summoned to bear witness against Moses. These objections have disappeared in the face of true science, but those were outstandingly wise who scorned them without examination, or who merely examined them to find the answer, without ever doubting that there was one.' Chateaubriand also equated innocence with ignorance. 'Innocence ... is merely a blessed ignorance; is it not the most ineffable of mysteries? Childhood is only so happy because it knows nothing, old age so wretched because it knows everything.' With views such as these, it was not surprising that the reactionaries should have regarded all popular education with suspicion. Barruel commended one of the Ministers of Louis XV for having revealed to the unsuspecting king that a proposal to increase the number of free primary schools was all part of the Great Conspiracy. 'Perhaps they are already too numerous. It is not books that form mechanics and ploughmen.' More breezily, the comte de Montlosier, a royalist deputy to the Estates General whose principles did not prevent him from accepting Napoleon – or Napoleon from accepting him, – declared that it was necessary to march 'well armed, and if possible with heavy artillery, against anything which nowadays calls itself spread of enlightenment, progress of civilization, spirit of the age'.

Palmer brings out the illuminating contrast between such attitudes and those of the Revolutionary Government in France. In 1798 the anniversary of the overthrow of Robespierre was celebrated in Paris by a procession headed by teachers and students from the Museum of Natural History, carrying rare plants, animals and minerals. Representatives of printing followed, with manuscripts, books and art treasures – some of them looted from Italy, such as the bronze horses of

St Mark's. After them came men from the *Collège de France* and the *École Polytechnique*. Amongst the slogans carried in the procession was a quotation from Seneca: 'To live ignorant is to be dead.' In the same month Bonaparte landed at Alexandria with the staff of *savants* who, amongst many other things, were to found Egyptology.

It was perhaps to be expected that the opponents of 'reason' should be distinguished by a 'holy fury' which their critics might be tempted to call hysteria. This was certainly true of Barruel and de Maistre, both of whom substituted abuse for argument. Barruel referred to 'a fiend called Condorcet', while de Maistre complained that Kant 'not content with suggesting that we learn German (which is quite enough in itself!) wanted to make us learn *Kant*'. Both indulged in the practice of guilt by association, which allowed de Maistre to dispose of Locke's *On Human Understanding* after a drum-head court-martial. 'As soon as you see it popularized by the Encyclopedists, translated by an atheist and praised to excess by the flood of philosophers of the previous century, take it as certain, without any other examination, that its philosophy is, at least as regards its general basis, false and dangerous.'

In view of de Maistre's condemnation of the Enlightenment as negative, one might legitimately expect him to offer some kind of a political and philosophical alternative. What emerges, as Sir Isaiah Berlin has observed, is almost nothing. Philosophically, he went back to the Cartesian belief in innate ideas and the conception of Leibniz and Pope of a world in which nature was bound by general laws from which man was exempted by his free-will. De Maistre made no serious attempt to deal with the problems which these conceptions raised. He dismissed the objections of the *philosophes* with the comforting reflection that the ways of God were inscrutable, and since almost everyone was guilty of something, there was no miscarriage of divine justice if a man happened to be innocent of the particular crime for which he was convicted. Underlying everything was the eternal war in nature and in human society and the need for perpetual regeneration by blood sacrifices which, however, seemed to be singularly ineffective as a means of propitiation.

De Maistre's version of the history of the human race was perfectly in accordance with his personal psychological needs. The Flood was a punishment whose enormity implied a sin so frightful that degenerate contemporary man could not even conceive of it. Some of the post-diluvian races had also erred, less catastrophically, but still in ways beyond our comprehension. They had therefore been reduced to the savage state in which one could still see them in every continent except Europe. De Maistre thus applied to all primitive peoples the theory of divine retribution of which the Jews had hitherto enjoyed the grim monopoly. 'One cannot fix one's gaze on a savage for an instant without reading the anathema written, not merely in his soul, but even in the external appearance of his body.' Conversion to Christianity offered the only redemption from the former, but not, presumably, from the latter. This was a far cry indeed from Uncle Toby. Where politics were concerned, de Maistre had nothing to offer but authority, punishment and obedience, especially punishment. 'All greatness, all power, all subordination rests on the executioner.' He commended the *ancien régime* in France on the ground that 'All influences were extremely well-balanced and everyone was in his place.' Since no one had thought so at the time, de Maistre's history was as unconvincing as his anthropology, and as we saw in his treatment of Galileo, a suitable past had first to be invented before one could risk appealing to it for support.

*

From these nominally Roman Catholic opponents of the French *Revolution* it is, on the whole, refreshing to turn to the

Anglican opponents of the *French* Revolution. The fact that the debate in the British Isles was on the whole less hysterical and visionary than on the Continent was not due to any superior merit of the islanders. When frightened, they could be as cruel as anyone else. There was not much moderation about the repression of the Irish revolt of 1798, or Nelson's insistence on the execution of 119 Neapolitan 'Jacobins' who had only surrendered in return for a promise that their lives would be spared. The British, as we have seen, were even prepared to dismantle some of the safeguards to civil liberty that had formerly seemed the most tangible proof of their superiority over all foreigners. Like the frightened nobility of Europe, the gentlemen of England were inclined to equate ignorance with political innocence. Windham affirmed in Parliament in 1792 that 'he saw no great loss to society from putting an end to the public house political clubs and alehouse debaters on politics'. Arthur Young, who had welcomed the Revolution in 1789 and even made unkind remarks about the British Constitution, struck a very different note four years later. 'Where the licentiousness of the press is in any degree allowed, the general instruction of the lower classes must become the seed of revolt, and it is for this reason that the friends of reform and zealous admirers of French equality are strenuous for Sunday and charity schools.' An opponent of Whitbread's Education Bill of 1805 was as uncompromising as any continental reactionary.

It would teach them to despise their lot in life, instead of making them good servants in agriculture and other laborious employments to which their rank in society had destined them; instead of teaching them subordination it would render them factious and refractory, as was evident in the manufacturing countries; it would enable them to read seditious pamphlets, vicious books and publications against Christianity; it would render them insolent to their superiors.

The general principle of immobility was preached as energetically by Gibbon as by anyone in Europe. 'If you do not resist the spirit of innovation at the first attempt, if you admit the smallest and most specious [*i.e.* plausible] change in our parliamentary system, you are lost.' 'If you begin to improve the constitution, you may be driven step by step from the disfranchisement of Old Sarum to the King in Newgate, the Lords voted useless, the Bishops abolished.' Faced by the unprecedented challenge from France, even diplomats lost their detachment and gave way to the kind of xenophobia that had previously been attributed to the lower classes. The British Minister to Switzerland wrote in 1795: 'It may truly be said that the world is inhabited by two sets of human beings, by men and Frenchmen.'

Attitudes of this kind certainly added to the general mass of human suffering, but they concealed from both reformers and reactionaries the fact that, by European standards, they were agreed on fundamentals. At the literate level at least, the entire British debate on the French Revolution might be described as 'variations on a theme by Locke'. At one extreme, the conservative Burke had made his reputation in part as the champion of representative government; at the other, the radical Tom Paine was scathing in his denunciation of those who entertained dreams of an *economic* revolution and a redistribution of property. Even Barruel might have hesitated before enrolling Dr Johnson amongst his 'Jacobin' conspirators – but Johnson was only a Tory because he believed that despotic government was inconceivable in England. The most authoritarian of Anglican bishops could scarcely follow de Maistre to the extent of blaming the whole trouble on the Reformation. In fact, the British were all, or almost all, committed to the defence of the Revolution of 1688 when a legitimate monarch had been dethroned and his successor chosen and circumscribed by Act of Parliament. As Burke himself put it in 1777, 'The people at that time re-entered into their original rights . . . at that ever-memorable and instructive period, the letter of the law was suspended in favour of the substance of liberty.' When he came to write his *Reflections on the Revolution in France* in 1790, he described more delicately a revolution which, however 'glorious', had become somewhat inconvenient. It is now 'a small and a temporary deviation from the strict order of a regular hereditary succession'. It was still a deviation, and to the divine-right purist, Burke's excuse was that of the girl whose illegitimate baby was 'only a little one'. The very terms in which Burke defended prescription – 'It is a guarantee of the long-continued approval of God and man' – implied that its sanction rested, at least in part, on individual consent. His peculiarly British insistence on the ultimate sovereignty of the individual distinguishes him from both the Roman Catholic reactionaries and the German Idealists. As he expressed it in 1782, 'By *nature* there is no such thing as politic or corporate personality; all these ideas are mere fictions of law; they are creatures of voluntary institution; men as men are individuals and nothing else.' Burke might insist that the compromise of 1688 was a contract whose terms were unalterable. By the very act of doing so he legitimized revolt against a king who might be unwise enought to call in question the purely human sanction behind his authority. Palmer has quite rightly insisted that Burke's appeal to prescription was similar to that of the continental absolutists, but in his case the *status quo ante* was one in which all the accused in state trials of 1794 could be acquitted in the teeth of Government pressure. Faced with a real threat to the rule of Parliament Burke's principles would have made him a rebel.

Burke was, in fact, the Montesquieu of a stable society. What made the Frenchman the oracle of revolutionaries and the Irishman the spokesman of British conservatism was not a difference in their principles, but of the societies in which they lived. The point was well taken by James Mackintosh, in his reply to Burke's *Reflections*, *Vindiciae Gallicae* (1791). 'The same Montesquieu, who thought as a philosopher of the eighteenth, was compelled to decide as a magistrate of the fourteenth century. The apostles of toleration and the ministers of the Inquisition were contemporaries. The torture continued to be practised in the age of Beccaria. The Bastille devoured its victims in the country of Turgot.' This was why all Burke's attempts to discover a formula that would legitimize revolt in England in 1688 and disqualify it in France a century later, were unsuccessful. By his own standards, a revolt in 1789 was justified if the Government refused peaceful concessions. What he really objected to was not the fact of revolt, but the programme of the revolutionaries. In a speech in Parliament in 1790 he objected to the frequently-drawn comparison between 1688 and 1789. In England, 'Aristocratic leaders brought up the corps of citizens who newly enlisted in this cause. Military obedience changed its object, but military discipline was not for a moment interrupted in its principle. . . . The nation kept the same ranks, the same orders, the same privileges, the same franchises, the same rules for property, the same subordination.' The French, on the other hand, had thrown away the opportunity of a similar 'revolution, not made, but prevented.' As Burke told them in his *Reflections*, 'You might, if you pleased, have profited of our example and have given to your recovered freedom a correspondent dignity. Your privileges, though discontinued, were not lost to memory. Your constitution, it is true, whilst you were out of possession, suffered waste and dilapidation; but you possessed in some parts the walls, and, in all, the foundations of a noble and venerable castle.' As the advocate of an organic conception of society, he should have realized that, in France, the image of a venerable castle meant not a stately home, but the Bastille and a kind of society that most educated Frenchmen in 1789 found intolerable. Burke himself almost provides the explanation why the English and French Revolutions moved in different directions. In his *Appeal from the New to the Old Whigs* (1791), he commended 'that state of habitual social discipline, in which the wiser, the more expert and the more opulent conduct, and by conducting enlighten and protect the weaker, the less knowing and the less provided with the goods of fortune'. Most of the French revolutionaries of 1789 would have been very happy to accept his proposed rule by a 'true natural aristocracy' since Burke defined this to include not merely the man of noble birth, but also the 'professor of high science, or of liberal or ingenuous art' and the wealthy merchant. If French society could have accepted these men as approximately equal in 1789, the French Revolution might well have taken a course that would have made Burke its champion. In other words, the British, as is their wont, had become involved in a philosophical argument and turned it into a political debate.

*

The Roman Catholic reactionaries saw the French Revolution as a warning that everyone should go back. Burke and his followers regarded it as proof that the British, at least, should stay where they were. Only the German Idealists tried to go forward from the Enlightenment to something that should supersede it. Where this led them can best be illustrated by a brief examination of the career and writing of Fichte. Fichte's thought sprang from the Enlightenment and throughout his life he drew on the legacy of Lessing, Rousseau, Kant and Herder. The French Revolution, which he welcomed, seemed to him the political counterpart to his own spiritual liberation of man from the tyranny of the world of phenomena. Less cautious than Kant, Fichte maintained that the external world was not real in the way in which the *noumenal* world of ideas could be regarded as real. Where Kant had merely asserted that one was the object of direct, intuitive knowledge, while the actual form of phenomena could not be known, Fichte claimed that objects did not exist except as perceptions, the only reality being that of the mind which perceived them. Man was therefore important only as mind. The individual mind was part of a universal mind, from which alone it derived its significance. Like his younger contemporary, Hegel, Fichte was much given to seeing the exciting events of his own lifetime as indicating a decisive stage in the evolution of this cosmic mind. His philosophical commitment to the French Revolution survived the deceptions of 1794. He offered his services to the Republic in 1799, writing in the same year, 'It is clear that henceforth the French Republic alone can be the country of the Just. It is to her alone that he can devote his strength. Henceforth it is not merely the dearest hopes of humanity, but its very existence that is bound up with her victory.' In the winter of 1804–5, Fichte gave a series of public lectures at Berlin, subsequently published under the title: 'On the characteristics of the present age'. With continental Europe in a state of precarious peace, and Prussia in particular committed to a policy of neutrality since 1795, Fichte took a lofty view of the balance of power: 'In this cosmopolitan frame of mind we may look with serenity on the actions and fate of nations.' What interested him was to locate the position of the revolutionary age in the story of the development of the world-mind.

Since the evolution of mind naturally proceeded by a logical process, the essential course of history was both pre-determined and predictable. 'Time rolls on in the steadfast course marked out for it from all eternity, and individual effort can neither hasten nor retard its progress.' The key to an understanding of this process was to be found, not in observation and subsequent induction, but by deductive reasoning. Where his method of enquiry was concerned, Fichte therefore rejected the Enlightenment for a return to Descartes. 'We have asserted nothing whatever upon the ground of experience, but on the contrary have deduced the different elements of our description from principle alone. If our deduction has been correct and rigid, we have no occasion to enquire whether these things are so in present reality or not.' He was not here denying a correspondence between logic and observable fact, but merely asserting that if what was logically necessary did not yet exist it was bound to do so at a later date. Fichte was insistent that the individual must sink himself completely within a collective mind, which was not that of humanity as a whole, but the mind of the 'race'. 'The individual life has no real existence, since it has no value in itself, but must and *should* sink to nothing, while on the contrary the race alone exists, since it alone *ought to be* looked upon as really living.' To avoid fathering upon him more than his share of the sins of his disciples, it is important to realize that for Fichte, as for Herder, race was not a biological concept, but described a community of people sharing common traditions and culture, and above all a common language.

In the beginning there had existed a Normal People, to whom reason and rational conduct were effortless and intuitive. These fortunate ones had been driven from their original home to mix with a totally barbarous surrounding population. The interrelation of these two peoples made up the content of all recorded history, which was the story of a phased return to the state of original virtue and wisdom. The evolution of man was therefore a matter of going *backwards*, and Fichte had to reject any suggestion that it might operate in the opposite direction. 'There is nothing from which history, as well as a certain half-philosophy, should more carefully guard itself, than the altogether unreasonable and fruitless attempt to raise Irrationality to Reason by a gradual lessening of its degree, and, given only a sufficient range of centuries, to produce at least a Leibniz or a Kant as the descendant of an orang-outang.' Idealism could be as intransigent as faith when it came to shouting down scientific evidence, and it is very striking to see how, at this early date, all the opponents of the Enlightenment, from de Maistre to Fichte, saw the need to dispose of the bogey of evolution.

After the initial diaspora of the Normal People had come

the second stage in world history, when 'heroes' descended from them had imposed their civilizing will on the recalcitrant barbarians. Fichte quoted Alexander the Great as a good example of those who saw that 'the civilized must rule and the uncivilized must obey, if *Right* is to be the *law* of the world.' He went on, in words that have a disconcerting sound to the modern ear, 'Tell me not of the thousands who fell around his path; speak not of his own early ensuing death – after the realization of his Idea, what was there greater for him to do than to die?' For Fichte, unlike Chastellux and Condorcet, human progress was achieved, not by the material development of society resulting from improved technology, but by the personally disinterested action of martyrs and heroes. He therefore broke with the Enlightenment in praising the Crusades and developed a view of the relationship between Europe and the other continents that was later to become the 'white man's burden'.

The third age was that of the revolt of reason against merely *de facto* authority, which had reached its culmination in the Enlightenment. The achievements of this age were of value in their specific historical context, but must inevitably be superseded by later developments. The gains of the Enlightenment, such as the abolition of torture, were therefore good in themselves, but to be considered as stepping-stones towards something better, not as ends. Fichte, as Lessing had done before him, regarded Christianity in the same relativist way, its essential contribution to civilization being to liberate man from the fear of God and from attempts to propitiate him by barbarous sacrifices – this was a little hard on de Maistre, whose religion still consisted of virtually nothing else. The third age, having reached its climax in individualist anarchy, must 'inevitably' give way to the fourth age of 'reason as science', in which individuals would subordinate their separate wills, by an act of deliberate self-discipline, to the collective will of the community. At this point Fichte's argument leaned so heavily on Rousseau's as almost to amount to a paraphrase of *Du contrat social*. As always, he then hesitated before the totalitarian implications of his own logic, and after making the state the custodian of individual morality, he drew back and denied that 'the higher branches of the culture of reason – religion, science and virtue' could ever become the purposes of the state. Towards the end of his course of lectures he therefore found himself in the uncomfortable position of arguing simultaneously that the development of the state towards a universal monarchy on European and Christian lines was the 'sole animating principle' of modern history, whilst at the same time asserting that religion provided a system of values by which the state could be judged.

When Fichte gave another series of lectures in 1807–8, which were published as 'Addresses to the German nation', he responded with a somewhat unphilosophical lack of detachment to the progress of the European war and the destruction of the Prussian state after Jena. There was no pretence now of looking with perfect serenity on the actions and the fate of nations. Jena, said Fichte, had ended the third stage in the history of humanity. Enlightened self-interest – the motive principle of the Enlightenment – would incline Germans to collaborate with a French occupying power which Fichte expected to remain in control of Germany for a long time. Since armed revolt was demonstrably futile, the Germans must make themselves morally ready to become the vehicle for the achievement of the fourth stage, in which the individual would seek his satisfaction in the moral welfare of the community as a whole. Fichte, in other words, called for German resistance to the domination of Europe by what he considered to be the Enlightenment Militant. His insistence on the special role reserved for Germany in the historical process deserves precise definition. It was not based on any racial theory, since he regarded as Germanic all the peoples who had once broken through the defences of the Roman Empire to conquer and colonize most of Europe. But it was only in Germany proper that these peoples had retained their original language, relatively uncontaminated by classical borrowing. By doing so, they retained a living culture, accessible to the people as a whole, whereas the French, for example, had both a mandarin and a popular language, the latter incapable of poetry and philosophy and the former sterile, in the sense that it could only express its higher thoughts in the form of alien abstract terminology that had no organic roots in the national consciousness. 'The German alone, because he is a living race, has a *true native land*.' More ominously, 'We appear to be the elect of the universal divine plan.'

It is almost inevitable – and perhaps not wholly unjustifiable – that we should read this in terms of the conclusions that later generations were to draw. It is therefore worth emphasizing how far Fichte, despite all his own efforts, belonged to the 'third age' which he was trying to outgrow. His romanticized view of the German trading communities of the Middle Ages reads like a transposition of Rousseau's idealized Geneva. The educational system which he saw as the means to public regeneration was extraordinarily similar to that imagined by Saint-Just. Fichte's 'We must form men so that they can only will what we wish them to will' echoes Saint-Just's 'It is for the legislator to make men into what he wants them to be.' This is understandable enough, since both derived their inspiration from Rousseau. One suspects that neither of them would have felt particularly flattered if he could have foretold that his ideal of an educational system based on public service, social conformity, plenty of healthy exercise, military training and a rather vague identification of religion and patriotism, was to be most faithfully realized in the English public schools of the nineteenth century! Historical inevitability was a more devious process than Fichte imagined.

Once again, as in his earlier lectures, Fichte saved his humanity at the expense of his consistency. After excluding from the civilizing process all who had not been brought up in the German cultural tradition, he suddenly added, 'Whoever believes in super-sensible culture, in his liberty, whoever desires to establish this super-sensible culture by means of his liberty, whatever his birthplace and his language, is of our race and will become one of us.' Perhaps with the unreliable trimming of the Hohenzollerns in mind, he also reaffirmed that the state was merely a means towards the advancement of civilization, not an end in itself. 'Patriotism must dominate the state itself and be regarded as the superior power.'

If one abstracts from Fichte's thought the saving vices of his own self-contradictions, one is left with the basic elements of the belief that was to be developed with fewer inhibitions by Hegel. History was a logical and inevitable process which the individual might recognize but could not alter. His existence, as mind, was determined by, and only meaningful as a part of, a national community. The age of anarchic individualism and endless interrogation was giving way to an age of action in which the enlightened individual would realize himself in proportion to the extent of his surrender to the state. History advanced by conflict and during the next stage of the struggle the German people would constitute the chosen vehicle of the historical process. The bases of German nationalism and, with suitable modifications, of National Socialism and Marxism, had already been established as part of the reaction against the Enlightenment that arose from the Napoleonic wars.

*

Both the Roman Catholic reactionaries and the German Idealists, from their very different points of view, were agreed in identifying the Revolution with the Enlightenment and in rejecting both. For the former, the Enlightenment was a modern heresy, to be countered by a return to blind faith and the acceptance of authority. For the latter, it had been a necessary – and therefore a justified – phase that had been outgrown; to revive its values and outlook was impossible and to wish to do so the sign of a retarded individualism that had no place in an age of collective action. Over a hundred and fifty years later, we have seen the consequences of both philosophies and are unlikely to be attracted by either. Nevertheless, their condemnation of the Enlightenment as negative and superficial has often been accepted, even by those who reject their alternative solutions to the eternal problems of God, man and history. I hope this book will have done something to suggest that their verdict on their own immediate past was as misguided as their influence on the future was to be pernicious.

Appendices

Appendix 1

THE EIGHTEENTH-CENTURY LIFE SPAN OF SOME OF THE MORE IMPORTANT WRITERS OF THE ENLIGHTENMENT

1700	1710	1720	1730	1740	1750	1760	1770	1780	1790	1800

Locke

Leibniz

Newton

Pope

Vico

Montesquieu

Maupertuis

Voltaire

Linnaeus

Buffon

La Mettrie

Hume

Rousseau

Diderot

Helvétius

Condillac

d'Holbach

Adam Smith

Kant

Lessing

Burke

Beccaria

Condorcet

Herder

Goethe

Appendix 2

SOME OF THE MAIN WORKS
OF THE ENLIGHTENMENT

WHEN the date is in italic type this indicates the year of composition of a book not published until later.

MULTI-VOLUME WORKS, PUBLISHED OVER A PERIOD
OF TIME

Pluche: *Spectacle de la nature* (1732–50)
Réaumur: *Histoire des insectes* (1734–42)
Buffon: Histoire naturelle (1749–89)
Encyclopédie (1751–72)

A CHRONOLOGICAL LIST:

1721   Montesquieu: *Lettres persanes*

1725   Vico: *New Science*

1733   Pope: *Essay on Man*
1734   Voltaire: *Lettres philosophiques, Traité de métaphysique*
1735   Linnaeus: *Systema naturae*

1738   Voltaire: *Éléments de la philosophie de Newton*

1740 Hume: *Treatise on Human Nature*

1745 Maupertuis: *Vénus physique*
1746 Diderot: *Pensées philosophiques*
1747 Voltaire: *Zadig*; La Mettrie: *L'Homme machine*
1748 Montesquieu: *De l'esprit des lois*; de Maillet: *Telliamed* (written at an earlier, unknown date); Hume: *Enquiry concerning Human Understanding*
1749 Condillac: *Traité des systèmes*; Diderot: *Lettre sur les aveugles*; Rousseau: *Si le rétablissement des sciences . . .*
1750 La Mettrie: *Anti-Sénèque, Système d'Epicure*; Maupertuis: *Essai de cosmologie*
1751 Maupertuis: *Système de la nature*
1752 Voltaire: *Micromégas*

1754 Condillac: *Traité des sensations*; Diderot: *De l'interprétation de la nature*
1755 Morelly: *Code de la nature*; Rousseau: *Discours sur l'origine et les fondements de l'inégalité*; Winckelmann: *On the Imitation of Greek Painting and Sculpture*
1756 Burke: *Origin of Our Ideas on the Sublime and the Beautiful*
1757 Hume: *Natural History of Religion*
1758 Helvétius: *De l'esprit*; Rousseau: *Lettre à d'Alembert sur les spectacles*
1759 Voltaire: *Candide*; Johnson: *Rasselas*

1761 Rousseau: *La Nouvelle Héloïse*
1762 Rousseau: *Émile, Du contrat social*

1764 Beccaria: *Of crimes and punishments*; Rousseau: *Lettres écrites de la montagne*

1766 Lessing: *Laocoön*
1767 d'Holbach: *Le Christianisme dévoilé*; Herder: *Fragments of the New German Literature*

1769 Diderot: *Rêve de d'Alembert*

1770 d'Holbach: *Système de la nature*

1771 Bougainville: *Voyage autour du monde*

1772 Diderot: *Supplément au voyage de Bougainville*; Raynal: *Histoire philosophique des deux Indes*; Chastellux: *De la félicité publique*

1773 Helvétius: *De l'homme*

1774 Goethe: *Werther*

1775 Herder: *Philosophy of History and Culture*

1776 Adam Smith: *The Wealth of Nations*

1777 Lessing: *Hamburg Dramaturgy*

1779 Lessing: *Nathan the Wise*

1780 Lessing: *On the Education of the Human Race*

1781 Kant: *Critique of Pure Reason*

1782 Rousseau: posthumous publication of first six volumes of *Confessions*

1783 Kant: *Prolegomena to Any Future Metaphysics*

1788 Kant: *Critique of Practical Reason*; Hutton: *Theory of the Earth*

1790 Kant: *Critique of Judgment*

1793 Condorcet: *Esquisse d'un tableau historique des progrès de l'esprit humain*

BIBLIOGRAPHICAL NOTE

THE subject of this book is so wide-ranging and so ill-defined that any pretence of offering the reader a representative bibliography would clearly be absurd. In any case, the most important books, and the ones he is likely to find most conducive to original ideas of his own, have already been listed in Appendix 2. Some eighteenth-century texts, however, are not easily obtainable and some modern studies are too perceptive to be passed over in silence. What follows is therefore a brief note about some of the books which I myself have found most useful or illuminating. If it will not give the reader a balanced view of the present state of eighteenth-century studies, I hope it may nevertheless guide him towards some enjoyable reading. More detailed bibliographical information is to be found in J. S. Bromley and A. Goodwin: *A Select List of Works on Europe and Europe Overseas, 1715–1815* (Oxford University Press, 1956), and in S. Pargellis and D. J. Medley: *Bibliography of British History; the Eighteenth Century* (Oxford University Press, 1951).

On European history as a whole, an excellent comprehensive introduction to the whole period is to be found in W. Doyle, *The Old European Order 1660–1800* (Oxford University Press, 1978). There are also two useful and inexpensive volumes in the Fontana series: O. Hufton, *Europe, Privilege and Protest, 1730–1789* (1980) and G. Rudé, *Revolutionary Europe, 1789–1815* (1964). For a stimulating look at ancien régime society, see C. B. A. Behrens, *The Ancien Régime* (Thames & Hudson, 1967). There is a rather nationalistic view of French influence on European civilization in Volume V of the *Histoire générale des Civilisations* by R. Mousnier, which also includes a survey of the revolutionary and Napoleonic period by E. Labrousse and M. Bouloiseau. See also P. Chaunu, *La Civilisation de l'Europe des Lumières* (Arthaud, Paris, 1971). *The European Nobility in the Eighteenth Century* (Black, 1953) looks at the aristocracy in its different national contexts. For the demographic history of the period, see M. Reinhard and A. Armengaud, *Histoire générale de la Population mondiale* (Domat-Monchrestien, Paris, 1961). For the last quarter of the century, R. R. Palmer's *Age of the Democratic Revolution* (Princeton University Press, 2 volumes, 1959, 1964) is indispensable.

For preliminary reading on French history, see A. Cobban, *History of Modern France* Volume I (Penguin, 1957) and J. Lough, *Introduction to Eighteenth-century France* (Longman, 1960). P. Sagnac, *La Formation de la Société française moderne* Volume II (Presses Universitaires, Paris, 1946) and H. Carré, *La Noblesse de France et l'Opinion publique au dix-huitième Siècle* (Champion, Paris, 1920) are still useful, but should be supplemented by G. Chaussinand-Nogaret, *La Noblesse au dix-huitième siècle* (Hachette, Paris, 1976). For the early period, see H. Rothcrug, *The Opposition to Louis XIV; the Political and Social Origins of the French Enlightenment* (Princeton University Press, 1966). On the reasons for the outbreak of the French Revolution there is nothing to compare with W. Doyle, *Origins of the French Revolution* (Oxford University Press, 1980). For general surveys of the revolutionary and Napoleonic period see the works of G. Lefebvre, *La Révolution française* (Presses Universitaires, Paris, 1951), *Les Thermidoceans* (Colin, Paris, 1937), *La Directoire* (Colin, Paris, 1946) and *Napoléon* (Presses Universitaires, Paris, 1941), all of which are available in English translations. For shorter accounts of the French Revolution, consult M. J. Sydenham, *The French Revolution* (Batsford, 1965), N. Hampson, *A Social History of the French Revolution* (Routledge, 1963) and M. Lyons, *France under the Directory* (Cambridge University Press, 1975). A. Cobban's *Social Interpretation of the French Revolution* (Cambridge University Press, 1964) began the criticism of Lefebvre's view of the revolution. A different view of its role in European history is expounded in F. Furet's *Penser la Révolution française* (Gallimard, Paris, 1978), which is available in an English translation. The best account of the expansion of revolutionary France is in J. Godechot's *La grande Nation* (Aubier, Paris, 1956). F. M. H. Markham's *Napoleon* (Weidenfeld, 1963) is a convenient brief biography, but readers should also consult P. Geyl, *Napoleon, For and Against* (Cape, 1949).

For eighteenth-century England, see J. H. Plumb, *England in the Eighteenth Century* (Penguin, 1950), *The Growth of Political Stability in England* (Macmillan, 1967) and W. A. Speck, *Stability and Strife, England, 1714–1760* (Edward Arnold, 1977). G. E. Mingay's *English Landed Society in the Eighteenth Century* (Routledge, 1963) is also very useful. There are introductions to Scottish and Irish history in T. C. Smout, *A History of the Scottish People* (Fontana, 1972) and J. C. Beckett, *The Making of Modern Ireland* (Faber, 1966).

The social history of Germany as a whole may best be approached through W. H. Bruford's *Germany in the Eighteenth Century* (Cambridge University Press, 1935, paperback) and the second volume of F. Hertz, *The Development of the German Public Mind* (Allen & Unwin, 1962). F. L. Carsten, in his *Princes and Parliaments in Germany* (Oxford University Press, 1959) provides a good deal of useful information about constitutional conflicts in the minor German states. For one particular example see T. C. W. Blanning, *Reform and Revolution in Mainz, 1743–1803* (Cambridge University Press, 1974). There is a general survey of the Habsburg Empire in E. Wangermann, *The Austrian Achievement* (Thames & Hudson, 1973). For the later period, see T. C. W. Blanning, *Joseph II and Enlightened Despotism* (Longman, 1970) and E. Wangermann, *From Joseph II to the Jacobin Trials* (Oxford University Press, 1959). Two older but still important works on the non-German territories of the Habsburgs are E. Denis: *La Bohème depuis la Montagne Blanche* (Volume 1, Leroux, Paris, 1903) and H. Marczali, *Hungary in the Eighteenth Century* (Cambridge University Press, 1910). E. Link's *Emancipation of the Austrian Peasant, 1740–98* (Columbia University Press, 1949) provides a useful account of one of the central aspects of Habsburg policy. On the social history of Prussia, H. Rosenberg's *Bureaucracy, Aristocracy and Autocracy, the Prussian Experience, 1660–1815* (Harvard University Press, 1958) describes the functioning of the state machine, and H. Brunschwig's *Crise de l'État prussien à la fin du dix-huitième siècle et la genèse de la mentalité romantique* (Presses Universitaires, Paris,

1947) explores the social and cultural tensions to which it gave rise. The plentiful literature on the reform of the Prussian state after 1806 is not sufficiently relevant to the present volume to justify its inclusion.

There are general histories of Russia by V. O. Klyuchevsky (Volumes IV and V, Eng. trans. Dent, 1926, 1931) and by P. Miliukov, C. Seignebos and L. Eisenmann (Volumes I and II, Leroux, Paris, 1932). Miliukov's *Outlines of Russian Culture* (Philadelphia, 1942) is also useful. H. Rogger's *National Consciousness in Eighteenth-century Russia* (Harvard University Press, 1960) is essential reading for an understanding of the repercussions of the Enlightenment in Russia. Two biographies are also worthy of note: D. M. Lang's *The First Russian Radical, Alexander Radishchev* (Allen & Unwin, 1959) and M. Raeff's *Michael Speransky, Statesman of Imperial Russia* (Nijhoff, The Hague, 1957). R. Portal's *L'Oural au dix-huitième siècle* (Institut d'Études Slaves, Paris, 1950) is an important contribution to the economic history of Russia. On Catherine the Great, see J. de Madariaga, *Russia in the Age of Catherine the Great* (Weidenfeld, 1981).

Other countries may be dealt with more summarily. Spain has been the subject of three excellent works: J. Sarrailh, *L'Espagne éclairée de la seconde moitié du dix-huitième siècle* (Klincksieck, Paris, 1954), R. Herr, *The Eighteenth-century Revolution in Spain* (Princeton University Press, 1958) and R. Carr, *Spain, 1808–1939* (Oxford University Press, 1966). J. Fabre's *Stanislas-Auguste Poniatowski et l'Europe des lumières* (Les Belles Lettres, Paris, 1952) provides an excellent account of Poland during the second half of the century. Poland was also the subject of a whole issue of the *Annales historiques de la Révolution française* (June–September 1964). Italy has been somewhat neglected by historians of the eighteenth century, but E. P. Noether, *The Seeds of Italian Nationalism, 1700–1815* (Columbia University Press, 1951) should be consulted. Brief accounts of the history of the Netherlands are to be found in G. J. Renier: *The Dutch Nation* (Netherlands Government Information Bureau, 1944) and B. H. M. Vlekke: *The Evolution of the Dutch Nation* (New York, 1945). On Scandinavia, see B. J. Hovde, *The Scandinavian Countries, 1720–1865* Volume I (Cornell University Press, 1948).

The best analytical work on the thought of the century as a whole is still E. Cassirer's *The Philosophy of the Enlightenment* (English trans., Princeton University Press, 1951, Beacon Press, Boston, paperback), and the same author's *Rousseau. Kant, Goethe* (Hamden, Connecticut, 1945) is equally illuminating. C. L. Becker's *Heavenly City of the Eighteenth-century Philosophers* (Yale University Press, 1932, paperback) is urbane and provocative. The best general survey of the movement is to be found in two books by P. Hazard, published in 1935 and 1946, whose English translations appear under the titles of *The European Mind* and *European Thought in the Eighteenth Century*; both are available in paperback editions (Penguin). The volume of essays edited by P. Francastel, *Utopie et institutions au dix-huitième sièle: Le Pragmatisme des lumières* (Moutan, Paris, 1963) contains some interesting material, and F. E. Manuel's *The Eighteenth Century Confronts the Gods* (Harvard University Press, 1959), is a useful account of the search for a sociology of religion. See also P. Gay, *The Enlightenment, an Interpretation* (Weidenfeld, 2 volumes, 1967, 1969) and *The Enlightenment in National Context*, edited by R. Porter and M. Teich (Cambridge University Press, 1981).

The most reliable account of the thought of the Enlightenment in France itself is still D. Mornet's *Origines intellectuelles de la Révolution française* (Colin, Paris, 1933). J. P. Belin's *Le Mouvement philosophique de 1748 à 1789* (Paris, 1913) is still well worth reading. Two recent works of outstanding scholarship are R. Mauzi's *Idée du bonheur au dix-huitième siècle* (Colin, Paris, 1960) and J. Ehrard's *Idée de nature en France dans la première moitié du dix-huitième siècle* (2 volumes, S.E.V.P.E.N., Paris, 1963). R. R. Palmer's *Catholics and Unbelievers in Eighteenth-century France* (Princeton University Press, 1939) is one of the few books to investigate the Church's reply to the Enlightenment. The symposium edited by G. Bollème, *Livre et société dans la France du dix-huitième siècle* (Mouton, Paris, 1965) contains much interesting information and R. Mandrou's *De la culture populaire au dix-septième et dix-huitième siècles* (Stock, Paris, 1964) describes the literature available to the majority of the population. P. Gay's *The Party of Humanity* (Knopf, New York, 1964) is particularly good on Rousseau, besides showing the importance of Genevan politics to an understanding of the political thought of both Voltaire and Rousseau. The political implications of one aspect of Rousseau's thought are the subject of a brilliant, if one-sided analysis in J. L. Talmon's *Origins of Totalitarian Democracy* (Secker & Warburg, 1952, Heinemann paperback). On Mesmerism see R. Darnton, *Mesmerism and the End of the Enlightenment in France* (Harvard University Press, 1968).

An interesting book on the penetration of French ideas into Germany is R. Mortier's *Diderot en Allemagne* (Presses Universitaires, Paris, 1954). On Germany itself, see E. Purdie's *Studies in German Literature of the Eighteenth Century* (Athlone Press, 1965) and R. Pascal's *German Sturm und Drang* (Manchester University Press, 1953). The symposium on *Art and Ideas in Eighteenth-century Italy*, published in Rome in 1960, contains much interesting material in addition to Sir Isaiah Berlin's outstanding essay on Vico. Works on England are too numerous and easily accessible for their inclusion here to be either practicable or necessary. I will therefore merely refer the reader to B. Willey's useful introduction, *The Eighteenth-century Background* (Chatto & Windus, 1940, Penguin paperback) and to A. Cobban's *Debate on the French Revolution* (Kaye, 1950).

Those interested in studying a particular author may find the following useful:

Montesquieu: R. Shackleton, *Montesquieu* (Oxford University Press, 1961)

J. Starobinski, *Montesquieu par lui-même* (Éditions du Seuil, Paris, 1953)

Voltaire: H. Mason, *Voltaire* (Elek, 1981)

I. O Wade, *The Intellectual Development of Voltaire* (Princeton University Press, 1969)

R. Pomeau, *La Religion de Voltaire* (Nizet, Paris, 1956)

P. Gay, *Voltaire's Politics* (Princeton University Press, 1959)

La Mettrie: A. Vartanian, *La Mettrie's 'L'Homme machine'* (Princeton University Press, 1960)

Helvétius: D. W. Smith, *Hélvétius, a Study in Persecution*
                  (Oxford University Press, 1965)

d'Holbach: P. Naville, *Paul Thiry d'Holbach et la philosophie
                  scientifique au dix-huitième siècle* (Gallimard,
                  Paris, 1943)

Rousseau: J. Guéhenno, *Jean-Jacques* (2 volumes, Galli-
                  mard, Paris, 1948, English translation by J.
                  and D. Weightman, London, 1966)

Chateaubriand: L.   Martin-Chauffier,   *Chateaubriand   ou
                  l'Obsession de la pureté* (Gallimard, 1943)

De Maistre: J. Lively, ed., *The Works of Joseph de Maistre*
                  (Allen & Unwin, 1965)

Hamaan: R. Gregor Smith, *J. G. Hamaan* (Collins, 1960)

Herder: F. M. Barnard, *Herder's Social and Political
                  Thought* (Oxford University Press, 1965)

Kant: S. Körner, *Kant* (Penguin, 1955)

Goethe: R. Friedenthal, *Goethe, his Life and Times*
                  (English trans. Weidenfeld & Nicolson,
                  1965)

Burke: A. Cobban, *Edmund Burke and the Revolt against
                  the Eighteenth Century* (Allen and Unwin,
                  1929)

Condorcet: K. M. Baker, *Condorcet, from Natural Philosophy
                  to Social Mathematics* (University of Califor-
                  nia Press, 1975)

Necker: H. Grange, *Les Idées de Necker* (Klincksieck,
                  Paris, 1974)

A good introduction to eighteenth-century science is to be
found in A. R. Hall's *Scientific Revolution, 1500–1800* (Longman,
1954). More detailed treatment is available in the three-volume
survey, *The Ancestry of Science*, by S. Toulmin and J. Goodfield,
of which the first two volumes, *The Fabric of the Heavens*
(Hutchinson, 1961) and *The Architecture of Matter* (Hutchinson,
1962), are available in paperback editions. The third volume,
The Discovery of Time (1965), seriously underestimates the extent
to which eighteenth-century writers had liberated themselves
from a biblical chronology. Two outstanding works on biology

are *Les Sciences de la vie dans la pensée française du dix-huitième siècle* (Colin, Paris, 1963) by J. Roger, and the collection of essays edited by H. B. Glass, under the title, *The Fore-runners of Darwin* (Johns Hopkins University Press, Baltimore, 1959). F. E. Manuel's *Isaac Newton, Historian* (Princeton University Press, 1963) presents an unfamiliar side of Newton's career – and a warning of the perils of applying scientific techniques to the solution of historical problems. For the status of science in France see R. Hahn, *The Anatomy of a Scientific Institution: the Paris Academy of Sciences, 1666–1803* (University of California Press, 1972).

INDEX